The Art of Making Peace

The Art of Making Peace

Lessons Learned from Peace Treaties

Edited by

Steven van Hoogstraten, Nico Schrijver,
Otto Spijkers and Anneleen de Jong

CARNEGIE FOUNDATION
PEACE PALACE

Universiteit
Leiden

BRILL
NIJHOFF

LEIDEN | BOSTON

Library of Congress Control Number: 2016960588

Typeface for the Latin, Greek, and Cyrillic scripts: "Brill". See and download: brill.com/brill-typeface.

ISBN 978-90-04-32123-6 (paperback)
ISBN 978-90-04-32124-3 (e-book)

This book is printed on acid-free paper and produced in a sustainable manner.

Contents

List of Abbreviations

AU	African Union
AUHIP	African Union High Level Implementation Panel for Sudan
AUPD	African Union Panel on Darfur
CPA	Comprehensive Peace Agreement
CSCE	Conference on Security and Cooperation in Europe
DDPD	Doha Document for Peace in Darfur
DDR	Deutsche Demokratische Republik
DPA	Darfur Peace Agreement
ECOWAS	Economic Community of West African States
ESPA	Eastern Sudan Peace Agreement
EU	European Union
GDP	Gross Domestic Product
IAEA	International Atomic Energy Agency
ICC	International Criminal Court
ICJ	International Court of Justice
IFOR	Implementation Force
IGAD	Intergovernmental Authority on Development
ILO	International Labour Organization
ITLOS	International Tribunal for the Law of the Sea
LSE	London School of Economics
NATO	North Atlantic Treaty Organization
NGO	Non-Governmental Organization
OPCW	Organization for the Prohibition of Chemical Weapons
OSCE	Organization for Security and Co-operation in Europe
PCA	Permanent Court of Arbitration
SADC	Southern African Development Community
SPLA	Sudan People's Liberation Army
SPLM	Sudan People's Liberation Movement
UN	United Nations
UNCITRAL	United Nations Commission on International Trade Law
UNDP	United Nations Development Programme
UNESCO	United Nations Educational, Scientific and Cultural Organization
UNFICYP	United Nations Peacekeeping Force in Cyprus
UNHCR	United Nations High Commissioner for Refugees
UNMIBH	United Nations Mission in Bosnia Herzegovina

UNSC	United Nations Security Council
UNTAC	United Nations Transitional Authority in Cambodia
UK	United Kingdom
US	United States
WHO	World Health Organization
WTO	World Trade Organization

Preface

The Centenary of the Peace Palace in 2013 provided an ideal opportunity to hold a conference of academic and policy experts about the role of, and practical experience with, international peace treaties. While the University of Utrecht wished to devote its full attention to the Treaty of Utrecht of 1713, and organised a high-level day on 19 September 2013 in the historic Academy building of the city of Utrecht, the Carnegie Foundation and the University of Leiden agreed to hold a one-day conference on the theme of "The Art of Peace-making, Lessons Learned from Peace Treaties" on 20 September 2013.

This conference took place in the Academy Building of the Peace Palace and was attended by some 150 participants. The conference was firmly chaired by Professor Jaap de Hoop Scheffer, former Netherlands Minister of Foreign Affairs and also former Secretary-General of NATO. The format of the conference was a roundtable of some 40 invited persons, while the remainder of the audience grouped around that roundtable as a participating group of listeners. Some of the participants of the Utrecht day were also present in The Hague.

The general theme of the conference in the Peace Palace was – after much preparatory debate – divided into four key building blocks: 1) the Treaty of Versailles of 1919, which was the end of World War I; 2) the Dayton Agreement of 1995, which meant the end of the war in the former Yugoslavia; 3) the Darfur Agreement of 2006, which brought peace to the Sudan, at least on a transitional basis; and 4) situations of absence of any peace agreement, more particularly situations in which the intervention and law-making of the United Nations are warranted in case an agreement between the parties is impossible to find (e.g. Iran/Iraq). Each part involved an intervention by two speakers (one main speaker and a commentator) and was followed by an extensive debate by the roundtable.

The general tone of the conference was that of a critical review of what the cited peace treaties had brought to the world. How difficult was it to come to an agreement? Was the agreement always the winners' will? What was conveniently forgotten? Which elements were too strongly implied? Was it a just treaty after all? In that respect, the first peace treaty of Versailles was the subject of overwhelming negative judgment. One speaker called this treaty a "disaster, the consequences of which are still being felt today". But the negotiations for the Treaty of

Versailles had run on for some six months, and involved the highest representatives of the Allied States at the time. Ultimately, Germany was only allowed to sign on the dotted line. The betrayal Germany felt was exemplified by a documentary drama, called *Paris 1919*, a short version of which was shown on screen.

This book is a reflection of the conference in the Peace Palace, enriched with some interviews with the major intervenors: the historian Professor Adam Roberts from the United Kingdom, and the lawyer Barney Afako from Uganda, who was deeply involved in the drafting of the Darfur Agreement. And a special debate was organised between a number of Judges of the International Court of Justice, a representative of the Permanent Court of Arbitration and some mediators/negotiators of international conflicts, in order to look at the parallels, but also at the differences involved in the employment of these techniques. We learned that the participation by NGOs was not always seen as helpful, even if sometimes the NGO could play a deciding role due to its knowledge and financial means to hire experts.

We look back with immense satisfaction on this meeting about *Lessons Learned from Peace Treaties*, and the only inadequacy we can see was that it lasted only one full day. So much more could be added to the debate. Nonetheless, we feel that major issues were addressed at the conference, and that some form of justice was done to a century of conflict and of conflict resolution. Once again the essential wisdom was emphasized that the parties in the conflict need to show a form of respect to each other when finalising the details of a settlement. For victors' law will be unmasked as the victors rule some day and resentment will lead to renewed conflict. On this particular point, history is our uneasy witness.

This book wishes to give a central place to the role of history in the lessons we learned from analysing peace treaties. This is how we understand the movements of the past, and their direct link to the challenges we face today. International law is both an instrument in guiding these processes and for directing future developments. It is an instrument that comes out of continuous negotiation and debate, of intense academic effort and political influence. But it is just as much an instrument of speech, and largely a product of oral history. In this book we chose to present these lessons learned in that way, each lesson referring to the author that presented it, framing it as his or her authentic view. We almost literally transcribed the contributions of the speakers at the conference, the interviews and the roundtable on mediation versus adjudication. In the texts, we did not include references or bibliographies. Instead, we tried to bear witness to the views and visions on peace treaties and peace processes as they were presented by some of the most eloquent academics of our times, at the global symbol of peace and justice, the Peace Palace.

Our unreserved gratitude is expressed to the two co-editors of the book: Anneleen de Jong (Carnegie Foundation) and Otto Spijkers (University of Utrecht). Without their continued interest in the conference theme and their belief in the result this book would not have seen the light of day. We also greatly acknowledge the work of our friend and colleague Alfred Soons (Emeritus Professor of international law at Utrecht University) for his cooperation in making this joint endeavour possible. We know that his Utrecht conference will lead to an academic publication, and we look forward to that book with interest. Our Hague-based book has the function of gliding over the issues with a certain distance, with a sudden focus here and there, which means that we have not reproduced all the words of the speakers, but rather have given a summary of what they said. We express our thanks to the Chairman of the Foundation, Dr. Bernard Bot, who gave a fine concluding comment at the end of the day on 20 September, but also participated fully in all preparations. His personal support for the whole operation was invaluable for us.

Nico Schrijver
Professor of International Law
Leiden University

Steven van Hoogstraten
Former General Director
Carnegie Foundation

From Utrecht's Peace to Modern Times: Introductory Words by Martti Koskenniemi, University of Helsinki, Treaty of Utrecht Chair at Utrecht University*

Greetings from Utrecht, and from a conference examining the Peace of Utrecht 300 years ago. The Peace of Utrecht is often regarded as the founding moment of the *droit public de l'Europe*, European public law. It was to be followed up by many other European locations: Vienna, Paris, Geneva, The Hague. No doubt it exemplified something like a "European tradition". At our conference yesterday on the historical aspects of the peace of 1713, we examined, among other topics, the enduring *Eurocentrism* of international law. And we made a note of the fact that the war of Spanish succession was not a war to end all war. Utrecht would not be the last peace negotiation, quite the contrary. The diplomatic history of the 18th century was peppered by peace negotiations. We also noted that the 18th century was a century of monarchic absolutism, and that the Peace of Utrecht, as well as those that had preceded and would follow it, manifested forms of peace-making between absolutist monarchs. There was not a single intellectual in the 18th century who would not have been suspicious of monarchic diplomacy, and doubted whether permanent peace between such men was at all possible.

The Abbé de Saint-Pierre published his *Plan for Perpetual Peace* in Europe at that very time. At our conference, we made many references to the plan of the good Abbé. The plan was based on what we would today call "realist" premises, namely that it would be in the interest of those absolute monarchs themselves to be at peace with each other. In this way, they could perhaps not only perpetuate peace but also their dynasties. Other people, such as Rousseau and Voltaire, were more sceptical. If the monarchs were such irrational creatures as

* This was an address designed to build a bridge between the conference "The Art of Making Peace. The 1713 Peace of Utrecht and its Enduring Effects", that had been held at Senate Hall of Utrecht University on 19 September 2013, and the Hague Conference on the following day.

Van Hoogstraten, Schrijver et al. (eds.), The Art of Making Peace: Lessons Learned from Peace Treaties
© 2017 The Editors. Printed in The Netherlands. ISBN *978-90-04-32123-6. pp. 1-7.*

they thought monarchs were, why would they see their own interest in peace? Instant gratification, after all, was at the heart of absolutist monarchy. This, too, is an enduring feature of European politics.

One of the intellectuals commenting on the peace was Abbé Mably, whose 1757 *Droit public de l'Europe* suggested that there should be what Mably called a "science of negotiations." Now I know that today's agenda is about the "art" of negotiations, and I leave it up to you to think about the difference between the "art" and "science" of diplomacy. But in the 18th century, what men of experience and intellect wanted to enlist were the recent advances in natural sciences also to contribute to diplomacy. This would be, Mably wrote, a science free of intrigue, and thus wholly unlike the old one. It would teach each nation to measure its projects in accordance with its forces, and to attain through peace what they could never gain through war. There is one simple rule of negotiations, Mably wrote, and that was the following: "*Toutes les négociations d'une puissance peuvent être entreprises et conduites relativement à son intérêt fondamental.*" Their fundamental interests... What an optimistic view! As if the interests of everybody would always be best served by peace.

I have been requested by this address to provide a bridge from our talks yesterday to the conference of today. Yesterday, we concentrated on three themes that were prevalent in the 18th century, and more specifically in Utrecht 300 years ago. There were three above all:

- First, the question of the balance of power;
- Second, the relationship between Europe and the colonial regimes, with a focus on the relationship between peace-making and trade;
- And third, the intellectual aspects of the peace, the way it inspired – or perhaps did not inspire – ideas about a standing peace arrangement between sovereigns, perhaps in Europe, perhaps in the world.

Three hundred years ago, Turkey was a big problem. Is Turkey today a big problem? I assume that this will be something you shall debate today.

The agenda of today's meeting makes reference to one European location – Versailles – and then other locations outside of Europe, especially Dayton Ohio and Sudan... The world has changed quite a bit. In Utrecht, no non-Europeans were represented. At Versailles in 1919, there were already some non-Europeans among the 34 delegations – China, Japan, Siam, Liberia, many Latin-American countries. But apart from the US, of course, they played no role whatsoever in the important decisions, namely decisions on what to do with Germany. And they were not too successful, either, with respect to their efforts to influence the drafting of the Covenant of the League of Nations.

One remarkable contrast between Utrecht and Versailles was that in the latter, there was no question about who were winners and who lost. The Allied Powers negotiated the conditions of the peace notoriously without the presence of Germany, and then handed over the draft of the peace treaty to the German delegation, to be accepted in the space of 48 hours. No wonder that the pacifist socialist international lawyer, Walther Schücking, who was among the German delegation, was disgusted at allied behaviour. Utrecht, by contrast, was negotiated among dynasties that were familiar, indeed, even related to each other. And they were friends. There was no existential hatred between the negotiators. Who won? Who lost? Well, hard to say. War was tragic three hundred years ago, as it is today, and many people suffered. But at Utrecht three hundred years ago, few people would have regarded the war of Spanish succession as a war between good and evil. It was about relative power and resources, but not about good and evil. By contrast, in the trenches of the First World War existential opposition could develop. "Hang the Kaiser!", people in London and in Paris exclaimed. This was an altogether different sentiment to that which reigned at Utrecht, three hundred years ago.

Versailles realised one of the objectives that many intellectuals since the 18th century had wanted to attain, namely a permanent organisation to see not only to the administration of the peace, but more grandly to the future of European and world order. Utrecht was about the balance of power – balance of power was a bad word in Versailles. Everybody present in the peace of 1919 remembered the July crisis five years earlier when diplomats rode trains across Europe, desperately trying to redress the balance that had been lost. And, of course, all those hectic manoeuvres came to naught, war commenced. And thus we saw the establishment of the League of Nations, and the idea of collective security. Everyone should bind their hands with a legal arrangement never to go to war again. In retrospect – somebody said this yesterday – this was just a starting point of the "second European thirty years war".

The second panel today will be about the talks that led to the ending of the Yugoslavian civil war. Europeans, three hundred years ago, did not yet possess the expression "the Eastern question" – they would have it very rapidly. But the Balkans had been, and would continue to remain a difficult area; how was the relationship between central Europe and what central Europeans always thought as the margins, to be organized? Again the issue of Turkey, and how Europeans were to think about Turkey's place and their relations with Turkey, became crucial. Replace "Turkey" by "Islam" and you will see how little we have been able to progress.

But the recent Yugoslavian peace would be different. Now the surrounding was not a European location but Dayton Ohio. What a change! A small location, albeit, of course, wholly global. Unlike Utrecht, but perhaps a little like Versailles, the negotiators had to be coerced to the negotiating table. And the great powers had to make sure that everybody signed neatly on the dotted line. We all remember those pictures from Dayton, with Bill Clinton, John Mayor, Helmut Kohl, Viktor Chernomyrdin, and Jacques Chirac, looking over the hostility still palpable in the mentalities of those who were compelled to sign. The Yugoslavian crisis, like all crises in Europe, would draw in the great powers. Was there an element in the Yugoslavian wars of the 1990s that made it actually a war between the great powers, carried out by proxy between small Balkan communities? What was the role of larger historical patterns?

The peace negotiations in Versailles and in Dayton Ohio were conducted under the shadow of accusations of war criminality. Unlike the emperor Wilhelm, Milosevic actually ended up in court, an unprecedented trial here in The Hague. What was the effect of the looming charges for the negotiations? Does the prospect of trials and war guilt make negotiation harder, as some suggest? That should be one of the issues that we will discuss today. It was certainly not a topic three hundred years ago. On the other hand, Dayton and Utrecht do resemble in that balance of power was the objective in both negotiations. The balance, and the Bosnian constitutional settlement tightly connected to it, were perhaps the most remarkable outcomes of Dayton. Notwithstanding Versailles, we seem unable to live without balance of power.

The comprehensive peace agreement of the Sudan of 2005 is very different from any of this. I was trying hard to think of the similarities between the peace of Utrecht and the process that led to the ending of the civil conflict in the Sudan. The differences are, of course, obvious. The background of decades of low-level violence, crisscrossing claims about natural resources, confrontations staged in ethnic and religious terms... All of that seems at least very different from what the negotiators in Utrecht had to face. To what extent was neo-colonialism an aspect of the Sudan negotiations? I was not present, so I do not know. I would like to hear about that. Like Dayton, the series of agreements that constitute the Sudanese comprehensive peace agreement are complicated, containing a great variation of items. So did the Utrecht peace agreement. Utrecht, too, was composed of many treaties, which dealt with territorial issues, commercial issues… But if Utrecht also dealt with slave trade, Sudan did not. What does that tell us? And then there was all the talk about transitional justice, post-conflict reconciliation… The diplomats in Utrecht did not have that vocabulary three hundred years ago. But I suppose those concerns were also on their minds, in a different vocabulary of course. For them, post-conflict reconciliation ought to be a failure.

"Art" of negotiations, or "science" of negotiations? I used to be a diplomat in my previous life, and was once invited to participate in a negotiation training seminar at the University of Columbia, led by the famous Roger Fisher and his negotiation team. The one thing that I have carried with me from that exercise was that you should always try to keep your eye on the BATNA. I am sure many in the audience are familiar with this. BATNA: Best Alternative to Negotiated Agreement. This is what one needs to keep an eye on so as to begin to negotiate successfully. This is part of the "modern" science of negotiation. It is a rationalist science, because it thinks of the men – nowadays also a few women – participating in those kinds of talks, as rational egoists. Now, St. Pierre, Mably, Rousseau, Voltaire… They did not for one second believe that the diplomats of the *ancien regime*, or indeed the monarchs, were rational. They were egoists, for sure, but the men of the Enlightenment did not believe that rationalism would go together with egoism. What a difference to some of our modern assumptions! So theirs must also have been a different science of negotiations, one in which "art" perhaps played bigger role than it does today.

History is not *magistra vitae*; it does not provide straightforward lessons. But we can – perhaps even must – interpret the narratives from the past in a fashion that makes the past speak to us, makes the past meaningful to us. It is therefore useful, I suggest, to read about Westphalia, Utrecht, Vienna, Paris… All those European locations that have staged grand peace-making efforts. One should be wary of anachronisms, historians tell us. But as a lawyer I am not sure we can heed to this warning. What else do we do when we dig into precedent, other than to prepare for anachronistic judgments? The stories of the past, in a conference like this, are perhaps best seen as narratives through which we can speak about contemporary events. Addressing the past is a neutral way to discuss problems that now preoccupy us, avoiding excess abstraction without having to point to what divides us in the present.

Let me finish this address by pointing to five series of issues that arise from the historical experiences of past peace-making, or from the narratives that we have of those past events. These issues may have significance, and even seem in some ways unavoidable in a conference like this:

- First is the question of who wins and who loses. And how does one deal with the fact that that is the way the negotiators often think about themselves?
- Second, the question of justice and war guilt. How does that fit into the negotiations? As Milosevic was indicted, many people were sceptical about mixing questions of criminal justice with peace-making. What can we say of the present experience?
- Thirdly, there are questions about balance or power and collective security. Must such a balance be always a predominant objective of peace talks? Or should the idea be rejected, and instead look for a common system of security?
- Fourthly, there are issues of transition and nation-building. What is the role of what we nowadays (perhaps too easily) call the "international community" in this?
- And finally, this is the lesson of Versailles: can peace perhaps hide another war inside it? Can it be that it provides only a breathing space, during which everyone can recover their forces?

I began by citing one Enlightenment intellectual, the world's first Communist, as Marx called him, the Abbé Mably. Much of what he had to say in his *Droit public de l'Europe* still speaks to us today, when we negotiate with stakes for our countries, but also to the world at large. There is another French intellectual from the Utrecht period with whom I want to end. This is François de Callières, whose *L'art de négocier sous Louis XIV,* from 1716, is often used in the training of young diplomats. De Callières was a member of the *Académie française* and former secretary of the cabinet of Louis XIV himself, an emissary, and a negotiator at the peace of Rijswick in 1679. He has still useful things to say to us. He does not, for example, think negotiators should use deception or dishonesty. On the contrary, he suggests that a good negotiator was to be an "*honnête homme*," with civilized manners and an ability to listen and persuade. De Callières had a special word for lawyers, les "*gens de Robe.*" These men were often more diligent and hardworking, more organised than courtiers or military men, also more in possession of the subtlety that was needed in courts. This is why they were necessary in making peace.

But they also have a professional burden, and De Caillières warned against relying on them excessively

> *Cette habitude de juger lui fait prendre un air grave et de supériorité qui lui rend d'ordinaire l'esprit moins liant, l'abord plus difficile et les manières d'agir moins prévenantes que celles des gens de la Cour, accoutumés à vivre avec leurs supérieurs et avec leurs égaux.*

PART 1

The Versailles Peace Agreement, Paris (1919)

FIGURE 1 *Poster in The Times breaking the news of Germany's acceptance of the Treaty of Versailles, 24 June 1919.*

Introduction

World War I officially ended with the signing of the Treaty of Versailles on June 28, 1919. The treaty, negotiated between January and June 1919 in Paris, was written by the Allies with almost no participation by the Germans. Faced with the overwhelming task of bringing order to a world shattered by four years of bitter fighting, the Paris delegates were convinced that they had fashioned a just and lasting peace. In The Treaty of Versailles, one reads how world leaders struggled to deal with the aftermath of the *War to End All Wars*.

The war had been so catastrophic and the losses had been so great, that there was a very strong feeling, first of all that someone should pay for it. Reasonable or not, it is human nature to want to find someone to blame, particularly after a great catastrophe, and to want to make someone or something pay. The difficulty with the Great War was that the damage was so great and the strength of public feeling so strong, that the potential bill to be presented to the losing side was astronomical. David Lloyd George, the British Prime Minister, and the French representative Clemenceau knew that they had little chance of extracting vast payments from the defeated nations, but they dared not say so in public for fear of losing political support. They also had to deal with US President Woodrow Wilson, who had made it clear in public statements that he would not support punitive fines.

The eventual treaty included fifteen parts and 440 articles. Part I created the Covenant of the New League of Nations, which Germany was not allowed to join until 1926. Part II specified Germany's new boundaries. Part III stipulated a demilitarized zone and separated the Saar from Germany for fifteen years. Part IV stripped Germany of all its colonies, and Part V reduced Germany's armed forces to very low levels and prohibited Germany from possessing certain classes of weapons, while committing the Allies to eventual disarmament as well. Part VIII established Germany's liability for reparations without stating a specific figure and began with Article 231, in which Germany accepted the responsibility of itself and its allies for the losses and damages of the Allies "as a consequence of the war imposed upon them by the aggression of Germany and her allies."

The German government signed the treaty under protest.

CHAPTER 1.1

Keynote: Sir Adam Roberts, British Academy for the Humanities and Social Sciences

Good morning, Ladies and Gentlemen. It is a privilege to follow Professor Martti Koskenniemi. I agreed very much with his remarks. Perhaps I could just mention two things that his remarks brought to my mind. One is a direct connection between the international politics of the 17th and 18th centuries and those of our own time. It was in the 18th century that a famous English poet, Alexander Pope, wrote a couplet which remained true in the 20th century, when he said:

> Now Europe's balanced, neither side prevails,
> for nothing's left in either of the scales.

So, criticism of balanced power is nothing new. I was also reminded of that extraordinary figure of the Abbé de Saint Pierre and his famous book about the organisation of peace. In some of its editions Turkey was to be included and in some of them it was to be excluded in what he incidentally called "European Union". So he was there long before the European communities existed, and here we are in the year 2013 still debating the 300 year old question whether Turkey should be included or excluded from Europe. And that is one of the issues that arose at the Paris Peace Conference, the issue whether extra European powers, as they were perceived at the time, were properly represented.

There were cheers on the 28th of June, 1919, the anniversary of the assassination in Sarajevo and the date the peace agreement was concluded. But there were also from the start doubts as to the effectiveness of the agreement reached. One of my favourite guides to the negotiations is a British diplomat Harold Nicolson who wrote to his wife at the time of the peace conference famously in a private letter on the 4th of May 1919. He said:

> But darling it is appalling these three ignorant and irresponsible men [by whom he meant his own Prime Minister Lloyd George, the French Prime Minister Clemenceau and President Woodrow Wilson], cutting Asia Minor to bits as if they were dividing a cake.

Van Hoogstraten, Schrijver et al. (eds.), The Art of Making Peace: Lessons Learned from Peace Treaties
© 2017 The Editors. Printed in The Netherlands. ISBN *978-90-04-32123-6. pp. 12-18.*

> Isn't it terrible the happiness of millions being decided in that way while for the last two months we were praying and begging the Council to give us time.

On the 28th of June 1919 he lamented in his diary: "It has all been horrible ... To bed, sick of life."

And that was his view of the treaty. Now I think, unless anybody in the room wishes to bravely raise his or her hand in disagreement, I think we all agree that the Versailles peace settlement was a disaster and a disaster in many different ways. But the question is exactly why these talented, able, knowledgeable people assembled in Paris made such a complete mess of the process? Now it is obvious that it failed in imposing a lasting disarmament regime on Germany. It failed to do anything for Germany's political stability. It failed to establish an acceptable basis for German relations with other countries, and it failed above all to implement the hopes for self-determination raised by President Woodrow Wilson. Now why?

During August 1914 the British author and social commentator H.G. Wells had written a book: *The War to End War*. The phrase caught on. And indeed it became axiomatic that the peace agreement also had to be a peace agreement to end war. This rhetoric and self-righteousness was a problem associated with modern warfare. The rhetoric of the war to end war contributed to the impossibility of the burden of those at Versailles. It was supposed to be the arbiter of a permanent peace and in fact it would not be unfair to call Versailles *the peace to end peace*. During the war many allied leaders and many others made impressive statements about the post-war order. I just mention two because they both address self-determination: V.I. Lenin, who took Russia out of the war, and Woodrow Wilson. Despite the differences between them, not least in their views of liberalism and democracy, both recognised the collapse of great empires as the central fact of their time. Both saw the power of self-determination as a rallying cry during and after the First World War. And if the collapse of great empires is the central theme of the day, the principle of self-determination is probably bound to arise as an alternative organising principle for international relations. Both of them, however, proved willing to ride rough shod over the principle that their rhetoric might have suggested. Neither of them can have been said to have developed a thorough and consistent theory about the place of self-determination in international politics, and least of all about how in practical terms it was supposed to be implemented.

I don't have time to go into the limits of the key visionary in this respect, who was Woodrow Wilson, who played such a key role in the conference, other than to say that although he stated the contrary, he did not have a clear vision of self-determination. In fact, the fourteen points did not mention self-determination at all. And some of his other proposals also did not mention it. It came to be mentioned as a principle in a diplomatic note that the United States sent to the Austro-Hungarian Empire indicating America's support for national self-determination of two peoples: the Czecho-slovaks and the Yugo-slavs. And of course in both cases it is deeply questionable whether we are talking of peoples in any meaningful sense. In both cases the States created on the basis of those hyphenated nationalities have since divided up, in one case tragically. So the principle of self-determination from the start was poorly articulated and theorized, and there was no sense of how precisely it was to be implemented. It was exciting rhetoric and appealed to peoples across the world, while contributing to the growing anti-colonial feeling in many empires. And yet because of its imprecision, because of the lack of awareness of looming tragedy in the resolution of many national issues, it contributed to the problem as much as to the solution.

Now, the story of the peace conference has been covered so well in many histories that I will pass over it hastily. Margaret MacMillan, in her wonderful book *Peacemakers,* has said that the German treaty was finished but many others were not, that there were many loose ends. Russia's borders were still fluctuating; it wasn't clear which States of Russia's periphery would keep their new independence: Finland, Ukraine, Georgia, Armenia. In the wreckage of empires in the center of Europe the borders were still disputed. One could go on about the lack of definitive conclusions of a range of issues. Not just in the Paris peace settlement itself but also in the many associated treaties that were coming up as the peace conference continued after the departure of Woodrow Wilson. Now, typical of the issues that arose at the peace conference and one that simply could not be resolved was the issue of Palestine. As Margaret MacMillan says: "No decision was made on Palestine, and it barely came up at subsequent meetings of the peace conference, as so often happened in Paris. An issue that was to cause increasing trouble over the years was scarcely treated at all."

One of my favourite figures in modern British colonial history is Gertrude Bell, an archeologist, spy and adventurer who revelled in the wonderful title that could have been dreamed up by Edward Said of *Oriental Secretary.* She attended the Paris peace conference and she wrote in a letter to a friend: "Oh my dear, they are making such a horrible muddle of the near East, I confidently anticipate that it will be much worse than it was before the war ... It is like a nightmare in which you foresee all the horrible things which are going to happen and can't stretch out your hand to prevent them."

Gertrude Bell was a considerable expert on Mesopotamia, modern Iraq, and she hung around the Peace Conference as part of the British delegation. However, she never got asked for her expert advice, and that of course was typical of the process.

The difficult issue of collective security was addressed inadequately at the Paris Peace Conference. As an English specialist on international relations Martin Wight wrote in his book *Systems of States*: "It is amusing and at the same time sobering to reflect that the League of Nations system of collective security was written into the Covenant of the League of Nations without any suspicion of knowledge on the part of Woodrow Wilson ... that it had been tried repeatedly in international history."

This idea had indeed been tried repeatedly in international history since the 15th century, and that is another criticism that can be made of the Paris Peace Conference: the lack of historical awareness. This at least can teach one a certain kind of prudence about how one addresses complex international issues.

First of all, the League of Nations Covenant's provisions were notoriously weak. The powers had been unable to agree on a procedure for decisive action so one can find weak phrases in many of the articles about what is to be done when there is a violation of the peace. But more than that, the League Covenant and the League system itself suffered from the dreadful problems that:

a) not all powers were represented. There were huge omissions in its membership, including of course the United States
b) it was perceived as, and it was to an extent, a European colonial project dominated by the British and the French which suffered from the limitations of their vision on how the world should be ordered.

From the moment the Peace Treaty was concluded it was heavily criticised, not just from the inside by Harold Nicolson, but from the outside. John Maynard Keynes, later to be famous as an economist, and whose ideas indeed we could do with a bit more often in Britain today, already in 1919 published *The Economic Consequences of the Peace,* which sold a 100.000 copies by the following July. Its focus was firmly on the question of the reparations that Germany was expected to pay. It was widely viewed as pro-German and therefore anti-French. The degree of criticism of Versailles was also itself a problem because from the moment that Versailles was tainted goods, there was a reluctance on the part of many of the powers, with the possible exception of France, to actually enforce implementation of its provisions.

And that is part of the tragedy that led to World War II. To summarise some of the awful effects of Versailles: in Germany it contributed to right-wing and militaristic approaches to politics, it led directly to the Kapp Putsch in 1920, happily defeated, but also of course to Hitlerism. Versailles was a center-piece of their criticism of the international order. It led to the Franco-Belgium occupation of the Ruhr and to the terrible German inflation which until modern time we didn't manage to excel. That inflation was astonishing. I have in my pocket a Reich banknote for 20.000 marks that has the precise date of issue on it of 20 February 1923. Within months they had to substitute millions for thousands. If anyone wants to give me 10 euros for 20.000 marks, they are very welcome.

Then, the effects in Asia were no less serious. In Japan, ever conscious of its achievements and its right to the same respect accorded to many white powers, the settlement got off to an awful start. Japan sought, partly for opportunistic reasons of its own, to include a racial equality provision in the League of Nations Covenant. In fact, Japan did at the time engage in racial discrimination of its own, both domestically and internationally. The proposal was vehemently opposed in Paris not least by the British and the French, but also by the Australians. The refusal to grant it was deeply damaging. It reduced the chance of full participation on the part of states that saw themselves as anti-colonial. And it had directly disturbing implications for the future of Japanese policy.

One of the Japanese representatives in the delegation was Prince Konoe. Prince Konoe had already written an article calling on the Japanese to reject the Anglo-American-centered peace. He was reinforced in his views by everything he experienced in Paris, particularly of course the failure of the racial equality proposal. He was in many ways a liberal-minded intellectual, very cultivated, very thoughtful as well. He was Prime Minister in Japan when it took the fateful decision to engage in military force in China in 1937, which was a direct link. In China too, there is a close link. As Rana Mitter has written in his wonderful new book about China's war with Japan. He said: "Under the Treaty, Germany had to give up its territories on Chinese soil. The Chinese assumed that the territories would be restored to the young republic as a reward of the efforts of nearly a 100.000 workers who had been sent to the Western front in World War I ... The Western allies turned out to have made simultaneous secret agreements with both China and Japan. In one of them Japan's actions on the international stage were wreaking havoc with China's internal politics." The effect of all this in China was a deep distrust because the provisions actually implemented reverted all the areas in China – internationally controlled areas – to Japan and not China. So the Versailles Treaty succeeded in inducing total distrust in both of those Asian countries.

Let me conclude by suggesting why Versailles was so disastrous in so many ways:

1. Where empires were collapsing all around, the problem of establishing a post- imperial order was inherently difficult and yet the inherent difficulties had not been drawn to the attention of the public in a way they should have been.
2. The fact that the principal powers in Paris were constitutional democracies did not help because it was popular opinion particularly in Britain that demanded punitive reparations.
3. The passivity of Woodrow Wilson on a wide range of issues including reparations meant there was a vacuum at the heart of the conference, and various rivalries between England and France came to dominate the conference. He was utterly vague about how self-determination was to be implemented in particular cases.
4. There was a disconnect between the rhetoric of self-determination and the procedures of the Paris Peace Conference. The continuation of the European empires in Africa or Asia was the most blatant example of that.
5. Despite Wilson's and Clemenceau's claims that Paris had attracted delegates from all the civilised peoples of the earth, this was far from being the case and contributed to the lack of legitimacy of the outcome.
6. The attempted device to create a constitution for the world was breaking new ground and was bound to be imperfect. It was unnecessarily weakened by being tied to a controversial treaty, rather than free-standing as the UN Charter is, and also by the facts that it was drawn up in ignorance of the problems of previous attempts and that it reflected the status quo and the interest of status quo powers.

7. From the start it was evident that there were difficulties in getting States to back up with force either the outcome of Versailles, or the international order more generally.
8. It was simply not possible for any conference to arrange such a vast array of problems. It was hubris on the part of the Allied leaders to think that it could be done.

This leads me to a simple conclusion, which is in the form of a question: Which post-war arrangement worked best: the one after World War I, carved out and made with massive publicity by a huge conference, or that after World War II, where there was no general peace agreement, at least not until the Helsinki Final Act of 1975, which was about as different as it could possibly have been in its structure, in its procedure and its contents from the Versailles settlement of 1919?

FIGURE 2 *Citizens of Paris celebrating the Versailles Peace Treaty, 1919.*

CHAPTER 1.2

Commentary: Randall Lesaffer, Tilburg University

My commentary will be rather on the Peace of Versailles than on the paper presented by Sir Adam Roberts. But by way of comment on his 8th point, I would like to share this thought. On 20 September some dozen people gather in a room not so far from the center of The Hague and by noon they start to sign a few documents. These documents constitute the Peace of Rijswijk, and the year is 1697, today exactly 316 years ago. They think they have ended all the major issues of the 9 years' war. A great conflagration among European powers. But 3, 4, 5 years later there is another great conflagration, the war of Spanish succession which will end in the Peace of Utrecht, because of one of the major outstanding issues they could indeed not cover in one single conference.

The Peace of Versailles is one of the most reviled peace treaties in diplomatic history, the peace to end all peace indeed. But strangely enough perhaps, the history often refers to it as epochal, as central in international law, but not with the same negative undertone. Perhaps this is another example of the discrepancy or *décalage* between law and reality that Martti Koskenniemi spoke about yesterday in Utrecht. Why do some historians of international law refer to the Peace of Versailles as an epochal event? Because in its first 26 articles it lays down the Covenant of the League of Nations, and thus starts a new era. It may be the false start of the institutionalisation of international society and the false or weak start at least of collective security.

I will look very briefly now at the place of the Peace of Versailles in the *longue durée* of peace treaties from a legal perspective. In the Western tradition, one can say roughly that there are two types of peace treaties: compromised peace treaties and punitive peace treaties, sometimes referred to as Carthaginian peace treaties. The Treaty of Versailles would, in great contrast with most preceding peace treaties of the 16th, 17th, 18th and 19th centuries, fall under the category of punitive or Carthaginian peace treaty.

From the perspective of law, one could also say, at least since the late Middle Ages, that in doctrine, and I claim also in state practice, there have been two conceptions of war and two conceptions of peace, which

Van Hoogstraten, Schrijver et al. (eds.), The Art of Making Peace: Lessons Learned from Peace Treaties
© 2017 The Editors. Printed in The Netherlands. ISBN *978-90-04-32123-6. pp. 19-23.*

are contingent to these two conceptions of war. The one conception of war, which originated from medieval Roman law and was then developed in the 16th, 17th and 18th centuries into, for instance, the work of Vattel: *La guerre en forme / War in due form*, the legality of war is a war that sees war as an instrument which serves as a substitute for legal trial. There is a conflict about an object, about a cause between two parties, and they cannot negotiate their way through it. In the end, war is a substitute for a trial in the absence of a higher authority or somebody having jurisdiction over them. War will, in the end, decide the dispute or the peace negotiations which are of course partly always based on the outcome of the war. War is indiscriminate in the sense that it doesn't oppose a just and an unjust side, but it opposes two sides that have a right to wage to war. They both benefit from the laws of war, they can make conquest for instance, and they can take booty. Peace is indiscriminate in character and it will in the end settle the issues on the basis of the outcome of the war and of the negotiation process, and not on the basis of the prior justice or injustice, legality or illegality of the claim, the territory, or whatever they were fighting over.

A just war, which of course goes back to theological and canonist traditions that are also assumed by Roman law in the late Middle Ages, sees war as sanction, war as a reaction to prior injury, to a prior immanently wrongful act by the enemy. War is here the enforcement action to sustain a pre-existing right. And war is discriminatory in this concept. In theory at least, only the just side can benefit from the laws of war and, for instance, make conquests. At the end of a just war should stand a just peace which is close to a punitive peace. A just peace according to Vattel has to attribute the object of contention to the just side, not necessarily the winning side, and make the unjust side liable for all the costs and damages of the war.

These are the two traditions of peace treaties and although it is sometimes said that in the 17th, 18th and 19th centuries the tradition of just war disappeared, it never really disappeared from doctrine.

Actually, as many have indicated over the last years in scholarship, the early modern law of nations is inherently dualist in character and the concept of war is that too. There is the concept of just war in the natural law, which in the end binds you in conscience and if you are a believer, it will lead to the last judgment in the end and will be enforced by God. And there is a concept of legal war, war in due form and its connected legal peace, which under the positive law of nations has legal effects in the here and the now. This duality is reflected in practice. All over the 16th, 17th and 18th centuries and to a large extent, though with major differences, in the 19th century, States or princes still justify their decision to go to war in formal declarations of war or in less legal texts, and justify them in a kind of vulgarized understanding of just war. But we see that they do not attach legal consequences of the war in relation to the application of the laws of war or in relation to peace-making. So you could briefly say that when princes went to war in the 18th century they went to just war, when they were waging or ending it they were waging or ending a legal war. Meaning that of course the type of peace was compromised peace. And as said before, Versailles breaks with this latter tradition.

Two brief remarks on the 19th century. First of all, you see that in justifications of war, which less and less take the form of a formal declaration, but might be press statements, political statements in parliaments, letters and so on and so forth, that the same structure is still used. But much more often there is a slip from reacting against a legal wrong to reacting against a violation of interest or even of honor. And a claiming that one acts in defense, that prior violence is on the other side, and that the other side commits aggression.

And aggression starts to become, over the 19th century, the major bone of contention, the major reproach made to enemies, without of course – and we international lawyers know that – having a clear definition of what aggression is, which is of course another matter.

If we then go to Versailles, is it a return to just peace under a conception of just war? There are certainly some strong elements to indicate that. There is the famous article that lays the sole responsibility of the war on Germany and its Allies, an attribution of guilt in the end based on aggression and the violation of the sanctity of treaties. Loss of territory is not legitimated in terms of punishment, at least not in the legal text, which you could call a more traditional way of phrasing it. Then there are the famous reparations, the liability for costs and damages which is then reduced to the military damages, which are the logical consequence of actually a kind of just war application. There is criminal prosecution, one-sided for the former Head of State of Germany for his role in having started the war on the basis of aggression and the violation of treaties, the neutrality of Belgium. And criminal prosecution, one-sided for war crimes for German officials. Then there is what is typical for Carthaginian peace, military restrictions, which are actually only justified in terms of a necessary step to come to general disarmament, and less a punition in legal phrasing of the text itself. Here I do not refer to political negotiations around them.

Is this a return to just war? And the logic of just war and just peace? One could say at least partially through the introduction of reparation and the idea of criminal prosecution. The idea of reparation is a very opportunist move, but in the end it does re-enter Versailles in the logic of just war and just peace. Criminal prosecution is pretty innovative but it enters to some extent also the logic of just war in its natural law guise: you will in the end, when you commit unjust war in the late Middle Ages or following centuries, be punished, not in the Courts of an international tribunal but in the highest Court ever, namely that of God. That is not a conscious decision.

I would like to add that it is often said that it seems that Versailles revolutionized the use of *bellum* by all of a sudden accusing and laying responsibility on Germany for starting a war of aggression. But this concept of aggression as the central bone of contention has been long in the making. You could say that it was already high on the agenda when Frederic of Prussia in 1756 committed what had been reviled by then as a great aggression, by his attack on Saxony and Austria. What is innovative is not the fact that aggression, how ill-defined it was, gets this central role. What is innovative is that legal effects are all of a sudden given to it, and that the old distinction between the tradition of just war and positive international law is collapsed. Some have described this as the re-entrance of morality into the field of law. Looking ahead beyond Versailles, I would like to very briefly draw a few conclusions on the questions: Did Versailles start a tradition? What is the impact of Versailles?

First, let me say that Versailles, and this is a technical point, broke with the traditional structure of peace treaties, the organisation of peace treaties, the international structure of the text, and that it never really returned after that in the same way it had been done for centuries. Secondly, if you look at peace treaties of a Carthaginian punitive character with elements of reparation and criminal prosecution, the closest you come are the treaties of February 1947 between the Allies and Finland, Romania, Bulgaria, Hungary and Italy where you have some of these elements. Sometimes references are made to the settlement of 1991 between the United Nations and Iraq after the now so-called 1st Gulf War, then still called 2nd Gulf War. Of course, there are some elements of it, but in general you cannot say Versailles started a tradition. Except perhaps that it acted to some extent as a precedent for the ideas of criminal prosecution and the shift from indemnifications, money payments of the loser to the winner of the war, to reparations on the terms of justice. But in a very different context. Reparation and criminal prosecution revived after Versailles in a context of a much more institutionalised international community and under a very different concept of war, a different *jus ad bellum*, which is now certainly after 1945 a *jus contra bellum* and a context of a stronger collective security. In that sense Versailles contributed to that by the false start of the Covenant of the League of Nations.

But it also contributed by basically breaking with the logic of legal war. Perhaps the biggest contribution from that perspective of Versailles is that it broke with the logic of a legal war, it broke with a tradition rather than starting a new tradition. It is a kind of revolving door, Versailles, where it takes some elements of justice of war through the revolving door, but not 360 degrees but into another room, a room of a more institutionalised international legal community. First under the League of Nations and then, of course, after the 30 years' war of the 20th century, under the Charter of the United Nations. What it also to some extent helped change in that respect is the fact that for almost 3000 years, peace treaties were the dominant way of ending wars. Over the 20th century that dominance became less and less, and alternative forms of ending war came to the fore. That has something to do with the Covenant of the League of Nations and the new *jus contra bellum*. As the new *jus contra bellum* has blurred the lines between a state of war and a state of peace, the traditional function of peace treaties of clearly demarcating the line between the two, by dealing with the legal consequences and restoring the peace, has become obsolete as these problems now need to be solved in a very different legal context as well.

CHAPTER 1.3

Roundtable Debate

Dr. Benno Teschke, University of Sussex: I have a question for Sir Adam Roberts. You kindly ask us whether anyone could disagree with the statement that Versailles was a failure. I thought maybe the question is wrongly posed, because it may have been a failure in terms of peace, but I would think that it was a superior project of the geopolitical management of space that underwrote the success of Versailles, which was certainly a success for the Western powers. Let me just tell you why I think it was a success in terms of geopolitics and power. The British and the French empires were preserved and extended, the United States fortified its Monroe Doctrine and its influence in the Western hemisphere; the Soviet Union, not Russia, was contained and hemmed in through the creation of the *cordon sanitaire* running down from Finland to Anatolia around Turkey. The old regime empires, Germany, Austria and the Ottoman Empire, were cut up, partitioned, parceled out and distributed. So in the light of these wider parts of Versailles, it seems to me that we need to look at this not in terms of the intention of creating peace, which was a sub-aspect of it, but in terms of reorganising the world geopolitically in favour of the victorious Western powers. If you look at it through the lense of power-politics I think we can say, yes, it was a full blown success for the Western powers.

Judge Bernardo Sepulveda-Amor, International Court of Justice: Sir Adam Roberts indicates that the treaty was a disaster and he asks exactly what went wrong in the negotiations themselves. I would wish to continue the quotations referred to Harold Nicholson. He says, and that may explain what went wrong in Versailles: "Lloyd George is trying his hand at reaching a settlement with the Italians on the Adriatic treaty. They all sit around the map. The appearance of a pie about to be distributed is enhanced. Lloyd George shows them what he suggests. They ask for a Scala nova as well. And then Lloyd George says: Oh no, you cannot have that, it is full of Greeks. Oh no, I whisper to him (that is Nicholson), there are not many Greeks here. But yes, he answer: don't you see it is colour green? I have been realising then that he mistakes my map for an ethnological map, and thinks the green means Greeks instead of valleys and the brown means Turks instead of mountains."

Van Hoogstraten, Schrijver et al. (eds.), The Art of Making Peace: Lessons Learned from Peace Treaties
 ISBN 978-90-04-32123-6. pp. 24-30.

Lloyd George takes this correction with great good humor, he is as weak as a kingfisher. I thought it was useful to bring this to our discussion in order to explain what went wrong. Surely the statement and the officials gathered in Paris were to blame for the disaster? But perhaps there are other explanations also. I think that in 1919 the international community was even more under pressure than what we see right now. It was a very primitive society with a lack of institutions. No institutions were working there in order to properly establish a world order. What I would say is that in spite of that, there were a number of important contributions that we have to recognise.

Of course, realising that there is a long process of institutional building in the international community, it is also true in the case of nation States. Let me say that as a result of all this process of institutional building, there is what we call the institution of arbitration. Thanks to the conference in The Hague in 1899 and 1907 arbitration has become part of a normal feature to settle disputes among states and also, in some instances, among investors and states. Then the construction of other important institutions such as the League of Nations itself which was something that made an important contribution to the establishment of institutions. The same is true in the case of the Permanent Court of International Justice, something that did not exist beforehand. By this I mean the judicial process by which there is a peace settlement. There were other international organisations also established as a consequence of 1919, by that I mean the ILO and some other organisations, predecessors of the WHO and UNESCO.

On the question of other contributions related to principles, I think that the question of self-determination is important and that perhaps one can explain the decolonisation process after the Second World War as a consequence of the notion of self-determination. The concept of collective security is again an essential feature, but nowadays has properly evolved. Another matter that I would like to point out is the question of international criminal responsibility. Something that now is amply recognised, but that certainly meant a possibility of bringing a Head of State to trial as a consequence of his individual criminal responsibility. And then one last feature has to do with a very impressive development of the institutions of international law. International law is certainly not the same nowadays as in 1919. It is very impressive indeed how the Permanent Court of International Justice and the International Court of Justice have developed a system of law that somehow imperfectly, I have to accept, provides a strong possibility of helping in any peace process. I would just want to say that in spite of all the problems that have been mentioned, for almost 70 years we have not had a global war. Unfortunately, we have a multiplicity of small little wars and of course a multiplicity of domestic conflicts, which will require nowadays the art of peace-making for domestic conflicts by the international community.

Ambassador Hans Corell, Sweden: I definitely belong to those who think that the Versailles peace was a disaster. And I think there are two important lessons to be learned from the last century, the Versailles peace, and the way the aftermath of the Second World War was handled.

When I understood, being a legal counsel in the UN, that the US and the UK would attack Iraq, I got hold of two books on Lucius Clay and McCloy, who were the Americans in charge of the civilian administration in the occupied zone in Germany. It was a really interesting learning experience to read those books and the way they interacted with the local population. The understanding in Washington then was that we must create a partner of our former enemy, the Marshall Plan was launched and so forth, and there you now have Germany as a major stabilizing actor in Europe. And then we have the Helsinki Agreement that I was as a lawyer a bit suspicious of, as they translated already legally binding elements into political declarations. But over time I changed my mind. The reason was that I saw the political commitment on the part of those who interacted in the Helsinki process that gave birth to the CSCE, now the OSCE.

But now I come to my major point, the Berlin Wall comes down in 1989. Everything was almost forgotten. Did the West go to Moscow, did they sit down with the Russians and say: Friends, we have one thing in common, one interest in common here, we should not get into an armed conflict with each other. How do you view the situation? This is how we see it. There were some attempts, but not really as I would have expected a determined intent to create a *détente* between Moscow and the Western world.

I am so sad when we know from what happened in the last century that they didn't understand how to do this in a better way. On the contrary, it did not take long and I sensed that in the corridors of the UN that if they're not on board we will go for it alone and they started building rocket ramps in Poland and Czechoslovakia. As if they never heard about the Cuban crisis, the same thing, building rocket ramps, the enemy *côte à côte*, very close to the borders of your own country. I was so disappointed to not see enough statesmanship there, and then just by coincidence when I left Stockholm yesterday I was informed of a new edition of the publication called *New routes: Peace agreements, learning from past experience*, (3/2013), issued by an institute in Uppsala in cooperation with a peace research institute there, their website is www.life-peace.org.

Professor Laurens Jan Brinkhorst, University of Leiden: I think we are talking about two subjects: one is peace on the worldwide level. But directly following Versailles was the Second World War. We should pay attention in this framework also to the regional impact in Europe. We had the Morgenthau Plan, to reduce Germany to an agricultural power, we had Bideau who wanted to permanently structure in four powers, dividing Germany, and it took the Schuman Plan and Monnet to realise that within the European Union we come to the end of a road and the idea of revenge should once and for all be finished. We created the European Court of Human Rights and the individual as subject of international law was created there. So between Versailles and Helsinki and Dayton there is the creation of the European Union, in this present time maybe no longer so popular. The essential political dimension is one that has caused the EU to stand behind criminal justice, to stand behind Helsinki. I was at the time involved in the Helsinki process, which would not have succeeded without the active participation of Germany looking for a new future. It was not America, it was Germany and as a result also the European Union as such. I think we should not underestimate the European dimension with all its difficulties as a statement for the future of a new structure.

Mr. Sacha Obradovich, Serbia: Article 227 in the Criminal Indictment of the German Emperor was known as the beginning of the end of impunity of the Head of State, but at the same time was known in international criminal law as a missed opportunity for the early development of an international criminal judiciary because the formal indictment was never issued, as the German Emperor found shelter in the Netherlands, a neutral country. I am interested in learning about the aftermath of that affair. Whether the international community imposed some pressure on the Dutch government for his extradition? Or simply, was he left alone and forgotten? Maybe this is a question for Professor Lesaffer.

Professor Jaap de Wilde, University of Groningen: To the long list of failures I would like to add one which I think has still a lot of contemporary value: the problematic reliance on rational choice. With hindsight we can come up with these lists of things that go wrong. If you think of the analysis of the causes of World War I by the historian H.A.P. Taylor, who read really every diplomatic step that was taken. All these steps were rational, and the outcome was irrational. If we now listen to Professor Adam Roberts' analysis of the end of World War I you can say the same, all the steps were rational, but the outcome was irrational. There is something problematic with rational choice. People active in the processes think they are following a logic of consequences, that they have of course cost-benefit analysis, they look to what are the options, what are the chances etc. Whereas in fact they are following a logic of appropriateness. What is in their normative make-up in their institutional background that forces them to take some specific decisions and call them rational, whereas in the end they turn out to be something completely different?

Response by Sir Adam Roberts:

I have listened carefully to all the comments. I agree with a very large part of most of them. I shall just comment on two suggestions.

The first: Dr. Teschke about the superior geopolitical management of space at Versailles. If the prime aim of the British and French was the preservation of empires, then of course, yes, you could say they did ok, in the short term at least. They obtained League of Nations Mandates to govern several territories. The British found themselves saddled with what we now call Iraq, but they quickly found that they did not have a clue how to govern it and had to pass off the administration on the nearest group of Iraqis they could find. They had difficulty in seeing how it could operate as a State. Shades of 2003 were already there.

Actually it was a failure even in those terms. The preservation of empires, at least in the longer term, could not succeed. This was partly because the unleashing of the idea of self-determination at Paris contributed, as one of the other commentators said, to the anti-colonial movement. Think of Ho Chi Minh, hiring a suit, turning up at the Peace Conference, distributing a leaflet, but failing to get any access and reaching the same conclusions as the Japanese and the Chinese did. Whatever the talk of self-determination, you are never going to get any justice from this lot. Think of the tragedies, the anti-colonial wars that ensued because of this huge failure. So I am sceptical and actually from the point of view of the populations of Britain and France, maintenance of empire was considerably less important than the prevention of war, in which the conference failed.

And finally, I would like to comment on the interesting point about rational choice. I have to confess at this point that the historian whom you name, A.J.P. Taylor, was a tutor of mine when I was a student at Oxford University. He certainly impressed on me his philosophy that small acts can have big consequences, that accident has a big role in history and that pseudo-rationality of the kind that was described doesn't always produce rational conclusions. I completely concur with that and it is a warning for our own times. Think of the original, the beginning of the war that resulted in this rolling catastrophe. The Habsburg monarchy, faced with assassination of the Archduke, says they will stamp out terrorism at source in Serbia. They will strike at what they call the hornets' nest. Many of our governments, including my own, are committed to the doctrine that it is always best to strike out terrorism at source. I have not heard any of them mention that actually that was attempted in 1914 and it did not work out terribly well. We do need that historical awareness and I think overall the comments really reinforce this conclusion. If we have to be grateful to Versailles for anything, it is because we learned by bitter experience how not to do things. And Hans Corell was right to say that that lesson has impressed itself on many diplomats, including in the United Nations. There is a wonderful West Indian expression for this, which I think is, alas, true of how we all learn: *Learning by burning.*

Response by Randall Lesaffer:

Briefly three things. The major cause for the failure of Versailles in my view is the lack of consent, that the three winners brought overpowering force to the negotiation table, and partly from the American side also strengthened by a feeling of justice. The lesson from this is that if you make a punitive Carthaginian peace, you either will have to enforce it permanently, as the Belgians and the French did in the early 1920s but then failed of course, or you will need to have a regime change and have the new regime at the table at some point, which did not work either.

Institutionalisation yes, I think the great contribution of the 20th century in terms of institutionalisation of power politics of war and peace is in the Council of the League of Nations and the United Nations Security Council. However, in a sense this was not innovative as the Congress of Europe did the same thing, but only with great powers. The great change in the long run was the admission of smaller powers at the table who spoke the language of right over might. In the long run I think that socialised a lot of power politics.

Briefly then, Kaiser Wilhelm: was there much pressure put on The Netherlands? Let's say, not much, clearly. Just to illustrate, it was never in jeopardy according to the British, who were officially pressuring for the former emperor's extradition, that the Permanent Court of International Justice would be housed in this house.

FIGURE 3 *Children's tea party in London, 1919; festive occasion for the Treaty of Versailles.*

CHAPTER 1.4

Interview with Sir Adam Roberts

Otto Spijkers and Anneleen de Jong

Professor Sir Adam Roberts is Senior Research Fellow at the Department of International Relations of Oxford University. From 1986 to 2007 he was Professor of International Relations there. His research interests include international law, and the role of civil resistance against dictatorial regimes.

We asked Sir Roberts about the enduring impact of Versailles, in the broadest sense. What lessons can we learn – and have we learnt – from the disaster at Versailles? We discussed the need for peace agreements to have local legitimacy. And we discussed how calls for cease-fires, and actual cease-fire agreements (as distinct from full peace agreements), are often very problematic and controversial. Sir Roberts further linked processes of civil resistance against dictatorial regimes to events in Versailles and beyond.

AdJ: How did your academic career develop and lead to the insights that you gave us in the conference on the Treaty of Versailles? Who were important thinkers, what were important moments, that changed your ideas? Describe your development.

My development was very unorthodox. It began with a strong sense I had even at school that international issues were the ones that interested me. I remember I had a history teacher who encouraged me to write about any subject I liked to write about, provided I did it well. He was a heretic. I decided to write about the Crusades. Of course that theme of Western attempted imposition on the extra-European world, the theme of the Crusades, is very similar to a lot of what we have seen in recent years. As a student I was very dissatisfied that at university we could not do very much international history. It was mainly one king after another, one English king after another. I became somewhat of a rebel. I was very active in the anti-nuclear movement.

But gradually it dawned on me that it was no use opposing a defence policy if you did not have something to put in its place. People need some sense of security and there are some real threats out there. So I became

Van Hoogstraten, Schrijver et al. (eds.), The Art of Making Peace: Lessons Learned from Peace Treaties
 ISBN 978-90-04-32123-6. pp. 31-42.

interested in two big themes: one was the theme of civil resistance against foreign occupation regimes, non-violent resistance in which connection I got to know people studying the Netherlands resistance; another landmark theme was *defense in depth* against foreign occupation regimes, defense strategies planned by Switzerland, Yugoslavia and others.

So those were among the guiding moments in my development and of course there were many events connected with them, such as, I wrote a book about civil resistance against foreign occupation one year before the invasion of Czechoslovakia. And I was in Czechoslovakia immediately after the Soviet-led invasion because I was so interested in the Czech and Slovak resistance to it. Of course all these interests and the interest in Yugoslavia convinced me among other things of the curious role that international agreements, including peace agreements, play where for example there was an agreement in Czechoslovakia between the Czechoslovak leadership and the Soviet Union, an agreement for so-called normalisation, but it was a completely unequal agreement. The Czech negotiators had been arrested and taken as prisoners to Moscow to agree it. That is a classic example of an agreement that does not work. My interest in Yugoslavia confirmed my interest in international legal issues, not least because there was the difficult question, what is the international legal status of resistance to occupation regimes?

But above all I always had an instinctive preference for studying small countries rather than big ones, for looking at the position of the underdog, if you like. And that meant that I was by nature particularly suspicious of agreements whereby the great powers decide things, but without consultation of smaller parties. They usually don't work, I won't say they never work, but they usually don't work.

OS: One of the themes you have talked about is the connection between political transition and peace agreements. I am trying to make a link with Versailles. Is there such a link that this peace agreement helped establish political change in Germany for example, or maybe in Europe, or in the whole world? Can you make this link, that political change or the transition that is going on is somehow reflected in the peace treaties?

Absolutely. Peace treaties both reflect changing political ideas and forces, and then in turn contribute to those forces. The Peace of Versailles of 1919 did both. It very much reflected a belief that there had to be a grand new scheme. That after the *War to End All Wars* there had to be a peace that would be enduring, that would last. Otherwise, was it worth fighting the First World War if there was no enduring result? So there was that very strong vision of having to create a better world but also a lack of real interest in small states.

Some of the representatives of small States at Versailles, as well as some of the small States that were not represented at Versailles, felt badly betrayed by the peace settlement. There was Ho Chi Minh who was turned away from the Peace Conference at Versailles, and there was of course Germany that was not a negotiating partner and that was dragged in to accept the treaty. Many of the peace negotiators and President Woodrow Wilson of the United States used the rhetoric of self-determination. And yet if you were a citizen of Germany or Vietnam you would feel that you would have been left out of the party, that the festival of self-determination might be happening, but that you were not invited. In that way the Peace Treaty had dramatic effects on politics as well as on the frontiers and diplomatic arrangements.

And of course the biggest problem of all with Versailles was that the talk was the talk of self-determination, but the ongoing reality was that the colonial powers, mainly Britain and France, sometimes in the new guise or disguise of being the custodians of old imperial territories, were the leading powers in the League of Nations, and that was deeply damaging to the view of the post- World War I settlement. It was still seen as basically a carve-up by colonial powers.

OS: Especially if you look at the League of Nations' Covenant one tends to say that the old ideas won, they prevailed in the end. There is some evidence of new ideas, self-determination and independence of small states, but also there is a lot of this idea of empires, of mandate territories. Who do you think won, the old ideas or the new?

I think in the end the new ideas would triumph, but not in 1919, much later they would triumph. In the end it did prove the case that the old colonial system was meeting more and more opposition from within the empires and there was also some friction between colonial powers, but that was less serious. In the end the logic of self-determination prevailed in many of the European overseas empires. By the time of the 1950s and 60s, independence was being granted left, right and center to many of these countries. So in the end, these ideas that it was said were only one third accepted in Versailles, did come out on top.

OS: So this process started in Versailles?

It started before, one can find the idea of self-rule as being preferable to distant rule very strongly expressed in the 19th century in Italy, in Ireland the movement for home rule began in the 19th century not in the 20th. So the idea was around, but basically there was one part of its application by Versailles for which one has to have some sympathy. That is the breaking up of the Ottoman and the Habsburg and the German empires and the Russian, all the territories that were then left to be dealt with. What was the principle you could adopt as a basis for dealing with them? The idea of self-determination was obviously a natural principle. So if, let's say, Czechoslovaks or Hungarians were now in a position where they were abandoned by a collapsing empire and wished to set up their own independent states, self-determination is a good basis for doing that.

So it wasn't completely empty or hypocritical of Versailles to do that and of course many of the States that were set up at Versailles, they have been through endless difficulties since Versailles, but they do still exist in one way or another. Some have been divided up as Czechoslovakia has become two States, but on the whole they still exist. That is evidence that it was not a completely frivolous exercise.

AdJ: If you mention your interest in civil resistance, and put it next to your critique of the Treaty of Versailles, could one say there should have been in the Treaty of Versailles more attention to public information, to having the people involved in making the decisions and not having these made by those in power and imposed? Or was the time not ready yet?

I think the time was ready and it was necessary to ensure that any peace agreement had some degree of legitimacy from below as well as from above. And in some cases that was done through the means of plebiscites or referenda. There was that validation from below. It is not always easy because somebody has to make the arbitrary decision of what is an appropriate unit of self-determination. Is it right that the self-determination of the Saar area should be decided by the inhabitants of the Saar alone or by the inhabitants of the Saar and the French or the French and the Germans? These are not simple questions, but the principle of needing support from below seems to me to be absolutely clear.

There is a fault in a good deal of Western thinking about the whole subject of peaceful change, which is the fault that associates peaceful change largely with negotiated settlements, with arbitration, legal mechanisms, appearing to Courts, to the International Court of Arbitration, and so on and so forth. The idea of peaceful change has not generally encompassed popular movements and activities. In my view we had in 1989 an extraordinary example of peaceful change with the movements in Poland, East Germany, Czechoslovakia, Hungary, they contributed to, I won't say they caused, the end of Communist rule in those countries and that is not a form of peaceful change from the Court of Arbitration, or from on high through international negotiation, it is peaceful change basically from below and that seems to me one much neglected factor in international relations.

AdJ: So that could be one of the very important lessons learned?

Absolutely.

OS: Is that the kind of process that is typical of Europe or if you look at the Arab Spring today, is it an universal thing that oppressed or dissatisfied people suddenly go for their own government, at least have a say in how they are being governed? It is kind of striking that these sorts of revolts always appear in one region of the world and then everyone does it, and then there is another region in the world, and so on.

I am absolutely not one to say that there is a region of the world that is immune to Western political ideas or indeed to any political ideas. Likewise I would not say that there is a region of the world were civil forms of resistance are impossible, on the contrary. There is a long history of people who have said that there can never be democracy in Catholic countries, or in Asian countries. History has proved these people wrong. I wouldn't dream of going down that road or one like it.

What I do think is true is that every movement, just like every democratic system has to develop its own local roots and relate to its own local culture. Many of the successful popular movements against totalitarian rule have happened in cultures very different from our own. I am thinking of the revolt in South Vietnam in 1963 against the rather autocratic rule of a Catholic ruler who had been imposed on them, President Diem, and who regularly claimed in elections to have 99 % of the votes on his side, just like Communists did. And this was a popular movement caused by or sparked by the official act of violence of shooting in the central Vietnamese town of Hue, and it became a mass movement and resulted ultimately in the unseating of the president. And likewise in the Philippines in the 1970s, President Marcos was kicked out by a popular movement, after he had had one of his potential opponents assassinated. It's often an act of official violence that sparks these movements. It was a very effective movement of non-violent resistance against dictatorial rule. So my view is that these things can happen anywhere, but that they need to relate to local causes and local cultures, and that they do not just operate by copycat methods.

OS: Can you say anything general about how civil unrest starts and how it evolves? Are there any general rules that seem to apply to it in the Arab Spring or in the overthrow of Communism? Is there anything general you could say about these processes?

I think there are three things one could say about this.

1. These processes often follow an act of what seems to be an illegitimate act of violence by the regime. In Poland, for instance, there had been a number of workers killed in the Baltic ports in 1971 that led to the 1st wave of revolt because of trouble between the Baltic ports and the Polish Communist regime. Then again, in the mid-1980s, I remembered visiting in Poland the shrine of a Catholic priest who was killed by the regime, a man called Popieluszko. This killing of a priest had huge political consequences. An element of official recklessness and violence often contributes to opposition movements.
2. Another factor is that the outside world may in some cases provide a more favourable environment for change than it does in the case of a regime that has the unchanging support of outside powers. In the American imperium, the tendency is to support rather authoritarian figures because they are convenient, reliable, stable. But then if there is an impressive popular movement of civil resistance, then American opinion tends to sway against the previous supported ruler. I would say that in Russia's imperium, for example, as we see currently in Syria, there is more willingness to go on supporting an authoritarian ruler than there is in the American empire. That shows that in the Arab Spring that we have regimes thrown out, in Tunisia, and in Egypt. Whereas in Bahrain, with strong outside support for the regime from Saudi Arabia, it is much harder to get rid of a regime.

3. A third factor is that there has to be some notion of what kind of regime could be possible after a change. If there is a democratic tradition to fall back on, if there are well-recognised politicians who are not compromised by the previous regime and are plausible candidates for taking part in government, then the possibilities are much stronger than in cases were those factors are not present.

OS: Do they always end in a text, like a new constitution or some agreement between the warring factions? We lawyers like these things to end in proper texts.

Very often movements of popular resistance can only bring about a stalemate and then there is need for negotiation and hence the roundtable is a very common phenomenon of these movements. Roundtable talks in Poland in 1989, roundtable talks in South Africa towards the end of the Apartheid era, the roundtable conference in which the British government conversed with Gandhi in the early 1930s. These negotiations do sometimes lead to clear agreements, such as, for example, the roundtable meeting in Poland led to a new sort of constitution arrangement whereby there was a semi-free election and Solidarity candidates could stand. It wasn't in itself an enduring, new relationship because semi-free elections are only halfway to where Solidarity wanted to be. But they were quite right to accept that and to build a future on the basis of that significant concession. It turned out to be a compromise that needed to be made.

All of which means that it is actually very important that these popular movements have leaders because there has to be someone who can negotiate and sign, and make the necessary compromises and that can bring his followers with him. All of that is difficult but needs to be done. One of the many problems in Egypt has been a lack of clarity as to who exactly represented the Tahrir Square demonstrators. There was a very serious and powerful series of demonstrations, continuous set of demonstrations, and yet the leadership was always a bit of a tricky question. It made subsequent negotiations on the constitution more difficult because that does involve compromises, as constitutions always do involve compromises.

AdJ: If we describe the process as we do as a collective behaviour then there is a dominant from one side and resistance against, and a reorganisation of power relations. What do you think of preventive peace negotiations, or preventive diplomacy as one of the roundtable members of the conference, Professor Pronk, mentioned? Do you think that is possible or should we just let the organic process happen, occur, so to say?

There was a lot of discussion on preventive diplomacy various times in recent years. The idea is a very understandable one: not to wait until the crisis erupts, but instead to try and tackle problems at source. There are some difficulties attached to the idea of preventive diplomacy. One of which is that sometimes it is very hard for those involved in an exercise of preventive diplomacy to make concessions because they haven't tested the limits of their strength in any outside forum.

So, for example, everybody knew in former Yugoslavia in the 1990s that there was risk that Kosovo could be the next trouble spot. Everybody knew that there was a majority in Kosovo that was discontented with Serbian rule and yet it proved very difficult to focus the minds of Serbians on the need to make concessions to this, and equally difficult to get Kosovars to recognise that they too might need to make concessions if there were to do a deal with Serbia. Sometimes, I fear, these crises have to be acted out a bit before they can come to a resolution. It is a classic problem, well-recognised in many conflicts, by many UN diplomats who have been involved in successful peace negotiations as, for example, in many conflicts in Latin America and Southern Africa in the 1980s: that you have to wait, choose the right time to intervene, to try and resolve such conflicts. And that often means a time when some of the parties do recognise that they may need to make concessions.

For example, over the regional conflicts in the late 80s or from the earlier 90s onwards, many of the UN negotiators who were involved in addressing these, recognised that the Soviet Union was no longer supporting some of the movements they had been supporting previously. Therefore there was an opportunity to reach a peace settlement because the logic of a withdrawal of total Soviet support was that there was more need to reach compromise. Also perfectly correct calculations contributed to peace deals of one kind or the other in Nicaragua, in Guatemala, in Namibia and in South Africa. Not to mention, in a manner of speaking, and a more difficult case, in Afghanistan. I think that the idea that there sometimes needs to be a drama and a stalemate before there can be a final settlement is not without force.

AdJ: And then the cease-fire would be the first step. So you let the conflict go on, you see too many people getting killed, you get a cease-fire and then you can start the negotiations.

That is right. However, a cease-fire isn't a necessary preliminary condition for negotiations, not every time. It is very striking in the war in Bosnia-Herzegovina in 1995 the cease-fire was concluded in September before the actual peace agreement was concluded in the subsequent months. So cease-fires have considerable importance. But where I do worry about cease-fires is where they become a sort of automatic response of the international community to almost any crisis. Advocacy of a cease-fire can be problematic. I'll give just two examples of how they can be problematic. One is they can have the effect of making the parties rush to achieve gains in a war before the inevitable cease-fire comes into effect. We know from the evidence of the memoirs of a number of Israelis, including General Dayan, that that was a motivation in both the 1956 and the 1973 wars in the Middle East, this desire to make gains very quickly before a cease-fire comes in. So they can have a slightly perverse effect there.

But I think the bigger worry is sometimes the call for a cease-fire reflects an assumption that the cease-fire will be the best route to peace in every case. In one instance where I fear that was a wrong assumption was in Sri Lanka around the time of the eventual Sri Lankan victory in very difficult and controversial circumstances, when from a Sri Lankan point of view the call for a cease-fire looked perverse. They had the experience of a war between the Government forces and the Tamil Tigers, which had been going on for a quarter of a century. And irrespective of how one attributes the blame for the cause and continuation of the war, there was clearly a prospect by 2009 of the war being brought to an end by victory by the Sri Lankan forces. At that point for outsiders to call for a cease-fire seemed to be taking sides with the Tamil Tigers, at least that is how it was interpreted by Sri Lankan government officials. Now I disagree with the Sri Lankan Government on many things, including the way in which the war was concluded, but I do think that the call for a cease-fire was somewhat easily made by Western politicians as the easy way of sounding well-intended and progressive in relation to the Sri Lankan conflict when there was no chance that the Sri Lankan Government would actually accept a cease-fire at that point.

So I think one has to be very careful before assuming that a cease-fire is the correct response to all conflicts. I wouldn't be one to say *Give war a chance* in any general sense, but there are times when a conclusion of hostilities, and a clearly defined peace, can be achieved more quickly by the use of armed force than it can by having a cease-fire with no clear political settlement accompanying it.

OS: You do seem to suggest that sometimes it is better to let the strong party defeat the weak one instead of bringing them together.

In the case of Sri Lanka I think this is what I am saying. If you are going to end a war that was the only way in which it could reasonably be ended and I put this against the background of something which is more fundamental and perhaps for us more difficult to cope with. Almost all the conflicts that we witness today are conflicts that might be called post-colonial in character. They are conflicts which are precisely about the lack of legitimate borders, lack of a legitimate political system, lack of legitimate political rulers, lack of settled relations with neighbours and these are all really difficult inherent problems of post-colonialism.

Sri Lanka was in a way an example of that. One of the fundamental problems of Sri Lanka has to do with the recognition of the Tamil language and the lack of recognition of it in official policy, which was trying to create a unified Sri Lankan state where the first language would be the fully recognised language of the majority: Sinhala. These language issues as we see in the Ukraine today are absolutely fundamental and it is very difficult for a new State to work out a balance between the understandable desire for a unificatory language and the need to recognise the rights of minorities. These are tough questions.

OS: It is interesting that they often look to their coloniser to sort of try and find a solution even though the period of colonisation is highly criticised. For example, when Mali or the Central African Republic was in trouble, they looked to the French. I always find it interesting that for some reason they expect the former coloniser to come to the rescue, they should expect some kind of responsibility based on the past.

And of course the history of colonialism is itself very complicated and often involves this exact process whereby there may be disagreement between two local rulers, one of them wants to call for the Dutch or the British or whoever to support their side, to give that ruler some advantage in a local dispute, and out of that grows a colonial pattern of relations and influence. In that sense, the world we see today is alarmingly like the colonial world that we thought we had left.

OS: Do you think, for example, that France has a special responsibility towards what is going on in Mali at the moment? Is that a reasonable way to argue?

I think there is discomfort with the idea of merely recreating old colonial patterns and that is one reason why so often the United Nations gets drawn in with their presence, legitimating mandates, mandates that may determine the length of the mission etcetera in order that this is seen to be distinct from early colonial patterns of behaviour. But nonetheless one has to note that it is a curious fact of our present day world that the very powers, the British and the French, that are widely perceived after the Treaty of Versailles as having carried on their own colonial ways, including within the new League of Nations Organisation, are now among the most active military powers acting outside their own immediate spheres in ways which are not very different from the old colonialism. We should not pretend that things are other than awkward in that regard.

AdJ: Do you think from that perspective, something that we can also read in the centenary book on the Peace Palace that we gave you, that it is very important to have different international perspectives on international law, taking into account more pre-colonial concepts of peace and international relations? Do you think there would be a possibility in establishing these criteria that we discussed for what peace agreements should look like, that it has this very diverse aspect to it in order to avoid the Eurocentric criteria?

Absolutely, I think that is very important. The recognition that there may be any different types of justice systems not all of which might seem perfect to a Western audience, that is an idea we need to take account of. Famously in Rwanda, many people involved in the genocide came before *gacaca* tribunals rather than Western-style tribunals and it is not for me to sit in judgment on these tribunals and say which was the better.

But at the same time one has to note some factors in the other direction, like the curious fact that of the African referrals to the International Criminal Court about half are self-referrals by a State asking the ICC to handle a particular issue rather than being the ICC charging in and insisting on its presence or being mandated by the UN Security Council on a specific case. So clearly, for some African States dealing with some types of issue, there is a role for an international Court. At the same time as there is quite a strong concern about the way in which the international Court has focused overwhelmingly on African cases. This has left many in Africa feeling disturbed at what they interpret as a bias of the Court. So I think that issue of sensitivity to local abuse of justice remains important and I have to say that the more you dig down into national legal systems, the more various and different they are. Sometimes our own system seems very strange to people from a different background and culture. So yes, there is a need to pursue that issue.

PART 2

The Dayton Peace Agreement, Yugoslavia (1995)

FIGURE 4 *Signing ceremony for the Dayton Peace Treaty at the Elysée Palace in Paris, France, 14 December 1995.*

FIGURE 5 *Sarajevo, 24 March 2016. People watch the verdict of the ICTY for Radovan Karadzic on television.*

Introduction

The violent break-up of Yugoslavia began in 1991, when both Slovenia and Croatia issued declarations of independence. The move by Croatia led to a violent clash between the official army of Yugoslavia, dominated by Serbs, and Croatian forces. In April 1992, another Yugoslav republic, Bosnia-Herzegovina, took the step to claim independence. The Serb leadership of Yugoslavia did not accept the unilateral move, and the Yugoslav People's Army now began to focus its military action on Bosnia. This led to the outbreak of the Bosnian War, which formally ended with the Dayton Agreement.

The Dayton Agreement is a General Framework Agreement for Peace in Bosnia and Herzegovina, which was signed by representatives of the Republic of Bosnia and Herzegovina, the Republic of Croatia and the Federal Republic of Yugoslavia, on 21 November 1995, in Paris, France. The latter also signed on behalf of the Republika Srpska, a non-State entity situated in Bosnia. In the agreement, the parties pledged to recognise each other as sovereign independent States within their international borders. The parties also pledged to abide by their international human rights obligations, and to cooperate with the investigation and prosecution of war crimes, and other violations of international humanitarian law committed during the conflict.

Besides this, the agreement itself basically consisted of a list of references to eleven annexes attached to the agreement. These annexes dealt *inter alia* with military aspects of the peace settlement and regional stabilization; the demarcation of the boundary between the Federation of Bosnia and Herzegovina and the Republika Srpska; elections in Bosnia and Herzegovina; the drafting of a new Constitution for Bosnia and Herzegovina; and the establishment of an Arbitration Tribunal, a Commission on Human Rights, a Commission on Refugees and Displaced Persons, a Commission to Preserve National Monuments, Bosnia and Herzegovina Public Corporations, and an International Police Task Force.

CHAPTER 2.1

Keynote: Abiodun Williams, The Hague Institute for Global Justice

Ladies and Gentlemen, it is an honour for me to discuss with you the peace-making and peacebuilding lessons provided by the case of Bosnia-Herzegovina. It is a country where I served as a UN political officer, and a country that remains close to my heart. I am most grateful to Nico Schrijver and Steven van Hoogstraten for their kind invitation and for their personal support since I assumed my new role in The Hague Institute for Global Justice months ago. It is a particular pleasure to share a stage once again with Marc Weller. My friendship with Marc dates back to our time at the Fletcher School of Law and Diplomacy, where we were Jessup Moot Court partners thirty years ago. So I trust that the discussions today will be equally lively.

Sir Adam's excellent presentation this morning on the Peace of Versailles evoked an era different in many respects from the mid-1990s. In the surroundings of the Peace Palace, the centenary of which we are marking with this conference, we are moved to recall that in 1919 the hope of peace provided through the international rule of law was in its infancy. In 1919, warfare was considered a matter between States, as the Great War had just demonstrated. And in 1919, my own country – the United States of America – was both a reluctant player in world affairs, and ultimately absent from the attempt to craft world peace. And yet, despite many of the differences, Sir Adam's speech reminded me of the similarities between these two moments: Dayton and Versailles. These were after all moments where the affirmative stance of an international community, ready to cooperate to avert the horrors of preceding confrontations, held real promise. These were eras where the US stepped into a leading role on the world stage, whether for the first time in the first decade of the twentieth century; or as the unrivaled global power, as in the wake of the Cold War. And both Versailles and Dayton represented and affected geopolitical change.

While the ramifications of the Bosnian peace cannot match in world historical significance those of 1919, the challenges which the implementation of Dayton presented to the international community fore-

Van Hoogstraten, Schrijver et al. (eds.), The Art of Making Peace: Lessons Learned from Peace Treaties
© 2017 The Editors. Printed in The Netherlands. ISBN *978-90-04-32123-6. pp. 46-53.*

shadowed many of the questions that have since confronted the UN, its leading member States, and countries affected by conflict:

- Should peace agreements in States that have experienced sectarian strife prioritize the retention of old borders or countenance secession?
- How should post-conflict States and their international guarantors sequence imperatives, such as providing basic security, fostering the rule of law and developing effective institutions?
- What was the role of the international community, both in enforcing the peace, and in terms of Bosnian long-term stability and reconstruction?

As a peacekeeper serving in the Balkans, both before and after the Dayton Agreement, I grappled with these and other questions. At the beginning of the Dayton process, US Secretary of State Warren Christopher gave a hint of the complexities that would follow the peace, by laying down some important conditions for a settlement. In response to the question on many lips, he affirmed that Bosnia had to remain one State. A settlement, Christopher argued, should take into account the special history and significance of Sarajevo, human rights should be respected, and those responsible for atrocities had to be held to account. Reconciling these sometimes contradictory aims would be no easy task, nor was the promise of action by the international community so strong at the conclusion of the Cold War. Holbrooke, who, together with former Prime Minister of Sweden, Carl Bildt, brokered the Dayton Agreement, later remarked that the international response to events in Bosnia had been at best uncertain and at worst appalling. The credibility of the UN had been so severely weakened by 1995, that it was not even invited to Dayton. Over the subsequent eighteen years, the record of the international community has continued to be mixed. But within the provisions of the Dayton Agreement, and in the manner in which it has been implemented, there are important lessons that can be discerned by international actors for future engagement in the wake of civil war.

In my remarks, after introducing the Dayton Agreement, I will consider the military, political and economic dimensions of stabilization and peacebuilding in Bosnia, both in text and in deed. I will conclude by offering some lessons of the experience in Bosnia, and by suggesting how the peace of Dayton, through commission as well as submission, can contribute to future peace-making activities.

What Dayton represents remains a contested issue. For some, the agreement was a minimalist one, essentially designed to put an immediate stop to a deadly conflict. For others, the accord established a wide-ranging mandate for long-term peacebuilding activities, with the aim of consolidating the peace and preventing relapse into violence. Was Dayton, in the words of former High Representative Lord Ashdown, merely designed to end war, not to build a State? Or did the multiple annexes to the agreement, comprising an agenda for State building, represent the heart of the accord? I will argue today that this apparent dichotomy draws us into a false debate. Dayton was designed to accomplish both ends, to provide an immediate end to conflict, and to realize the promise of long-term stability.

This forum is not the occasion for a lengthy overview of the conflict or its conclusion. So I merely note the context which drew in the international community in a decisive way. A military stalemate on the battlefield; the severity of continued campaigns of armed violence; and particularly the emergence of atrocities that shocked the conscience of the world. It was against this background that Operation Deliberate Force, the NATO bombing campaign which began in August 1995, served as the coercive instrument in support of ongoing diplomacy, spearheaded by US envoy Holbrooke, to force the parties to the table.

As many here will be aware, while the Dayton Agreement – the peace treaty that emerged from international diplomatic and military pressure – preserved the territorial integrity of the Bosnian State, the agreement created separate political entities, comprising the federation of Bosnia-Herzegovina. Though the State structure is highly decentralized, there remains a rotating State presidency, a central bank, and a constitutional Court. Moreover, no entity can leave the State outside the legal process.

Beyond establishing a new political structure, the other primary concern of the Dayton agreement was to allocate international responsibility for the implementation of the stabilisation and peacebuilding portfolios, detailed in various annexes. Responsibility was divided between five principal organisations, an arrangement which was at the root of subsequent criticism. Dayton provided the international legal basis for the deployment of a military presence led by NATO, in and around Bosnia, to ensure that conflict did not recur. The OSCE was charged primarily with running independent elections and advancing democratization. The UNHCR was responsible for humanitarian efforts, in particular the return of refugees and internally displaced persons. The UN mission in Bosnia Herzegovina, UNMIB, retained only a thin slice of the international mandate, albeit an important one: responsibility for police restructuring, police reform and assessment of the judicial system. And the office of the High Representative was charged with overall political and institutional coordination.

With the background to the agreement now established, let me first address the military dimension. Securing a safe environment on the ground was an obvious challenge for the implementation of a peace agreement. And the primary means were the tasks set out in the annexes of the accord. The requirements detailed included a ceasefire, the disarmament and demobilization of combatants, the promotion of confidence building measures, prisoner exchange, and most importantly: the deployment of a multinational military implementation force. This NATO mission became known as IFOR, and initially counted some 60.000 troops. It was established to ensure the compliance of the warring parties – Serb, Croat and Bosniak – with the provisions, and was granted a flexible but well-defined mandate. Despite some operational challenges, this force, now an EU mission, was instrumental in maintaining security and preventing recidivism upon the cessation of hostilities. The mandate given to IFOR was a strong one, and reflected the stake NATO had in ensuring that Bosnia did not relapse into conflict. Its general successes suggest some elements that should be repeated by similar forces:

- First, formulate a clear but flexible mandate with short and long-term goals;
- Second, demonstrate military resolve from the outset, and an ability to respond robustly (in Bosnia, this was initially hampered by the one year mandate which the USA originally imposed on the international force, providing incentives to spoilers to simply wait out the interveners);
- Third, establish disarmament, demobilization and reintegration programmes for the combatants;
- Fourth, reform the security sector, both military and police, to build capacity to resolve local disputes;
- And fifth, harmonise military and civilian operations, so that they reinforce each other.

It is this final recommendation, civil-military coordination, or at the very least effective communication between international forces and civilian bodies, which was the clearest weakness of the military dimension of the Dayton paradigm. Unable to count on the enforcement capacity of the military, civilian activities tended to rely on less powerful means of persuasion, including financial aid. The lessons of the civil experience in Bosnia have already been applied in other post-conflict contexts.

Let me turn now to the political and legal dimension of Dayton implementation. As the peacebuilding experiences of international actors of the past two decades have demonstrated, the consolidation of a safe and secure environment is dependent not only on military stabilization, but also on progress towards the establishment of accountable and equitable institutions, as well as the development of the rule of law. This was an understanding reflected in the annexes of the Dayton Agreement, which emphasised, as Christopher had done, the centrality of legitimate State institutions to sustainable peace. The prescriptions of the agreement are familiar to those engaged in post conflict situations: free and fair elections; constitutional revisions to ensure democratic institutions; and respect for fundamental human rights. Importantly, and at the heart of its legacy, Dayton also called for the establishment of a central State with representative constituent entities. Here again, the record has been mixed. The balance struck between the central government and respective entities has often been an uneasy one, with weak central authority, exacerbating progress towards reforms in other areas, such as fighting corruption. The popular acceptance of the rule of law, a concern not absent from Dayton's provisions, but perhaps not adequately prioritized, has been slow. An obstacle acknowledged by Lord Ashdown, who remarked in 2002 that in hindsight the establishment of the rule of law should have been put in first place. Everything else depends on it: a functioning economy; a free and fair political system; the development of civil society; and public confidence in the police and in the Courts. Ashdown added in 2002 that we would do well to reflect on this, as we formulate our plans for Afghanistan and perhaps Iraq. Yet in Bosnia, despite justified criticism, the achievements of the political settlement set down by the Dayton Agreement should not be too readily discounted. Following a conflict where two million people had been displaced, the peace did after all facilitate the increased movement and return of internally displaced persons and refugees. Elections, though arguably held too soon, have since been generally free and fair, and have expanded political and social participation. Over time, the central government has expanded its functions. At the local level, police reform, first undertaken by the UN international police task force, and later by the EU police mission, have made significant strides towards developing an effective professional and accountable police presence in Bosnia. And despite a slow start, justice has been served to many of those responsible for the most egregious human rights violations and international crimes, in large part thanks to the tribunal based in this city (The Hague). Political and legal successes, as well as failures, suggest lessons which have become familiar for peace-builders, but which have but all too rarely been implemented in practice:

- Rule of law promotion should take priority, once minimal security conditions have been achieved. Reconciliation between the former warring parties depends on this, and on the advancement of a culture of criminal justice.
- Free and fair elections are important, though rushing to the ballot boxes can be counterproductive. The result has been the consolidation of ethnic identities and the growing propensity of Bosnians to vote for nationalist candidates, undermining the development of a cohesive multiethnic state.
- More important than full and immediate representation is the effectiveness of political and judicial bodies as well as public confidence in them.

The final dimension of the Dayton Agreement is the economic one. Conflict, as Collier has famously stated, is development in reverse. And the imperative of rebuilding Bosnia and stimulating growth was an evident one for the international community. The conflict had left local infrastructures degraded, and financial institutions no longer functioned, or operated solely in support of a war economy. The economic reconstruction, which was undertaken in Bosnia, underpinned by international donors, and with the lure of EU accession as an ever present beacon on the horizon, tackled some of the stagnation that resulted form conflict. Prior to the global financial crisis, both real wages and real GDP increased steadily. A common and stable currency was established, a custom system was integrated, and substantial banking reforms were undertaken. Today however, the general feeling in the region is that activities undertaken in the wake of Dayton have done too little to foster genuine economic opportunity. Moreover, given the weak political framework within which economic reforms were undertaken, the gains of growth have too seldom been enjoyed by the Bosnian people at large, as corruption remained an endemic problem. The economic rejoinder to Dayton is an alarming unemployment rate, high levels of poverty, and a cumbersome environment for international investors, linked to ethnic divisions and the political arrangement between the central government and the separate entities. The absence of employment opportunities for erstwhile combatants is a matter of particular concern, as are the roadblocks to efficient provision of basic goods and services linked to the investment climate. Economic setbacks in Bosnia are a structural conflict risk, which ought to be addressed. International actors could have done more to create employment opportunities, and to open the economy to outside investment.

As my remarks have suggested, the military, political, legal and economic lessons of Bosnia since the Dayton Agreement have been an important source of learning for the international community, which continues to engage in peace-building activities. It has been heartening to see wider agreement on the interlinkages between development, security and rule of law; a relationship which was stressed by my former boss Kofi Annan, in the landmark report *In Large Freedom*. The report memorably asserts that there will be no development without security, and no security without development. And both development and security also depend on respect for human rights and the rule of law. Working in Bosnia during the post-Dayton years with Kofi Annan and the UN, and in other contexts affected by conflict including Haiti, I have been struck by the lessons that the Bosnian peace provides for those confronting post conflict situations. Indeed, it is for this reason that the institute I now head, *The Hague Institute for Global Justice*, launched, here in the Peace Palace, two weeks ago, the *Hague Approach*: six principles for achieving sustainable peace in post conflict situations. The Hague approach draws on the lessons of Bosnia, as well as situations like Afghanistan and Iraq, that Ashdown identified would be presented with similar challenges. In suggesting tools to prevent the recurrence of conflict, foster a rule of law culture, work through networks and engage the private sectors, the principles will, I hope, be of use to those planning international peace-building operations like the mission in Bosnia.

To my mind, there are four key lessons from Bosnia which have informed the Hague approach, and which peace-makers and peace-builders should bear in mind:

- First, get the timing right. As the initial one year mandate granted to IFOR demonstrated, stakeholders in Bosnia discovered that attaching unrealistic deadlines compromises the integrity of certain undertakings.

- Second, ensure that the resources are sustainable. Peace-building in Bosnia has cost billions of dollars. We spent seven billion dollars in the first years after Dayton. International partners must be prepared to commit both human and financial capital willing to sustain their efforts.
- Third, strike the right balance in international engagement. The Office of the High Representative was criticised for excessive involvement in domestic matters, but on other times it was needed by local partners to make the necessary substantive changes. International engagement ought to be balanced judiciously with demands for local ownership.
- Fourth, coordinate effectively. Dayton's biggest handicap was the institutional arrangement it bequeathed to actors in Bosnia, whereby separate organisations were given responsibility for each annex of the Dayton accords. Exacerbating this was the overall institutional weakness of the civilian side, which coordinated poorly with the military. The High Representative was given no real coordinating role or independent authority, creating a leadership vacuum. This diminished both the legitimacy and effectiveness of international action. Far better would be to work dynamically through a peacebuilding network, avoiding arbitrary silos. Determining clear leadership, backed by an international mandate, creates accountability for peace-building activities.

Ladies and Gentlemen, Dayton, as I alluded to in my introduction, was the product of a unique moment in history. It ended the fighting through negotiation, not capitulation. The price of this negotiated peace was that a protectorate could not be imposed, even though with hindsight a protectorate of limited duration would have been the most effective and quickest way to implement peace and bring war criminals to justice. Although Dayton experiences problems in its implementation, and was in certain ways flawed in its conception, it was nevertheless a historic achievement. After three years of horrific violence, the maintenance of peace in Bosnia, since 1995, has been more than many had hoped for. And that is, in the final reckoning, the ultimate test of the agreement's effectiveness. It is my hope that with continued effort, as well as commitment of more time and resources, the aspiration of Bosniaks, Croats and Serbs to live in peace will be consolidated and that the menace of conflict will soon be as alien in the Balkans as it is in the rest of this continent (Europe) which is now my new home.

CHAPTER 2.2

Commentary: Marc Weller, Cambridge University

Thank you very much, Chairman. Thank you to the magnificent Nico Schrijver. I thought this was going to be a conference about the art of peace-making, but I now understand it is a class reunion. So thank you so much for bringing me together with my friend Dr. Williams, after about 30 years. And I am particularly pleased that it has fallen upon me to offer some brief comments in relation to his excellent presentation.

I propose to say a few words on Dayton particularly, but you have all received what I think the organisers call "the reader", where in fact I have stolen my own thunder by telling you everything one could possibly say about Dayton. And I know that you have, over the coffee break or possibly overnight last night, been studying the documents sufficiently vigorously that it will not be necessary for me to go through all of that. Also because Dayton really is one of the most overstudied episodes of peace-making in some ways. And I fear that some of the conclusions I offer in the short paper in the commentary may not be entirely unfamiliar to you. But in the first part of the presentation I shall pick out some of these points very briefly. I shall then turn slightly more generally to the other two aspects: first, the science of peace-making, and then the art of peace-making, based on the Bosnian experience.

The Chairman reminded us at the outset that for some decades the organised international community has committed itself to preventative and early action in relation to conflicts of this kind. Dr. Williams has described what kind of conflict this was, involving extreme violence, and techniques of warfare that are horrendous and entirely unacceptable. After some months, it could have been possible to anticipate that a conflict of this kind would not be easy to settle through conventional means. Nevertheless, the traditional international adherence to the doctrine of non-intervention, and the attempts to engage in diplomacy of quite a traditional kind, manifested by Lord Carrington – and later we had my own efforts and those of others – proved fruitless. By the time that NATO decided to intervene forcibly, it was something like an intervention of limited scope of five days that ended three plus years of intense human suffering, involving the destruction of 100.0000 lives

Van Hoogstraten, Schrijver et al. (eds.), The Art of Making Peace: Lessons Learned from Peace Treaties

ISBN 978-90-04-32123-6. pp. 54-59.

– there are various different estimates – and which left half of the population of Bosnia-Herzegovina displaced. So one of the issues that arise is not only early action, but perhaps confidence in the predictions of those who try to analyse conflicts of this kind, as to whether traditional means of settlement may be appropriate, and the willingness to consider other means. The Dayton peace conference in itself did not really bring peace. It was the use of force that changed the calculations of the actors on the ground, to the extent that they could be forced into a peace settlement under very unusual circumstances, locked up in a faraway air-force base for weeks on end, with the only source of food the hamburger joint of the ever hungry air-force crews. This was clearly very different from the experiences of Rambouillet, where at least they gave us a château.

Next, I will address the issue of the substance of the settlement. We heard that it was a geopolitical realignment of borders, or of the balance of power in Europe, that was at issue. I am not so sure whether that was the key issue in relation to Bosnia-Herzegovina, and the Dayton settlement. For me, it was an issue about international rules and principles relating to statehood. Can ethnic groups become States? It was an issue of denying territorial change, brought about by ethnic cleansing and other grave violations of the international legal order; of insisting on the maintenance of the territorial integrity and political independence of a State so threatened; and perhaps an issue of trying to deny the principle of the ethnic constitution of States. Dayton succeeded, at least in a kind of shell form, to try to remain committed to those principles, although the paper argues that underneath that shell, perhaps the implementation of the settlement did not quite achieve those aims. I already mentioned the unique tools that were employed in this context: the pressure cooker of Dayton that resulted in the agreement, the unusual composition of the participants – it was not really the protagonists who were represented, but the external sponsor States that had to come to an agreement. This is in itself already an interesting and telling comment in relation to those who argue that Bosnia-Herzegovina was a civil war, strictly speaking.

These were a number of unusual features and factors that come out of Bosnia-Herzegovina. Now let us turn to the other issue of the substantive approach to the settlement. We heard a moment ago that Dr. Williams referred to the bipolar nature of making international peace, but at the same time establishing the constitution for a new State. Being at an air-force base in America, it sounded sort of slightly far-fetched that this could be achieved. Perhaps the lesson to be drawn is that, if at all possible, you should try to divide the tasks of conflict settlement and State-building. Yes, by all means one could outline principles that a necessary constitutional element has to address. But perhaps we ought to delay the actual constitution-making, and allow those directly concerned a larger voice in the process. What kinds of tools were deployed in this venture of defining a constitution for a fundamentally divided State?

Conflict-settlement through power-sharing – and this was the great moment for the theoreticians of ethnic conflict. This was the great moment for con-sociationism: the idea that the visions they had been proposing of quite an extreme form of power-sharing could now be deployed and prove themselves. And the lesson that comes out of Dayton is that you may have to start with a consociationist type of settlement, but you need to make it dynamic and allow it to develop into a more integrationist mode over time. You do not want to be locked forever more in a settlement that emphasises ethnic division rather than providing incentives for inter-ethnic cooperation.

The issue of accountability arose in relation to the implementation. Dr. Williams referred to the role, not of the UN really, but of the Peace Implementation Council. This was a kind of self-appointed body of States, that granted powers to the High Representatives of Bosnia-Herzegovina. These were powers of international governance, which on the one hand the local actors were criticising, but on the other hand the local actors were also demanding that in the end somebody at the international level should resolve the issues that they were unable to resolve themselves. So if such action was taken internationally, I think Bosnia-Herzegovina was the kind of point when the international debate moved to the question of accountability in relation to international governance. What kind of mechanisms are there to control, to make accountable, to establish the rule of law? So yes, we did manage to conclude the most violent and desperate armed conflict that had been raging in Bosnia-Herzegovina. And all of those, including myself, criticising aspects of the Dayton settlement, must remain mindful and really thankful for this. On the other hand, the underlying issues of ethnic relations have not really been addressed to this day. Last time I was in Sarajevo, there was a palpable kind of tension. There were issues of constitutional reform that revealed that the ethnic sides had principally remained within the kind of positions they had held some twenty years ago.

But let me now move on to a few lessons on the science of peace-making, and then the art of peace-making, which are based on the Bosnian experience, but also drawn in part from my involvement in other peace settlements elsewhere. Talking about the science of peace-making, of course, as Martti Koskenniemi this morning indicated, we immediately have to visit the East Coast of the USA, and start using acronyms like BATNA and ZOPA: Best Alternative to Negotiated Agreement (BATNA), and Zone of Possible Agreement (ZOPA). Peace-making is not the same as trade negotiations. It is somewhat different because war is the BATNA. War is, in view of the actors, the best alternative to negotiated settlement. And that of course does raise issues that are of concern to the organised international community as a whole. It is quite a special element of peace negotiations. And what is the zone of possible agreement? What if the one side says: "I need to remain the president;" and the other side says: "We accept any settlement providing you don't remain the president"? It is difficult to see how you can have a zone of possible agreement there.

But, of course, the trick is to *create* a zone of possible agreement, to bring the actors to see that they have interests that are not merely manifested in those two opposing and perhaps unresolvable positions. The trick is to convince them that there are issues that, in the longer term, they want to see safeguarded. For example, the right of their constituencies always to be represented in the State, irrespective of who is the president; or the ability to be safe, to have access to economic opportunities, not to be disenfranchised and perhaps even at a later stage to retain a political structure that can capture power peacefully through elections. So one of the tools of the trade is to reframe the issue, in order to try and move out of what appears to be unresolvable antagonistic positions. That would be the East Coast, or Harvard kind of approach to peace negotiations. But that requires rational actors, actors who follow us, actors who we try to explain why it is that their true interest is not reflected in the position they are desperately clinging to in the negotiations we are trying to encourage.

The answer has to be to change the BATNA, to change the calculation that war is the best means of implementing the interests of the constituents. This can be done ideally by building incentives. The organised international community can hold a large conference, saying "If only you sign on the dotted line, billions of dollars will flow your way which you can use for reconstruction, for development; a glorious future awaits you!". On the other hand, to remove Allies that help to sustain the conflict, to reduce the availability of weapons, or to change – through military means. as happened in Dayton – the calculation that a particular side will win the conflict, if only it persists in the use of force. The issue, and here we are coming closer to the *art* of peace-making, is an emotional one. At the level of the social entities involved, where nationalism has been used to fuel and sustain a conflict, how do you engage the thing that has been built up during a conflict and that no peacemaker, that no leader of that respective group, will want to violate? It is the thing that they have to somehow respect. But also in relation to the individual leaders, to somehow give them the dignity that allows them to take the decisions that are very difficult for them. How to explain to, say the President of Yemen, that a mere forty years of him being president have brought untold benefits to his country, but perhaps now would be a useful point in time to "take my hand and walk with me over this bridge," and allow new elections to take place where perhaps he would not stand as a candidate?

So this leads us into the kind of personal relationships that the mediator would need to build, in relation to those who the organised international community sometimes might not wish to embrace or even consider particularly attractive. And finally, if nothing works, we need to mobilise alternative constituencies for peace. We need to try and build the middle ground, and include those who actually suffer the actual effects of violence, and those who might not be represented by what sometimes are leaders representing quite a small segment of often their own economic interests, and who wish to remain in power because they fear what will happen to them if they are no longer in power. Sometimes refusing an agreement is a means of trying to ensure that personal safety and wellbeing is not endangered.

Let us proceed a little further within the one minute that the Chairman indicates I have, to address the art of peace-making. Holbrooke famously said: "Peace-making is like jazz, you have to listen to the other instruments and improvise." Well, I do think it is a mixture between jazz and carefully crafted composition. You do need to pay attention to some of the analytical requirements, in terms of conflict analysis, the understanding of the environment of the conflict, and the personalities of the mediators.

What other factors? The leadership. Who defines the core needs or interests of the relevant constituency involved in the conflict? Where you have a Dr. John Garang, who is powerful and respected as a national leader, and has a clear vision, it is possible to make peace in the Sudan. When you have an ever-proliferating number of armed opposition movements that purport to represent Darfur, it is probably very difficult to achieve a similar result.

External actors. There is the international community, the Security Council. I am now rushing through points I would otherwise have expanded upon.

The style of the mediation. Must you choose a consensual or a more dictatorial style? This must be matched to the relative demands of the situation.

Must you always insist on one single mediation route? In the Libyan case, we had a competition between the UN and the African Union, which inhibited the ability to generate one clear strand of mediation.

And finally, the impact of lawyers. What do we as lawyers contribute? One of my own experiences has been that early drafting of elements of agreements helps. They may never be used, but they give tools to the mediator which he or she will certainly be able to utilise. It is better than just presenting options if you put something into a draft which you would not share with anyone. And if they ever leak to the press, it would be a disaster. In several cases, we found it extremely useful, and in some cases the lawyer's draft actually did in the end become, with modifications, the agreement.

What is also useful is the ability of advisors, or lawyers such as us, to draw in experiences of other cases and to try and see how this episode fits into a broader pattern of development. You see the development from Dayton, through power-sharing, through Rambouillet, through the constitutional framework for Kosovo, to finally the so-called Ahtisaari-document. We can identify a learning process of how to manage power-sharing and consociationist techniques in a way that they can be more productive. And finally, of course, the legal advisors insist on calling on principles that must not be violated through a settlement. In the UN context, we have UN principles we would rely upon. But also fairly firm guidance on issues that need to be pursued. And we need to be mindful of lines that cannot be crossed, for instance in relation to amnesties and accountability, in relation to women's issues, treatment of the vulnerable, etc.

CHAPTER 2.3

Roundtable Debate

Dr. Paul Meerts, The Hague: I would like to probe a little bit further on the question of peace and justice. The problem is if you want Mr. Kony of the Lord's Resistance Army in Uganda to have a peace agreement with us, and he knows we are going to take him to the International Criminal Court, then he would probably walk away into the woods, and peace will not be signed. How do you deal with that? We gave Ben Ali of Tunisia an apartment in Paris, and this solved some problems in Tunisia. Are we also going to offer an apartment in Moscow to the Syrian President Mr. Assad?

Professor Djamchid Momtaz, University of Tehran: J'aimerais revenir sur la disposition figurant à l'annexe de l'Accord de Dayton qui interdit aux parties d'accorder l'amnistie aux personnes soupçonnées d'avoir commis des crimes au cours des conflits armés qui se sont déroulés sur le territoire de l'ex Yougoslavie. Il s'agit là d'une nouveauté puisqu'elle va à l'encontre de la disposition pertinente du deuxième Protocole additionnel aux Conventions de Genève relatif aux conflits armés non internationaux. Cette disposition recommande en effet aux autorités au pouvoir d'accorder la plus large amnistie possible aux personnes qui auront pris part au conflit armé, ceci en vue de favoriser la réconciliation et garantir la paix. L'inclusion de cette disposition dans l'Accord de Dayton se justifie par le souci de lutter contre l'impunité des personnes responsables des crimes les plus odieux. Impunité, qui, selon le Conseil de sécurité, constitue une menace pour la paix. Cette idée, sous-jacente à la mise en place par cet organe du Tribunal pénal international pour l'ex Yougoslavie, a été reprise six ans plus tard par les rédacteurs de l'Accord de Bonn qui mettait un terme à l'ère des Talibans en Afghanistan. Néanmoins, le président Karzaï, considérant que la lutte contre l'impunité constitue un obstacle à la réconciliation, sera amené à accorder l'amnistie générale à toutes les personnes présumées avoir commis de tels crimes. La question qui se pose en définitive est celle de savoir si la justice à tout prix peut être considérée dans tous les cas comme une garantie de paix ou si des assouplissements devront y être apportés compte tenu des circonstances qui prévalent dans chaque cas particulier dans le but de tourner la page et favoriser la réconciliation.

Van Hoogstraten, Schrijver et al. (eds.), The Art of Making Peace: Lessons Learned from Peace Treaties
 ISBN 978-90-04-32123-6. pp. 60-66.

Sir Adam Roberts, United Kingdom: Just three points that have emerged from listening to these two excellent presentations. Both presentations really were informed by what was going on in Bosnia-Herzegovina.

The first thought I have is: one principle might need to be added to what you said about negotiations. This is the need to avoid the leopard spots approach to territorial settlements. Think of all the hours, days, weeks that Lord Owen and others spent trying to work out a territorial arrangement within Bosnia, and with different zones looking like the leopard's spots. It was very similar to what had been attempted by UN intermediaries in Palestine in 1948 and 1949. It just doesn't work, and I think it was well forgotten at Dayton. Thank goodness.

A second conclusion is that when you mention that timing was all-important, as indeed it is, it is not just the timing within the settlement, but it is the timing of the negotiations. You implicitly accepted this point already in your presentation – but I think it needs underlining. After all, these negotiations happened not just after Operation Deliberate Force, but also after the Anglo-French deployment of the rapid reaction force outside Sarajevo, which actually ended the siege of Sarajevo. And also we have to mention the expulsion of Serbs from Croatia, which contributed hugely to the Serb sense that they were facing defeat. It is only when a party to a conflict begins to realise that its ambitions cannot be achieved, that there is an opportunity for peace. So there is the timing lesson that comes in.

And the third lesson I would draw, and this really adds to what the presenters were saying, is the quality of the detailed follow-up. This is all-important in a wide range of issues. I was very struck – I took part in some election observation missions myself, including one in Bosnia-Herzegovina – by the quality of the OSCE's work in this particular area. The OSCE may not have a wonderful record overall, but they certainly do know how to organise and monitor elections. And you could see and feel how the rigor of the method of election monitoring actually impressed itself on the people, who actually were carrying out the elections in Bosnia-Herzegovina. And that detailed quality, the attention to a wide range of practical matters, is what makes the follow-up work.

Mr. Hugo Siblesz, Permanent Court of Arbitration: I think I have been invited to this conference as Secretary-General of the Permanent Court of Arbitration. But my question and comments relate more to my experience as a former Dutch diplomat, involved in the early nineties in the conflict created by the breakup of what is now the former Yugoslavia.

My question is: do you believe that Dayton provided the proper tools to address the underlying issues, or was it more a matter of implementation? I am stealing the thunder in a way of Dr. Barney Afako, who is going to speak later today on the Sudan, by taking a very important line out of his presentation, which reads that "No peace process can be indifferent to the history of the conflict that it seeks to resolve." Well, the history of Bosnia-Herzegovina goes back further than 1991 or 1992. In my view, what happened in 1991 and 1992, in the context of the breakup of Yugoslavia, was a decision taken by outside actors – the EU, OSCE, UN – who decided that the former constituent republics of Yugoslavia would become, under certain conditions, independent states. Some say that this had to do, at the time, with the possibility of the breakup of the Soviet-Union. The breakup of Yugoslavia, other than by recognizing the republics as independent States, would have set a very infelicitous precedent. In any event, what was then decided by outside powers, was an outcome that was contested by some in Bosnia-Herzegovina, and defended by others. To sum up: I think what is at stake was the refusal to live under the same roof. Peoples claiming different ethnicities, for one reason or another, were refusing to live under the same roof. So my question is: do you believe that Dayton provided the tools to lead to that cohesive multiethnic state?

Ambassdor Hans Corell, Sweden: Maybe in this context I should first mention that I was a War Crimes Rapporteur in Bosnia-Herzegovina back in 1992 and 1993, and we presented the proposal for the statute of the Yugoslav tribunal that was handed over to the UN. I have three quick points.

The first point is personalities. I cannot stress that enough. One of the problems with the Dayton agreement was that there was one person involved who wanted to make a name for himself. When I look at peace negotiations, and those who assist in such negotiations, I think the real contributors are the ones people may not even know of. They just simply disappear into the woodwork. Your task is to bring the parties together, and when there is an agreement, it is the parties and their representatives who should shake hands in front of the TV cameras, because that gives legitimacy on both sides to the agreement. I cannot stress this enough, and I have seen this in different contexts. Also: the sooner you start drafting, the better. I have one personal experience of chairing a committee in a completely different continent. Four members of that committee, and I was chairing that group, immediately started drafting, and then they told me whether they agreed or not, and used the square bracket method. It took just three days until we had a paper that was so solid that it could be brought to the attention of the principal negotiators at the top level, who could then come to an agreement. I cannot stress this enough: the personalities, and the ability to bring them into the forefront, not the negotiator or those who tried to get involved.

Number two: the protection of minorities. This was part of the Helsinki process of 1975. And when the Berlin Wall came down, what had become priority number one on the agenda was the protection of minorities. I cannot stress this enough either. Once you change borders, you have to look after the minorities, because they are the ones that suffer. If you draw new borders, there will be a new minority that needs protection. I think of the Kosovo situation, for example. When Serbia was governing, there was a minority of Albanians. If you turn it around, you have a minority of Serbs in Kosovo.

Lastly, Dr. Williams mentioned the rule of law. When I look back at my years on the bench, in the Ministry of Justice and the Foreign Office, and ten years as Legal Counsel of the UN, if I look at any conflict in the world, the issue is always the same: there is no democracy, there is no rule of law. And this, I think, is the most important element that we have to address for the future. There was a topical discussion among former heads of state and government in 2008. This gave birth to an idea to develop a guide for politicians on the rule of law. And since we are in The Hague, could I say that this was an excellent cooperation between the HiiL and the Raoul Wallenberg institute in Lund in Sweden. This Guide has now been published, and it is now being translated into between ten to fifteen languages. It is available online at: http://rwi.lu.se/wp-content/uploads/2012/09/Rule-of-Law-a-guide-for-politicians.pdf.

Mrs. Ida Van Veldhuizen, Netherlands Institute for Multiparty Democracy: What you hear sometimes is that the Dayton Agreement should be revised, or maybe it should be supplemented. So my question is: is there a necessity, or is it feasible, to change or amend the Dayton agreements? Or is it so that Bosnia-Herzegovina will have to live forever, or at least for many more years, with the present text and the annexes?

Dr Sarah Nouwen, University of Cambridge: Dr. Williams moved us from peace-making onto peace-building. But that also opens up a whole range of questions. Let me ask just one: what do we mean by "peace"? When there is reference made to the *Hague Approach* to peace-building, what frame of peace underpins this approach? In the current literature on peacebuilding, there are three dominant approaches. One is the liberal peace-building model, which, for instance, underpins Dayton. Keywords are: rule of law, the State, human rights, individual rights, and Statebuilding. But peace-building and State-building are not necessarily the same. In Somalia, we have seen that the pursuit of building a State did actually the opposite of peace-making. Somaliland did not pursue a State, and was quite successful at peace-making.

A second approach, which we see in our Ministries of Foreign Affairs, where peace-making units now being transformed into stabilisation units, is to equate peace with stabilisation. Here the keywords are: anti-terrorism, law and order. But this may be accompanied by the suppression of all kinds of liberal institutions. So the two paradigms of peace clash.

The third paradigm of peacebuilding could be seen as promoting social justice. But social justice and law and order, or the liberal peace model, do not always coincide either.

So my question is: considering that there is a *Hague Approach* to peace-building, does it fit with any of these three frames? The references you made are mostly within the liberal framework. But how is attention being paid to the other two? And how does the *Hague Approach* recognise that peace itself is a hugely contested concept?

Response by Abiodun Williams:

I just want to say that I am grateful for all the comments and observations and questions. I cannot do justice to all of them. Let me just highlight that I agree with much that has been said. Let me touch on three points.

The first was about the tension between peace and justice. I think ultimately, of course, there is a realisation that it is two sides of the same coin, really. You cannot have peace without justice. And you cannot have justice without peace. But having said that, it does not take you all the way. And what one sees now, and I am struck by it, having just moved to The Hague, is the growing tension that one sees between the international criminal prosecutors on the one hand, and the peace negotiators on the other. The international criminal prosecutors believe that there are certain people who have blood on their hands, that cannot be negotiated with, and should not be negotiated with. And then there are the peace negotiators who understandably believe that sometimes you have to deal with really reprehensible characters in order to get a peace agreement. So there is a challenge, a task to bring these two communities together. They are both in a sense trying to achieve the same objective, but in separate ways.

The second point I would just touch on is about Dayton and whether it really provided a basis to create a multiethnic State. I think here I would just say that the record is mixed. It is the question which faces many post-conflict States: do you have secession, or do you keep the territory as it is and maintain territorial integrity? Dayton succeeded, of course, in preserving the territorial integrity of the Bosnian State. But I think, because the rule of law in particular was not a top priority at the outset, what has happened is that the result has been the consolidation of ethnic identities. And you see it in the growing tendency of Bosnians to vote for nationalist candidates, which is undermining the development of a cohesive multiethnic state.

And then just the third point: about the conception of peace. What is the conception of peace that underlies the *Hague Approach* which I mentioned? I would just say that I think a narrow conception of peace would hold that peace is only about the preservation of order. But I think the view that underlines the approach is a broader conception, which says that peace is not only about the preservation of order, but also about the promotion of justice, which involves protecting and promoting a fabric of rights and responsibilities relating to human rights.

Response by Marc Weller:

Three quick points. First about the relationship between peace and justice. Amnesty: for the UN, the issue is quite clear. The guidelines which the UN has issued say that there cannot ever be UN involvement in, or endorsement of, a blanket amnesty relating to crimes against humanity, war crimes, genocide, sexual violence and other widespread violations of human rights. That does limit what UN mediators can do, but the guidance is very clear. There are occasions where situations of awkwardness arise. For example, in Yemen the Gulf Cooperation Council proposed a peace deal connected to a clear blanket amnesty for President Saleh, and all those who worked with him. This is quite a broad category. The UN was involved in the implementation mechanisms for that initiative, which in the end led to the cessation of violence. That was really only possible because the amnesty was included in a separate instrument. The UN could not have endorsed that particular instrument.

And then about leopard spots. Yes, it is odd to stand up for the principle that the ethnic composition of a population should not equate to a claim to territory in accordance with that ethnic composition, but at the same time to divide the territory according to who lives in that particular pocket of territory. That approach appears discredited. This also shows the importance of minority issues. If you do assign territory on the basis of ethnicity, you need to remember that there will also be other ethnic groups within that territory. They need to be provided for, and their protection and advancement needs to be secured effectively.

And finally, timing. In Bosnia, other factors – besides those mentioned already – might have been: the military effectiveness of the Bosnian armed force; the creation of the Croat Muslim Federation; and also a crucial element was the imminent collapse of the arms embargo, which would have been the first instance when a mandatory Chapter VII Security Council Resolution was at risk of being disowned by key States who just could no longer bear complying with it. The negotiations must begin when the dispute is ripe for resolution. Perhaps we could say that, analytically speaking, some disputes are not quite ripe for resolution. Outsiders might say, for example, that in Syria neither of the sides is presently ready to come to a zone of possible agreement. The government thinks it has won, the opposition thinks in the long run it will win, or must win. Can they come to an agreement? But on the other hand, the level of violence is so high that a body like the UN cannot afford to stand by and wait for ripeness. You somehow have to try and help generate a peace process. And perhaps having a process can help bring the parties to seeing that a peaceful alternative might after all better preserve some of the core interests, which they are at present pursuing through the use of force.

PART 3

The Sudan Peace Agreement (2005)

FIGURE 6 *2005 Sudan Peace Treaty, which was meant to end the long civil war.*

Introduction

The conflict between the North and the South of the Sudan is at least as old as the country of the Sudan itself. Many attempts have been made to resolve the conflict. Sometimes the parties came close to realising this goal, for example in 1972, when the Addis Ababa Agreement was signed. This agreement formally ended the First Sudanese Civil War. Unfortunately, due to a failure to live up to this agreement, the parties resumed the fighting, and the Second Sudanese Civil War began. In an attempt to stop the fighting, the Intergovernmental Authority on Development (IGAD) initiated new peace talks in the mid-nineties. These talks ultimately led to the Comprehensive Peace Agreement (CPA) for Sudan, signed in Nairobi in January 2005.

The CPA essentially consists of six agreements, all signed between the Government of the Sudan (Khartoum) and the Sudan People's Liberation Movement/Sudan People's Liberation Army. The former represents the North, the latter the South. The first agreement was made in Machakos, Kenya, already in 2002. It was decided to tackle the difficult issues first, and thus this protocol dealt, *inter alia*, with the right to self-determination for the people of South Sudan (the organisation of a referendum). This first protocol was followed by five others, all made in Naivasha, Kenya, in 2003-2004. All these protocols needed to be brought together into a comprehensive peace agreement, which would then serve as a permanent cease-fire, and would thus constitute a formal end to the conflict between North and South (the Second Sudanese Civil War). After some setbacks, the Government of the Republic of the Sudan, represented by First Vice-President Ali Osman Taha, and the Sudan People's Liberation Movement/Sudan People's Liberation Army, represented by its Chairman John Garang, concluded the Comprehensive Peace Agreement in 2005.

CHAPTER 3.1

Prelude: Peace and Its Confluences, a Short Story by Jamal Mahjoub

Whenever I visit Khartoum I find I am at my most content when simply wandering the streets. The dust, the crazy, jigsaw geometry of decay, the broken pavements, the slabs of concrete that seesaw over the drains, the yellowed neem leaves that glow like golden embers in the sand. I've been writing about this country for almost thirty years and am still no closer to understanding the enigma of its malaise. It is a place that has grace and beauty. One that can produce greatness in art, in thought, in music. Yet these qualities seem condemned to bow in the face of the relentless, destructive forces of greed, race, religion and sectarianism. The cruel and the stupid triumphing over the generous and the sublime.

When I first came back, in 2008, after almost twenty years away, I had no idea what to expect. I imagined a city that I could no longer recognise. I was astonished to discover how much had not changed. Or so it appeared at first. The old centre had become a ghost town. The shops that weren't shuttered were dark and gloomy places, selling odd curios that spoke of another age; crocodile skin handbags and carved ivory animals for a non-existent tourist trade. The neon signs were cracked and faded, the letters thickly laden with dust. The elegant coffee houses had become dirty, neglected shells, their furniture reduced to plastic crates and broken stools. Around these lingering traces a new commerce had sprung up, quick and mobile. The arcades I recalled were now peppered with itinerant merchants, many of them from the South. They spread their shoes and belts, shirts and underwear out on the ground in the cardboard boxes that had carried them from the South China Sea.

On the way into town one day I noticed a couple of young girls working their way along the lines of cars waiting at a busy junction, one pushing the other. The eldest one, who sat in a wheelchair, was about twelve years old and had lost both her legs. They rode up and down, stopping beside each window to hold out their hands. What was striking was how carefree they both seemed, despite their situation. Their faces were bright and cheerful, as if this was some kind of a game, racing between the cars begging for change. They were a vivid reminder of a war whose consequences were rarely glimpsed in the capital.

Van Hoogstraten, Schrijver et al. (eds.), The Art of Making Peace: Lessons Learned from Peace Treaties
 ISBN 978-90-04-32123-6. pp. 70-76.

The 2005 Comprehensive Peace Agreement closed the book on twenty-one years of war that had cost millions of lives. It laid the steps towards consolidating peace and would culminate in national elections and, perhaps more importantly, a referendum that would allow the South to opt for secession. Over the six-year interim period the country was to be ruled jointly by a Government of National Unity, ostensibly preparing the way for a united nation at peace with itself. But already, three years into the interim period, it was becoming clear that little progress had been made. The taxi driver who was with me when I saw the girls at the traffic junction on Mek Nimr Street told me that the southerners had no business here and the sooner they went back to where they came from the better.

'What if they don't want to go back?' I asked.

'That's all taken care of,' he assured me confidently. 'The CPA gives them six years to sort things out, after that they are on their own. We have nothing to do with them and they have nothing to do with us.'

As we drove on, the two girls settled themselves down under a tree to wait for the lights to change. When I was a child we used to drive along this road every morning to go to school. A different age, and perhaps, in retrospect, a more tolerant one. The Addis Ababa Accords of 1972 put an end to the first round of the civil war. They provided the South with a degree of autonomy. At the time the star of Socialism ruled over the country and although it was not trouble free and certainly ended badly, it was a period that allowed the country to achieve something close to nationhood, albeit briefly. The failure of the North to fulfil its commitments and a gradual erosion of trust, led to the outbreak of hostilities again in 1983.

That taxi driver reflected the view of many in the capital. Northerners viewed Southerners as lazy inferiors who drank alcohol and fraternised with the opposite sex. As non-Muslims they were seen to lack the moral code of Islam. Added to that was the historical burden of times past, when Southerners had been traded as slaves. And that time had left deep traces. The common term for Southerners was still *abd* – the Arabic word for slave. The irony was that the country needed the South now more than ever. Without the revenue from oil exports Sudan's economy was non-existent, an unmitigated disaster weighed down by billions of dollars of foreign debt. Some 80% of the oil reserves lay in the South.

Since the CPA came into effect Khartoum had been riding a wave of unprecedented prosperity. An era of stability and steady economic growth that was largely due to the oil revenue. High prices on the world market and direct foreign investment in the country meant that GDP growth climbed to a peak of 10% in 2007. The boom years produced a new class of well-heeled Sudanese who were unrecognisable to me. Like second rate Gulf sheikhs they clogged the streets with their new cars and sat around in chic cafés that served overpriced cappuccinos to the new urbanites. The influx of a foreign labour force to serve them only reinforced local perceptions of superiority; Filipina waitresses served their food, Turkish constructors built their buildings, Chinese maids cleaned their homes, Egyptians cooked for them. The boom largely served to hide the almost complete absence of any long- term economic strategy. Over-reliance on oil money combined with a lack of initiative and investment in institutions, education, healthcare, infrastructure, etc. left the country in a vulnerable state.

And while the CPA recognised the existence of different cultures, the real task facing the Government of National Unity was reinventing the notion of Sudanese identity to encourage cultural, religious and ethnic parity. It never really happened. The CPA was commonly perceived as being less about consolidating unity than about finding a solution to the 'Southern problem'.

The first time I came back I didn't know anyone. My immediate family had gone and I had lost contact with all the people I knew. I stayed in a small, rather run-down and noisy hotel on the airport road owned by a Korean man. By chance it happened to be situated about five minutes walk away from the old house where we used to live. On that first visit the house was still there; a low, single storey villa that was more or less unchanged. In the coming years I would watch it being broken down and then replaced by an apartment block; the last testament to my existence here. The waiter who served me breakfast at the hotel was Ethiopian. When I explained where I was actually from, that I had lived close by, he laughed. He thought I was making a joke. I didn't look anything like his idea of a Sudanese.

I couldn't really blame him. Khartoum had changed. Over decades, as a consequence of war and natural disaster, people from every corner of the country had drifted steadily towards the capital seeking refuge. A circle of informal townships had sprung up around the old centre, like concentric rings inside a tree trunk, each one marking a new catastrophe, a different stage in the ongoing conflict. It sounded odd when people said that the city had become more African, but it was true to some extent. Khartoum was in the North and was mostly occupied by

Northerners. The new arrivals had come from the South, the West and the East of the country. They brought with them their own ways, their own history and their own troubles. One might think that being confronted by the fact of the nation's diversity on their own streets ought to have made Khartoum's population more aware of what was going on in their country. It didn't. Instead, it created fear. The interim Constitution stated that no effort should be spared to make unity an 'attractive option'. But it would take more than a few lines on paper to counter centuries of prejudice, and there was little evidence that anything real was being done. On the contrary, the police seemed determined to carry on persecuting the Southerners, raiding their churches and breaking up parties, arresting women for brewing home-made beer and whipping them in public.

It seemed to me that in this unwillingness to embrace the issue of diversity there lay a very personal question addressed to me. I heard it echoed in that hotel waiter's laughter, just as I had heard it many times before and in many other places in the world: What was I doing here? Why had I come back? What had I hoped to find?

In a way, I had been working on the answer to that question for a long time. For as long as I could remember I had been seeking to make sense of this country and my place in it. I had devoted my life to the task because somehow it seemed to me that my own fate was bound up with that of this country in a way that was intimate and complex. I could not write about myself without first writing about Sudan and vice-versa. And where does the impulse to write come from anyway, if not a desire to understand our place in the world, who we are and what purpose our lives serve?

I was born out of a very particular alignment of historical forces: the end of the colonial era and the dawn of independence, which had begun with all the promise of freedom and self-determination. My parents believed there was a place in the world for them and their offspring, who would be neither of this world or the other, but belong to both at the same time. It was the triumph of reason and modernity over prejudice and superstition. That may not have been so surprising considering the fact that they had grown up in the era that witnessed the defeat of Fascism. It is easy to see how, in a curious blend of optimism and innocence, they might have believed they were witnessing a new age of openness and enlightenment.

That was the spirit I had been brought up in and everything I had done up to this point had, in a way, been aimed at trying to achieve that promise. Not in a political sense, but personally, through the writing. To address the injustice and the ignorance that threatened to sweep us all backwards. It wasn't even a national struggle, but one which linked my life in this country to my experience elsewhere. I believed then and now that the fate of this country, which now hung in the balance, comprised something essentially universal. Something to do with how we learn to live in this world among people who look different to ourselves, who have other beliefs and customs. To me, the Sudan question was always really a world question.

If I was surprised at how little the city had altered in my absence it was because it felt somehow smaller than I remembered, though very much unchanged; the streets, my old school, even the sign over my mother's shop that was still in place. In time I realised that the old downtown area was a hollowed out carapace of what it used to be. The result of a metamorphosis. The old colonial-style buildings, the narrow roads laid out by Kitchener in the shape of a Union Jack (to better control unruly crowds), the cracked and extinguished neon signs, all remained as wretched reminders of a past that had never truly been shaken off.

Instead of addressing the core of it's soul that lay at it's centre, the city grew outwards, becoming more diffuse and dislocated as settlements the size of villages sprang up around the periphery, each of them home to displaced communities, people who brought with them their customs and ways, as well as a distrust of the city and its inhabitants. They formed a ring of poverty and resentment around the wealthier, more established occupants. Many of these satellites were unable to survive without support from the myriad international charity and aid organisations operating in the country. They had no water, no schools, no electricity, no healthcare. The city's authorities refused to recognise them. There was the hope that if they were ignored they might just go back to where they came from.

This agglomeration is a reflection of the national crisis. Over the last two or three decades the city had become a microcosm of the country as a whole. Problems that were once removed from the capital by great distances now rubbed shoulders with the country's ruling elite.

The civil war was the most pronounced of the conflicts ailing the country and the CPA provided not only the best chance for peace the country had seen in a quarter of a century, but also the last one. Billions of dollars in oil revenue were at stake and no ideological vision was available to challenge the sectarianism and prejudice, racial, religious and cultural that prevented the country from achieving national unity.

The diverse expansion of Khartoum held up a mirror to the complexity of the national equation – not simply a North/South divide, but a crisis that included Darfur, the Red Sea area, Kordofan and even Nubia. While these conflicts were of a lower intensity, they nevertheless stemmed from the same underlying issues of inequality and neglect, and threatened to erupt into violent confrontation at any moment.

Perhaps the dream of national unity died with John Garang, one of the last believers in the notion. His death, in a helicopter crash some six months after the peace agreement was signed, did not bode well for the future. It sparked off angry riots in the capital in which not only Southerners, but also disenfranchised young men from Darfur and elsewhere took part. It was an outpouring of frustration, triggered by the belief (never proven) that the regime had had a hand in his death. The riots bore testimony to the fragile balance that held the country together. Without Garang unity never stood a chance. He had the power and the authority to stand up to Bashir. In his absence the opposition was rudderless.

By 2011, the CPA had run its course. The Middle East was gripped by revolution and the mood in Khartoum was one of uncertainty. Right up until January's referendum nobody really believed the South would vote to break away. Not even the Vice-President, Ali Osman Taha, the man who had negotiated the CPA with Garang. The clause stipulating the South's right to hold a referendum was only included at the last minute as a mere formality, a concession to the secessionists in the southern ranks with whom Garang had long been at odds. As the truth dawned people were in shock, as the consequences of their inaction became clear. 'I never realised how much they hated us,' one woman, who was crying, told me. Inter-tribal conflict runs deep in the South, back into the founding myths and for years the North had consoled itself with the illusion that the South would never break away, that no matter how badly they were treated, most Southerners would prefer to take their chances in the North than live under the domination of the Dinka, the largest ethnic group.

In the West, the referendum results produced something akin to euphoria, as if the decision by the South to opt for independence was in fact a triumph of Western ideals, a moral victory over the dark forces massed in the North. Much of this, of course, stemmed from the simplistic notion that North and South constitute two distinct and easily divisible halves. Separate them and conflict will instantly end. At a distance, perhaps, but on the ground the situation is far more complicated.

I began to see that I had arrived at a water-shed in history, the culmination of an era, when the country stood at the point of no return and would choose in the coming referendum to either go on together towards lasting peace, or to separate and remain forever estranged. And it was here that that fate would be decided. Here where the two sides rubbed shoulders together, where government would make or break the notion of unity. This city, Khartoum, the confluence of the two great rivers. This was where the dividing line would stand or fall. There could not be a more appropriate setting.

FIGURE 7 *Kabul by night, illuminated mosque.*

CHAPTER 3.2

Keynote: Barney Afako, Former Legal Advisor to the Juba Peace Talks

It is a great pleasure to be here to discuss with you the Comprehensive Peace Agreement (CPA) that was signed in 2005 between the government of the Sudan and the Sudan People's Liberation Movement (SPLM) and Army. Also, I am particularly glad that my friend and colleague Sarah Nouwen is going to be discussing my paper. That frees me immensely to simply present an overview of some of the issues I thought we should reflect upon. And I do look forward to the roundtable discussion on this important African agreement.

Like all conflicts, as we were reminded earlier, the Sudanese war was steeped in history; a history that we cannot ignore, and a history that the negotiators and mediators had to face up to. One of the little known facts in Africa, especially sub-Saharan Africa, is that Sudan actually attained its independence on the 1st of January 1956. I say that is a little known fact, because for a very long time, when we were commemorating the trend of independence in Africa, a lot of States tended to start with Ghana, which of course got its independence after the Sudan. Part of the reason for that, I think, is that the independence of Sudan was shrouded in some controversy. In fact, the first Sudanese war, a civil war, broke out before independence, and continued until 1972, when the parties reached the Addis Ababa agreement. So quite clearly, from the onset, Sudan was a nation that was not at ease with itself. Part of the reason for this was that Southern Sudanese aspirations for greater self-government, in a federal Sudanese State, had not been realised for various reasons. It was thought that it was inopportune, in 1955, for Sudan to be split into two States. And the fall-back position of having a carefully framed federation, where the Southern Sudanese would have virtual self-government, was not realised. Once the war started, it went on until the parties were forced by the circumstances, the sheer length of the conflict, and the devastating effects of the war, to reach an agreement. In 1972, in Addis Ababa they concluded that agreement, which provided for self-government and other Southern demands, including absorption of Southern fighters into the army and a range of other issues. However, that agreement was later to be abrogated, shortly before the second Sudanese conflict.

Van Hoogstraten, Schrijver et al. (eds.), The Art of Making Peace: Lessons Learned from Peace Treaties
© 2017 The Editors. Printed in The Netherlands. ISBN *978-90-04-32123-6. pp. 77-84.*

It is this second conflict that we will focus on today. It ultimately led to the negotiation and signing of the Comprehensive Peace Agreement. In 1983, Dr. John Garang, the leader of the Sudan People's Liberation Movement, went back with his colleagues to the bush to launch another war. Why were the Southern Sudanese fighting? Why was Sudan not at ease with itself? The analysis has been made that the problem of Sudan was that it had failed to manage the diversity of the peoples within its borders. The Sudan, which was Africa's largest State until two years ago, was diverse in social and religious terms. And economically it was diverse too, insofar as the economic strength, along with the political power, was concentrated in a narrow band around the capital Khartoum and its surrounding areas. Sudan's periphery was marginalized. In its analysis of the conflict in Darfur, the African Union Panel on Darfur (AUPD), headed by former South-African president Thabo Mbeki, categorized the conflict in Darfur as symptomatic of the general political condition of Sudan, where there was a concentration of power, wealth, and influence in a few hands.

For the years between 1983 and 2000, the world was changing around the Sudan, but the Southern conflict was not coming to an end. The humanitarian impact of the conflict was one of the worst to be seen in that part of Africa. So the world could not ignore the situation in Southern Sudan. In Northern Sudan itself, the conflict was taking its toll on the economy and politics. Of course, the fighting had a negative impact on communities, not only in the South, but also affected families of soldiers, and people who had been conscripted to support the war effort in the South. So there was a convening, if you like, of both internal and external factors, which led to the success of the initial efforts to bring the parties together. International and regional interests were invested the situation, as we say, especially because of the humanitarian impact, which was spilling over into neighboring countries. Southern Sudanese refugees were to be found in Uganda, Kenya, Ethiopia, among other States. More broadly, in the international community there was increasing concern about the position of what one may call political Islam in Africa. Some of those motivations brought Sudan, and the Southern Sudanese problem, on the top of the international agenda. Of course, the events of September 11 2001 also accentuated these fears. And so, coming together were not only the African neighbouring States and the African Union, but also representations of Western countries, including the United States, the UK, Norway, Italy and the European Union among others.

The parties came to the table with different views on how to resolve the Southern problem. For the Sudan People's Liberation Movement, the old agenda of deriving a settlement that would ensure self-government was very high on their list of priorities. Of course, the government of the Sudan wanted to maintain the integrity and unity of the Sudan, and to bring an end to the conflict that was costing it immensely. At this time, oil had been discovered in Sudan, and most of the reserves were in Southern Sudan. So it was important for the government of the Sudan to ensure that its access to this important resource would not be interrupted by the conflict. So these factors meant that the mediation of the Intergovernmental Authority on Development (IGAD) was able to bring the parties to the table, and to frame an agenda which would begin to reflect some of their aspirations. They seized the moment that presented itself about thirty years after the Addis Ababa agreement. But how did they go about this process of solving one of Africa's longest and most bitter conflicts?

Many people came together for the negotiations, and not only the key IGAD mediators, but also representatives from neighboring States, acting as observers. Many States, besides Kenya, sent observers to sit in the talks. There were regional representatives from African Union as well as international community representatives. Of course, this posed a challenge, because of all the different regional and international interests involved in the process; specifically, how to facilitate the coalescence of this diverse group of supporters of the process, and ensure they are coherent in their interventions with the parties. I think the fact that Kenya took the lead, and nominated a single mediator to oversee the process, was crucial. It also helped that the supporters of the process, including the observers and the others, had the discipline to respect that arrangement. One of the benefits of this is that one did not experience the kind of forum-shopping that is often the case in peace talks, which can lead to derailment or the distraction of parties from solving the problem before them. Apart from the consensus from the supporters of the process, more importantly was the fact that the parties themselves had reached the conclusion that it was important to engage with each other in order to resolve this conflict. So it fell to the mediator to manage the process in such a way that the parties' priorities and aspirations were reflected in the process, and that they were able to negotiate to their maximum advantage.

Now, from the point of view of Southern Sudan, one of the key issues that was very prominent in the negotiations was their demand that they would have the opportunity to choose their future; the right to self-determination. At the same time, that demand, of course, had been behind the prolonging and the manifestation of the conflict within Sudan. This was a difficult issue because, obviously, the North would have felt that this would set a precedent, which would be damaging to its efforts to deal with other crises within the Sudan, not least in the East and also in Darfur. This was a difficult issue, but one that could not, given the history of the conflict, be ignored. And it is to the credit of the mediation that it grasped this nettle, and did not duck the point of self-determination. And so the Machakos Protocol (signed in Machakos, Kenya) of 20 July 2002, which is the very first protocol of the comprehensive peace agreement, is a crucial one because it sets out, if you like, the ballpark within which the rest of the negotiations would be carried out. That protocol is explicit on the right to self-determination. It also provided that there would be an interim period, a period within which the Sudanese parties would do their best to ensure that a secession of Southern Sudan would not be inevitable. In the words of the protocol; to 'make unity attractive'. Of course, the Southerners had felt aggrieved since before independence. They had felt betrayed by the abrogation of the 1972 agreement, and therefore needed a fairly solid guarantee that their right to govern themselves would be reflected in any arrangement adopted in these negotiations.

The Machakos Protocol also dealt with the thorny issue of the place of religion in the State. Sharia would be retained as a source of legislation for the rest of the country, but in the South they would be free to adopt another system. It also set out the principles for federal political arrangement, but the detail of that was to be fleshed out in the power sharing agreement. So in the Machakos Protocol, which took everybody by surprise, because of its content and detail, the parties managed to frame the direction that they would take with their negotiations. One has the sense that, if the mediation had adopted a piecemeal approach, and had tried to negotiate each of those matters which featured in the Machakos Protocol independently, the course of the negotiations might have turned out to be quite different. So in terms of the tactics, they got that right. Once the Machakos Protocol was adopted, then the process evolved, and dealt with the details of the power-sharing, of wealth-sharing. The negotiations also dealt with the future of other regions where there was support for the Southern cause, like in the case of Abyei, and in what is called the "Two Areas" of Southern Kordofan and Blue Nile.

All of this was a very detailed agenda, which was designed to make sure that the Southern problem would be addressed, and that there would be a framework and a timeframe which would lead to a choice of whether or not to remain within the Sudan or to secede. Between 2002 and 2004, pretty much non-stop, the parties were engaged, at one level or the other, in the negotiations. But in-between, the parties returned to war. After the Machakos Protocol, with its promise, the war broke out again with quite some intensity, and there was a hiatus in the negotiations until a temporary cease-fire was signed, which was then eventually confirmed. But the negotiators held their nerve, and the mediators held their nerve as well. They were able to continue with the process after the parties returned to the table. Nowadays, any outbreak of hostilities during negotiations tends to be treated as a complete collapse of the process. At the time, there was ferocious military activity between the negotiations, but the ability to recover from that, and to bring the talks back to the correct trajectory, is a very important lesson. We are often very easily distracted by a return to hostilities in the process of negotiations.

In terms of the participants in the process, there has been a criticism that the Comprehensive Peace Agreement process failed to deal with all of Sudan's issues, and was not representative as to who it brought around the table. This is on the face of it a valid criticism. The proposition that, during talks, you must bring around everybody who might have a stake, so that once and for all the problem is resolved to everyone's satisfaction, is an attractive proposition. But it is only superficially attractive, because at that time, a lot of the issues and conflicts in Sudan were not yet ripe for being dealt with in Nairobi under those arrangements. And so again I would suggest that it was to the credit of the mediators that they stuck with the Southern issue, and allowed the parties to return to the broader Sudanese issues after they had completed the CPA. The Comprehensive Peace Agreement was in fact a process of constitution-writing, which set up a new constitutional dispensation, which ended in elections and then a referendum on the future of Southern Sudan. It was a power-sharing arrangement between the two dominant political forces (the Government and the SPLM). So even with the unsatisfactory political context of the focus on the interests of two parties, it seems to me that it was important at the time, and for southern Sudan, that the two parties should focus on that issue, and return later to the broader Sudanese issues. We shall come back to how the parties are currently doing that in a moment.

So by not attempting too much, the mediators and the negotiators gave themselves the opportunity to succeed in achieving some progress on one of the Sudan's main conflicts. Of course, it left the question of Darfur, other conflicts in the East, and other structural problems of Sudan, such as democratic deficits unaddressed in their totality. But it opened the door for those issues to be tackled. It did so by setting a precedent on how the central questions, and central problems, on the political constitution of Sudan could be addressed; including the question of managing diversity and democratization in its broad sense. So for the CPA mediation to succeed, they had to stick to the Southern issue. They had to assemble in Nairobi and other parts of Kenya the right people who would address the issues that had been identified in Machakos.

Of course, looking back now, it might not have been possible to secure the kind of agreement that became the CPA without two very key characters. The first of course was Dr. John Garang, the leader of the SPLM. Because of his political vision and charisma, he was able to carry the constituencies of SPLM into the talks and to speak with one voice on behalf of the movement. Had there been insurmountable leadership problems within the SPLM, it may well have been much more difficult to present a united front in the negotiations. On the side of the government of Sudan, after the Machakos Protocol, the then Sudanese Vice-President Dr. Ali Osman Mohammed Taha himself came to lead the negotiations. He engaged, in a one-to-one negotiation, with Dr. John Garang. This political clout that was brought to bear to the issue was critical for the progress that was achieved. But the political competence of the negotiators did not absolve the mediation from planning, and assisting the parties with the content of the agreements. We heard earlier some suggestions about drafting and putting forward proposals to the parties. I think that the mediation did an excellent job of striking the right balance in this regard: it presented proposals, but also allowed the parties to shape the talks, to shape the agreement. And that is a call that any mediator has to make: how much is too much, and when do you show restraint and allow the peacemakers, who can make the difference, the space to do their own thing without necessarily intervening at every turn?

So in the end, you had a comprehensive peace agreement. It was comprehensive to the extent that it set a road map for addressing the Southern Sudanese grievance. It was not comprehensive in the sense that the Sudan faced other challenges that required attention, and would require attention in the future. And one of the ways this has been addressed, is by the continuing engagement of the supporters of the CPA in the implementation process. And here I would highlight the role that the African Union has played. There was a whole range of countries and institutions supporting the implementation of CPA, including the UN. The parties had agreed to the establishment of an assessment or evaluation commission, which was much more of a soft oversight and support. The assessment commission provided some assistance with the implementation of the CPA. But the issues and politics were complex, and these measures were not sufficient, in the end, to guarantee progress, especially as the end of the interim period drew near. And that is the point at which the African Union stepped in and decided to assign a High Level Panel to assist the two CPA parties to navigate through the rest of the interim period of the CPA, leading especially to the referendum on Southern independence.

The African Union High Level Implementation Panel for Sudan (AUHIP) – a successor to the AUPD, and also chaired by former South-African president Thabo Mbeki – was now assigned the responsibility to support the parties in the democratization of the Sudan, in the processes that would lead up to the referendum, and in the implementation of outstanding issues in the CPA. It was an important intervention, in part because events elsewhere in Sudan, and particularly in Darfur, and the intervention of international criminal justice, had meant that a lot of the interlocutors – people who sat around in Kenya to help the parties reach an agreement – had ruled themselves out of being of any high level assistance to the government of Sudan after the indictment of the Sudanese president by the International Criminal Court. Fewer countries had the political possibility to engage robustly with the Sudan. However, the African Union did not have those restrictions. The AU's role in the Sudan, through the AUHIP, represents a model for assisting African countries with complex political situations internally and also in relation to external politics. The immediate aim in Sudan was to encourage and support the parties to stick to their commitments – which they have done – to carry out elections, and then the referendum on Southern self-determination, which led to the secession of South Sudan.

So how does one judge the CPA? I think it would be a mistake simply to judge it by the outcome of the referendum. I think the parties, once they signed the CPA, met their key obligations. Southern Sudan attained self-government, the wealth-sharing protocol worked, and eventually the government of Sudan respected the choice of the people of Southern Sudan to be independent. It meant that all the key issues that had been identified in the Machakos Protocol were addressed. Ultimately this was possible because of internal political commitments to peace between the two parties, but also because of strong external support after the signing of the CPA. Despite the fact that some countries were politically somewhat restrained in their engagement with the Sudan, they were able to express their support in other ways. The credit goes back to the process that delivered the CPA texts in 2005, because those involved in the drafting had skilfully identified the key issues at the outset, and the process had marshalled internal and external support and identified the right interlocutors to deliver results. They seized the opportunities that were presented. Today, one wonders what would have happened if the parties had not signed the CPA in 2005. It is quite likely that the process would have been derailed by the events that took place subsequently, particularly in Darfur. One of the things that you will note, when looking through the various agreements of the CPA, is that they are not overloaded with questions of what is now called transitional justice. And I think the reason for that was that the parties identified that their priority was to have a peaceful transition from war, and the possibility of making a choice for self-determination or a choice for Sudan to remain together.

By not attempting too much too early, they gave themselves the opportunity to reach an agreement with the right people around the table. And they left some of the outstanding questions about both Sudan and South-Sudan to the future. It seems to me that that was a sensible and realistic way of making peace in a complex situation such as the Sudan.

CHAPTER 3.3

Commentary: Sarah Nouwen, Cambridge University

If peace-making is an art, then Dr. Barney Afako is Leonardo, Elvis and Chinua in one. Having observed the Maestro working, quietly but relentlessly, like one of these people that Ambassador Corell referred to, never claiming "I did this" or "I did that", but effectively being one of the key drivers of peace processes in Uganda, Sudan and the African continent as a whole, I see my role today as someone who merely tinkers a bit with the frame, to allow the masterpiece to shine. For frames, in Sharath Srinivasan's words, "shape what is viewed and how what is viewed is interpreted". Our discussions today are shaped by the frame of the conference, "The Art of Peace-making". Let's deconstruct this frame and fit it onto the Maestro's painting of the Sudans. Let's begin with splitting the frame into two: peace-making and art. Let us begin with peace-making.

While our conference is dedicated to peace-making, most of our panels are dedicated to peace agreements. Since we simultaneously celebrate the 100th anniversary of the home of the ICJ and PCA, it is understandable that we focus on that element of peace-making that seems most relevant to international law – a text reflecting an agreement (or, at times more realistically, in Philip Allott's description of a treaty, "a disagreement reduced to writing"). Moreover, since the end of the Second World War, peace agreements have been one of the most fashionable ways of trying to resolve armed conflicts, and in particular non-international armed conflicts.

But let us contrast the fashion with the basics. First, peace-making does not necessarily require text. If we return to the Sudanese context, for any peace to last in the Sudans, the relations between the Misseriya and Ngok Dinka in Abyei, the Zaghawa and the Bani Hussayn in Darfur, the Rizeigat and the Maalia in Eastern Darfur, and the Nuer and the Murle in Jonglei are as important as the relations between the government of Sudan and the government of South Sudan. Improvement of these community relations usually does not require a text, but confidence-building measures and adjustments in practices related to land, arms and public services.

Van Hoogstraten, Schrijver et al. (eds.), The Art of Making Peace: Lessons Learned from Peace Treaties
© 2017 The Editors. Printed in The Netherlands. ISBN *978-90-04-32123-6. pp. 85-90.*

A peace agreement is not necessarily the right medium in the relationship between the State and a rebel movement either. Some of the armed conflicts in Sudan, and in particular in Darfur, are governed by the rules of the patronage market. As Alex de Waal has argued, "Sovereignty is a commodity to be bartered"; loyalty to the incumbent government is ended the moment that the cash dries up, or another party offers a higher bid. For peace-making in a patronage market, a business plan may be more effective than a peace agreement.

Secondly, even when peace-making does result in a peace agreement, the actual process of peace-making begins long before the negotiations on a text. Mr Afako's story has pointed out how, in the Sudanese context, various local, national, regional and geopolitical factors had to come together in order for an environment conducive to negotiations to ripen. Looking at ongoing armed conflicts today, the greatest challenge is not how to conclude peace negotiations, but how to begin them; in other words, how to ensure that all these influences point in the same direction, namely, that of a peace process.

Thirdly, once negotiations are ongoing, the obvious focus is to reach an agreement, to be written down in a text. But, as Martti Koskenniemi mentioned yesterday, the making of peace occurs as much in socialisation around the negotiations (in his example, in the Finnish sauna with some vodka) as in the ensuing text. Thus, while it is important to keep the momentum, the external imposition of deadlines for reasons other than the progress of the negotiations can kill the entire process. The deadlines of the negotiations of the Darfur Peace Agreement were imposed, not with a view to a successful agreement, but in order to have an agreement which the UN had set itself as precondition for "rehatting" an African Union peacekeeping operation into a United Nations mission. Consequently, the agreement was stillborn, and it took years to get new peace talks, none of which has been as promising for peace as the negotiations that were killed by deadline diplomacy.

Similarly, when international actors, losing patience with the pace of the process, take over the pen, that balance to which Barney referred, between inserting technical expertise and ensuring that ownership is maintained with the parties, is lost. The CPA maintained that balance; the Darfur peace processes have not. An entire florilegium can be composed of draft peace agreements for Darfur, some of which were designed in European universities. But agreements that were not negotiated by the parties themselves are unlikely to be adopted, signed and implemented. Zooming in on the text risks losing sight of the actual process of peace or war making that takes place around the text.

Finally, even when peace agreements are signed, this should not indicate the end of a peace process. In Sudan, the conclusion of the CPA merely indicated the beginning of a new period of peace-making, involving continued negotiations over interpretation, implementation and adjustment. That peace process continues today, now between two independent States and within the two States, under the leadership of the African Union High Level Implementation Panel. If a peace agreement is the end of a peace process, then it usually is with dire consequences. In Darfur, the signing of the Darfur Peace Agreement by only one of the armed movements, spurred further division and conflict, among forces opposing the government, but also, in their image, among the internally displaced persons. It shows, as in Versailles, that a peace agreement can also be an incentive for violence. This brings us to the second part of our frame: peace-making as an art.

Arts are usually contrasted with science. Art is validated by its results, science by its process; art intends to evoke subjective states, science tries to achieve objectivity; in art it is originality that counts; in science replicability.

In many respects the qualification of peace-making as an art is thus entirely appropriate. First, whilst process matters to peace, it is usually the outcome by which it is evaluated. Secondly, that outcome – a particular degree of "peace" – is to some extent subjective: whether it is evaluated as good or bad often depends on one's position. And finally, as Barney pointed out, the art of peace-making is that of having an eye for the originality of the situation – not the replicability of a peace agreement from elsewhere.

Let me illustrate the subjective evaluation of the outcome with the case of Sudan. After the rather unique historical occasion of the successful birth of a new State, beaming a sense of victory, joy and hope that was difficult not to be impressed by, the dominant discourse on the Sudans today is back to one of gloom. South Sudan is independent, but the conflicts between and within both countries have not ended. Some commentators have written off the CPA as "little more than an extended ceasefire." Indeed, others have argued that the CPA has emboldened rebellions elsewhere in the country.

Whether one assesses the CPA as success or failure, depends on the frame for the analysis of the conflict in the Sudans. The CPA itself was built on two contrasting and sometimes diverging frames of conflict analysis.

One of those frames reflected the center-periphery axis. The leader of the SPLM, Dr. John Garang, had argued that the SPLM liberated not just the South of Sudan, but the entire Sudan: all marginalized areas in Sudan. It was his vision of a New Sudan, in which the government would be representative of all its peoples, that had gained the SPLM political, and in instances even military support throughout Sudan. The Beja in the East, the Ngok Dinka in Abyei, the Nuba in Southern Kordofan, the Ingessena in Blue Nile, the Fur, Massalit and Zaghawa in Darfur, they all opposed Khartoum's attempts to organise Sudan on the basis of external ideologies, such as Arabism or Islamism. The SPLA's strong presence in some of these areas was thus not so much a sign of that army's military strength, as it was an expression of an indigenous rebellion against the government, fought in association with the SPLM, or sometimes merely following its example. This centre-periphery axis was reflected in the CPA's democratisation and federalisation agenda.

At the same time, the CPA was also built on a North-South axis. The parties committed to making unity attractive. But, as Barney pointed out, the Machakos Protocol already promised the Southerners the right to self-determination for in case unity would not have been made attractive in the six years' interim period. Northern regions in which some groups had fought with the SPLM, namely Southern Kordofan and Blue Nile, obtained their own CPA Protocol, but not the right to secede from Sudan. Only the region of Abyei was given the right to decide whether to stay in the North or join the South.

The peace negotiations, as Barney explained, reflected only the North-South frame, not the center-periphery frame. The Nuba, Ngok Dinka and Ingessena, were supposed to be represented by the SPLM, even though they had mostly fought with, rather than for, the southern cause. The regional groups that had opposed the SPLM, for instance the Misseriya in Abyei, were supposed to be represented by the Government. In reality, however, these ties of representation were at best weak. Several other marginalised regional groups in Sudan did not feel represented by either of the two parties. To them, the Machakos Protocol sent the signal that in order to obtain a piece of the national cake, one has to start one's own rebellion. The conflict in the West, Darfur, exploded shortly after the signature of the Machakos protocol. The conflict in the East was also pursued with a view to obtaining an independent peace agreement.

And these peace agreements came. Indeed there is an alphabet chain of peace agreements – CPA, DPA, DDPD, ESPA; many parts of the country have their own peace agreement. But these peace agreements did not necessarily bring peace. First, as we have already seen in Darfur, one party's signing of an agreement can cause further splintering of armed movements and their supporters. Secondly and more fundamentally, the paradox of Sudan's existing peace agreements is that they have all been framed as agreements between the center and one particular region, yet they hardly address region-specific issues. Instead, they all address national issues of the center-periphery relation. The result is a chain of peace agreements essentially all addressing the same issue. It is thus that the experience of exclusion in one peace process could become an incentive for the fight for inclusion in another. The chain of peace agreements sends the message that the road to rights is based on violence, not citizenship.

Meanwhile, in the implementation of the CPA, many of the efforts that were required to making unity effective did not take place, or at least too slowly, according to the 99.83 % of the Southerners who voted for independence. Of course, in hindsight one may speculate whether the outcome would have been different if Dr. Garang had not died in a fatal crash three weeks into the interim period, and if the SPLM had therefore focused more on the Sudan-wide democratisation agenda, instead of preparing for independence. But it is questionable whether even the leader of the SPLM in six years would have succeeded in convincing the Southerners to stay with the North after decades of war. The CPA had already promised the *ultimum remedium* of secession; implementing the lesser remedy of transforming Sudanese politics into an inclusive and democratic practice would always have been the more difficult option.

For Abyei, Blue Nile and Southern Kordofan, the end of the interim period proved also the end of an interim peace. In these areas, the struggle for the Sudanese identity continues.

Now, to conclude: is the CPA to be blamed for the present situation? Should it have been more inclusive? Was the frame wrong? Some argue yes to all three questions. But there are at least four caveats to this simple condemnation.

First, as Barney explained already, in many respects the CPA was a success for people in the South who wanted independence.

Secondly, the CPA could also have been more effective for peace in Sudan more broadly, if in the implementation phase the parties, and the international actors, had prioritised the center-periphery frame over the North-South frame. And if they had not furthered a piecemeal approach to peace in Sudan, thereby effectively dividing up the country.

Thirdly, as Barney pointed out, the mediators in the CPA negotiations in fact resisted the temptation to design an all-inclusive process, not unlike the Dayton negotiators consciously excluded Kosovo: inclusion could have jeopardised the entire process. The perfect would have been the enemy of the good.

Finally, the frame of the CPA, or that of any other peace agreement, is not a technical issue that can be "fixed" with sufficient "expertise" or a problem-solving mentality; nor is it a scientific "given": frames are part of the piece of art – they are inherently political, and reflections of the art of the possible.

FIGURE 8 *South Sudan wrestling competition at Juba Stadium, 23 April 2016.*

CHAPTER 3.4

Roundtable Debate

Professor Jan Pronk, The Netherlands: I have some minor points. Firstly, on process and outcome. Texts. Both are extremely important, I think the speakers will agree with me on that. But both are equally important. It is not the case that one of the two is more important than the other, in my view. If you have a wrong process… Very often peace negotiations are taking place in a form of a tragedy of blunders. Take, for instance, the whole procedure towards the Darfur Peace Agreement (DPA). You have a good text – and you may even say that the DPA was a good text in itself – but it is not going to be implemented because of the procedures leading up to the DPA. But if you have a very good process, like the whole procedure that led to the CPA, and you would not have had a good text, it would have been flawed in its implementation. I think we must be very lucky that we had a good process towards the CPA; finally, after forty years of fighting. And it was a good text. I am very strongly in favour of good texts, because, as a politician, I have become very much convinced of the need to have good legal texts. If you would have had a text with many loopholes – and the CPA hardly had any loopholes – these loopholes would have been used later on in the framework of the talks between the North and the South, as a justification for non-implementation. The agreement was as comprehensive as possible; in fact, I do not know of any other African peace agreement which is so comprehensive as the CPA. And that indeed has been a good basis.

But not everything can be dealt with in the agreement, because there are always deadlines. The deadlines, by the way, were set by Vice-President Taha and Garang themselves. They were not imposed from the outside. But as soon as they were set, the international community did embrace them, and told the negotiators: "Please, stick to your deadline." Not everything had been dealt with before the deadline. But the CPA also included provisions on how to deal with those issues which had not yet been agreed upon. And that made the whole peace treaty more comprehensive than otherwise would have been the case. I agree, if Garang would not have died, in particular those provisions would have had more concrete and precise political substance, because the succession of Garang was in the hands of those who were not themselves really good negotiators. You also need procedures for implementation, for ad-

Van Hoogstraten, Schrijver et al. (eds.), The Art of Making Peace: Lessons Learned from Peace Treaties
© 2017 The Editors. Printed in The Netherlands. ISBN *978-90-04-32123-6. pp. 91-99.*

dressing those issues which have not yet been dealt with. And you need procedures for review of the peace treaty which has been agreed upon, because it cannot be eternally just.

I have another point on deadlines. Deadlines are important. But only if they are being agreed upon by the parties. They should never be imposed by outsiders. This means that deadlines can only work if you have a process in steps. In this sense the Machakos protocol, plus the ceasefire which was dealt with later on, was crucial for a good CPA. And I agree very much with those who say that if there is a violation of the ceasefire agreement – and there are always violations of ceasefire agreements – it should not be seen by the parties or by the external mediators as a total failure. It is important to continue. We see at the moment a good example of this in the peace talks in Colombia. There are violations of agreements, but still the parties continue to negotiate. They do not leave the negotiation table. It is important for external factors, external forces, to call parties back to the negotiation table if such a violation of the agreements takes place.

Finally, on the frame. I agree with Sarah Nouwen that it is hardly possible to have a kind of overall model for peace talks and for peacemaking. All situations are different. But maybe the following suggestion could be offered: peace talks are perhaps more effective if they take place in stages. You do not have to deal with all the issues at the same time. The Machakos protocol, followed by the CPA, is a good example. But peace talks have to be comprehensive in terms of the inclusiveness of all parties. As soon as you leave out some specific stakeholders, you are lost. Because then you create another reason for those who have been left out not to accept the peace agreement. And that was the major mistake which was made – by external forces – in the CPA.

And a second element of the frame. I think that – and I say this on the basis of experiences with all types of negotiations – you would draw the conclusion that justice should always come after peace. Any effort, very often imposed by the external community (international organisations), to impose justice before peace will be counterproductive. You hardly will be able to reach justice, and you will not be able to reach peace. So you are creating your own deadlock. Justice, yes; no amnesty should be included in any peace agreement. But justice should be possible *after* peace, not before.

Mr. Mohamed Alawad, Organisation for the Prohibition of Chemical Weapons: The Sudanese Comprehensive Peace Agreement (CPA) is only eight years old, as opposed to the other agreements we have discussed earlier, which are much older. This one is very young. And around that young peace agreement, a history can be made.

Mr. Afako mentioned the IGAD. Initially, it was the initiative of the Sudanese government to ask this regional body to play a role in the peace mediation between Sudan and the movement of SPLA. And later the Netherlands took the initiative to have IGAD friends, and later they became IGAD partners. This is how the international pressure came.

I can mention two issues which were crucial for the negotiation teams of both the Sudanese government and the SPLA. The first issue was the referendum. The issue of the referendum first appeared in January 1992. By then, the IGAD itself was starting its role in the negotiations. In the North of the Sudan it was seen as a form of betrayal that someone could talk about a referendum. It was a very sensitive issue. It broke down the negotiations, and it came back again to the negotiation table after thirteen years of political dialogue in Sudan and other parts of the world. This issue, plus the issue of religion, was included in the first draft agenda made by IGAD. And that is the reason why negotiations broke down for thirteen years and then they came back again. I mention these two issues of the history, to show that the peace agreement in Sudan was comprehensive and it looked to the problem. By then Darfur was not there, the Eastern problem was not there, as Dr. Sarah Nouwen mentioned.

The issue of the war in Sudan started earlier. That started already in 1947, and Sudan was independent ten years later in 1956, and it carried over all the history. Negotiations started in 1972 and then broke out again in 1993. And all this time the war continued. At the start of his movement, Dr. Garang was fighting those who were asking for the separation for the Sudan. All the fighting was between the Southern Sudanese themselves; between Garang and his movement and others who were asking for the separation of the Sudan. In Southern Sudan the issue of the referendum was not an easy issue. It came after bloody wars within Southern Sudan. So the peace agreement was comprehensive because it addressed all the issues, and it took a long time to make.

The peace negotiations started in Nairobi, between 1991 and 1994. At all those meetings, the negotiating teams were in Nairobi, and they had all these papers with them, and the first time a referendum was mentioned was in 1994, when they suggested to organise a referendum within thirty years. Many years later, the referendum was mentioned again, and then it was said that the referendum should be organised within six years. This was included in the peace agreement for Southern Sudan, and it cannot be repeated for the other regions. It cannot be repeated in Darfur, because the situation is completely different; and it cannot be repeated in the Eastern Sudan, because that situation is also completely different. The Darfur peace agreement was signed, and now everybody is waiting for those who were not joining to accept what was achieved. Sudan has a culture of diversity within the community. I hope the comprehensive peace agreement will be seen as an example, and fortunately today we can see it is discussed among other important peace treaties.

Professor Hans Lammers, The Netherlands: The situation in the Sudan today is still very complicated, including the relationship between the North and the South. There are border demarcation problems in the South. And there is violence between the tribes. And there is the question of the oil transportation from the South to the North etc. But there is one particular aspect which has not been dealt with in much detail today. It is an aspect which the speakers could explore a little bit more, and about which they might give us somewhat more information. One protocol of the CPA dealt with the situation of Abyei. Abyei is an area between the North and the South. And it has a bit of a history. It is an area which was transferred by the British, in 1905, from the South to the Northern province of Kordofan. It has been my understanding that the reason to do this was to better protect the Ngok Dinka tribes, living in that area, from the Arabs from the North. On the day that the referendum on Southern independence took place, a referendum should also have taken place on the status of Abyei. In the latter referendum, the people should have been able to decide whether the area of Abyei should remain a part of the North with an autonomous status, or whether the area should become a part of the South.

But first there was the question of the exact delimitation of the area. That was a big problem. An international boundary commission, which consisted of five people from the South, five people from the North, and five international experts, was established. They came to a conclusion where the boundaries were of that area, which had been transferred from the South to the North by the British. The outcome was not accepted by the government of Khartoum, and it led to further violence in the Abyei area. And then the two parties fortunately decided to submit the question of the demarcation of that area to arbitration, which eventually took place in the Hague, in the Grand Hall of Justice of the Peace Palace. So I think that issue is now more or less decided.

But there remains the question of the plebiscite, the referendum. And up until now, it has not been possible to have this referendum. You have the Ngok Dinka, and the Misseriya nomads who go through the area. And I would like to ask the two speakers to explore the situation. Why was it not possible to have the referendum? How do they see the future?

Mr. Hugo Siblesz, Permanent Court of Arbitration: Just an additional remark. I thought Professor Lammers was going to make the point, but he has not. I think it is appropriate to point out that the arbitration which was conducted here in the Peace Palace on the demarcation of the Abyei boundary was an exceptional feature, in the sense that it was about settling a dispute between the central government and a liberation movement. This, I think, is without any precedent, and probably will remain without many successors. But it is an important innovative element in the whole peace process. I do not know whether it is an artistic or scientific achievement, but in any case I would appreciate comments from the speakers who put the Sudan question to us, especially on its role in the overall peace process.

Response by Barney Afako:

I associate myself with the proposal that text is very key, just as much as process is: text is the basis for a lasting settlement. Thank you, Ambassador, for those clarifications and additional information on the history. I think the point to take from that is surely that any peace process has to build on what has gone before. And indeed what was possible in the Machakos Protocol was a result of all of those efforts, including the elements that were in the 1972 Addis Ababa Agreement. So although we say that the 1972 agreement was abrogated, the aspirations contained in it lived on. And they were manifested again in the negotiations in Kenya. And I agree that the challenge to manage diversity is an ongoing one, and efforts are being made in that direction. This is not a typically Sudanese issue. Across the continent in Africa, we face that very same challenge: how do you manage these artificial States, which consist of various nationalities, bound together often by the accidental colonial history? I think we are seeing situations where, in the post-colonial stage the negotiations which should have preceded the nation-building exercise are actually take place later, as a kind of reaffirmation of a de facto situation.

Now to come to the Abyei issue; Abyei was the subject of one of the protocols of the CPA, and it was one of the difficult issues in the CPA. It is an unusual protocol in its history, because it is the one protocol where the United States government played a very prominent role. And speaking of preparing texts: it was the US government that prepared the text on the Abyei Protocol, which was subsequently adopted "as is." It also meant that some of the issues that arose in the text came to light much later, because the protocol did not have the benefit of going through a systematic process of proposals, followed by counter-proposals, and mediator's texts, etc. Maybe some of the interpretational issues arose because it was one of those "take it as it is" package-agreements. So it has an unusual history in the process of drafting.

So let us leapfrog to what is happening with the protocol now. It is true that the referendum on the future of Abyei did not take place as envisaged. The key point was a failure to agree on the criterion for participation in the referendum. There exist two opposing views on this. For each view there are strong constituents. The Ngok Dinka community is very strongly lobbying with the government of South Sudan to stick to their interpretation of the protocol. On the other hand, you have the community of the Misseriya who are also putting strong pressure on the government of Sudan to take a view on participation that is different from the Southern position. Both Governments have their own interests and stakes in the future of Abyei. The AUHIP made a proposal to the Parties, which the Peace and Security Council of the AU then endorsed. It also agreed that the two presidents in Juba and Khartoum should engage each other to resolve this matter either by going back to the text of the protocol, or by finding another accommodation which would allow the referendum process to go ahead. Today, the complication, of course, is that you no longer have one Sudan. You have two States. So you are no longer just implementing an internal text within one state. You now have to think about how you translate the content of the protocol into an arrangement for two sovereign States, together, overseeing an administrative process. So you may need to find supplementary language to clarify who makes the appointments to commissions; how do you fund the process; etc. And that is quite apart from the thorny issue of how to craft the criterion for participation in the referendum. Who determines the criterion? Do you leave it to a commission to decide, or do the two States agree on the criterion through another mechanism? Because the outcome of the referendum will be determined by the criterion of participation, this is critical. As soon as the criterion for participation is published, you will have a pretty good idea of how the referendum will turn out. That is why I think it is a difficult matter. There are very strong stakeholders who want to know what the referendum will look like and where it will leave them. I think that is still an ongoing conversation. It may require further mobilisation of political encouragement to both Khartoum, Juba and, crucially, the local communities. There is presently an agreement of temporary administrative and security arrangements for Abyei, which has been endorsed by the African Union and the United Nations. There is a UN force in Abyei, which is permanently there, and consists mainly of Ethiopian blue helmets, funded through the UN, to look after the security. You also have administrative arrangements, an additional tier of administration to look after Abyei issues in the context of two States. So you do have some express amendments of the Abyei protocol already. What remains will simply be the adoption of the criterion for participation in a referendum that needs to be reflected in new texts. You may have a new textual supplement to the Abyei agreement, but politically the matter is in the hands of the presidents for negotiations. It is coming up in the summits every so often. You see reports in the press that one side or the other is dissatisfied with the way it is being handled, but it is one to watch and to support the parties in their attempts to resolve it.

Response by Sarah Nouwen:

First, in response to the Ambassador. Some people consider the Machakos Protocol as a coup against Dr. John Garang. It was the secessionists in the SPLM who favoured self-determination, whereas John Garang fought for a united Sudan, a new Sudan, a democratic Sudan. The Machakos protocol granted self-determination. Some people who observed the proceedings say that Garang was furious with the negotiators, because of the way the Machakos Protocol had been phrased. So you are absolutely right in the sense that the South too was itself highly divided about the question of self-determination.

About the peace versus justice debate. I fully agree that "Justice before peace" can be quite problematic, but I am also quite sceptical about the very prominent sequencing argument: "First peace, then justice." Legal certainty is important in a transition. So you cannot first say: "Now peace without justice," and a few years later say: "Okay, let's do justice now." We have seen this happening with devastating consequences. During the Juba peace process, Joseph Kony read in the newspaper about Charles Taylor and Thomas Lubanga. Charles Taylor had been given asylum in Nigeria, but ended up in The Hague; Thomas Lubanga was promised inclusion in the government in the Congo, and also ended up in The

Hague. He queried whether he could trust signing an agreement with the government of Uganda, when there is such international pressure that ultimately he, too, could end up in The Hague. He never signed the Final Peace Agreement. In today's world, even Joseph Kony in the bush is totally aware of these developments. So "First peace, then justice" is too simple. The real answer is a broadening of our concept of justice. Why would justice just be criminal justice? There are so many dimensions of justice that have been totally ignored by the monopolisation of international criminal justice. So I think if The Hague has a role to play here, it should come up with a more diverse and universally informed concept of justice.

Just a few comments on Abyei and the role of the PCA. The PCA did help in resolving one of the issues, namely the question what is Abyei. Mr. Afako mentioned the fact that the still outstanding issue, which was not in the mandate of the PCA to address, is to identify who exactly the residents are of Abyei, and thus who has the right to vote in the referendum. That question is still outstanding. But in a way I am also glad that the PCA did not have the mandate to resolve it. Because to what extent can a judicial institution here in The Hague be able to resolve the relationship between the Ngok Dinka and the Misseriya, who will live together and have to live with each other in that particular area? I think what is needed is a much more locally informed peace process. A process which forces those entities that claim to represent the two sides, namely the SPLM and the government of Sudan, to negotiate in the peoples' interests rather than in the symbolic interest that Abyei has taken on.

And that is the second point I wanted to make. The Abyei issue has attracted so much international attention – Abyei this, Abyei that, Abyei such and so – and I think rightly so. It is indeed a very important area. But as a result, two other contested areas, the Blue Nile area and Southern Kordofan, have been ignored in the months before the South Sudan referendum. And everybody knew there was going to be a huge problem There, because in these areas there was an indigenous rebellion. There was a huge SPLM army there. Now of course when the CPA ended, the North did not want to have an SPLM army in its country, so the SPLM had to go South. These people said: "We are not Southerners, we are from here; we have fought our war, and with the secession of the South, our war has not been resolved, so we are going to stay." Of course, the North did not want to accept, because it did not want a second army in its country. The result is that now we have a civil war in Blue Nile and Southern Kordofan.

The Abyei Protocol has to be implemented one way or the other. But it is much more important to see Abyei in the context of the North-South relations more generally, including the implementation of the Addis Ababa Agreement, and the citizenship arrangements. What about all the Southerners that lived in the North? They are now suddenly foreigners in a country where they were born and raised. They only speak Arabic. Would they have to go South? Abyei should be resolved in that broader context.

FIGURE 9 *Billboard for National Reconciliation in South Sudan, April 2016.*

CHAPTER 3.5

Interview with Sarah Nouwen

Otto Spijkers and Anneleen de Jong

Sarah Nouwen is University Lecturer in Law at the University of Cambridge and a fellow of Pembroke College, Cambridge. She focuses in her research on the intersections between law and politics, justice and peace. Sudan plays a prominent role in her research. She wrote, *inter alia*, about the influence the involvement of the International Criminal Court in the Darfur situation has had the domestic criminal justice system in Sudan. Over the years, she has spent considerable time in the region, researching, teaching, and providing advice to various foreign ministries, NGOs, and regional organisations, in particular the African Union.

With Sarah Nouwen, we talked about the Sudanese peace process, and recent and related developments. In particular, we asked her to reflect on what had happened in South Sudan after the peace talks ended, and to link the peace talks and subsequent developments to Sudan's history in more general terms. We also spoke more generally, and in the abstract, about peace negotiations. And we asked her what lessons could be learned from the experience in South Sudan that could be applied in peace talks elsewhere.

OS: How has the work of the International Criminal Court (ICC) influenced attempts to find peace in the Sudan? It has been argued that it might have negatively affected such peace attempts, for example through the indictment of Omar al-Bashir, which made it difficult for certain international organisations to negotiate with him.

The primary research question in my doctoral dissertation was about the principle of complementarity, and whether this principle catalysed domestic proceedings. Nonetheless, the question you raise did emerge in my research. It is something you cannot avoid. There are several effects and impacts. First, as you mentioned, as the result of the ICC's involvement and the ICC's arrest warrants, some international actors felt that they could or should not talk to Bashir. Legally speaking, there is

Van Hoogstraten, Schrijver et al. (eds.), The Art of Making Peace: Lessons Learned from Peace Treaties
© 2017 The Editors. Printed in The Netherlands. ISBN *978-90-04-32123-6. pp. 100-110.*

not a strong basis for this: the Rome Statute does not prohibit talking to anyone. One is not prevented from talking with even indicted Heads of States. At the same time, there are of course political consequences attached to such ICC indictments. By following this self-imposed rule of refusing to talk to Bashir, some States have hugely diminished their influence on developments in Sudan. A lot of local foreign diplomats in Sudan were frustrated by this policy, because they felt that they could otherwise have had an impact on the peace process. In order to influence the peace process in Sudan, one must talk with Bashir.

But this is only a minor component of the impact. The biggest impact is that, as soon as you get the International Criminal Court involved and the Court issues arrest warrants against leaders on one side to the conflict, or sometimes two sides, or sometimes even three sides, the conflict as of then gets analysed through a criminal lens, *i.e.* the focus is on the individual criminal guilt of perpetrators. The conflict is explained through the frame of bad intentions of people – those identified as the criminals – rather than looking at the political features of the conflict. This poses a huge risk; the Darfur conflict is a perfect example, where the criminal lens for a long time replaced the political lens. This became a big obstacle to the resolution of the conflict.

OS: I believe you are right. To put it somewhat bluntly: in Europe, everything that has gone wrong is mostly blamed on al-Bashir, because he is depicted in the media as the principal villain.

And that is actually not an accurate picture of what is going on in Sudan. In no way do I want to plead in favour of Bashir. But the structural features of the conflict in Darfur were already visible under previous leaders; it escalated under Bashir, and the problem is more a lack of control by Bashir over militias that the government enabled, rather than too much control. The entire arrest warrant is based on Bashir being the mastermind and giving instructions, but that's not an accurate reflection of the situation in Sudan or the political system. That's one of my concerns about the relationship between the legal/criminal lens and the peace processes. That the former is not based on an accurate interpretation of the circumstances.

OS: Is a local justice mechanism a viable alternative, through which the Sudanese try to hold the perpetrators accountable?

It's the alternative to doing criminal justice at the *international* level, but I'm not sure that it is the only alternative. The first question should be: what does justice mean for people in that situation? I asked many Darfurians: "What does justice mean?" A frequent answer was: "Justice means the end of the war." Then the question is: "How do you end the war?," and the answer is: "By arresting Bashir." So this seems to support the ICC's approach. But many Darfurians referred to "real justice" as compensation and restoration in accordance with traditional judicial proceedings. Local justice mechanisms also have to be in balance with the peace efforts. The problem is the system that we have erected: with the ICC we have created an international institution that focuses only on criminal justice; the other elements that people value as "justice" are much less institutionalised and therefore marginalised. So both at the domestic and the international level we need a much more holistic approach to justice.

OS: Article 17 of the Rome Statute allows States parties to the Statute to organise criminal trials at the domestic level. If there are no such trials, then the ICC will step in. But if you use a more creative way to deal with such atrocities then it will not satisfy the ICC.

Exactly, so if you want to render cases inadmissible before the Court, you have to do precisely what the Court will do, but then at the domestic level. In the context of peace negotiations and peace processes, even without negotiations, I'm not sure whether this purely criminal justice approach fits in with the elements that you need for a successful peace process.

OS: Sudan is not even a party to the Rome Statute, but still the ICC manages to impose this criminal justice type of thinking on the Sudan. Is that not quite alarming?

It is the Security Council Resolution, and thus the UN system that imposes this on Sudan. This has had a big impact because when Security Council Members adopt the ICC system, they also begin to analyse Sudan through the criminal frame.

AdJ: But will this in the long run not have a positive effect? Perhaps not in relation to handling Bashir, but maybe it could deter future leaders?

The question with the positive effect of the ICC is: positive effect on whom? One can say: "Absolutely, by doing certain things in countries A and B, the ICC potentially has a positive effect on countries C, D, and E." But a question one should ask is: is it always appropriate to use countries A and B in order to set a precedent for countries C, D, and E, if this means making the resolution of the conflict in countries A and B more difficult? So the question is: do we have a sufficiently strong sense of community at the international level to do what the domestic criminal justice system does? In the domestic criminal justice system, we have such a society where you punish Mr. A and B and C in order to have a deterring effect on Mr. E, F, and G. Within that society we are all responsible to make sure that this justice system does not have negative consequences. We will suffer ourselves if it does. That is different at the international level. You can do justice in countries A and B, with the view to deterring criminal behaviour in other countries, even if this has disastrous consequences only for countries A and B.

OS: Can we anticipate a future role of the ICC also in the South Sudan? The Security Council might think about referring the situation in the South also to the ICC.

That's the interesting thing. One of the things I've been wondering over the past weeks is, why is it taking so long? I think it is because so far the Security Council has always used ICC referrals at the moment when it itself had confirmed who are the good guys and the bad guys. Libya and Sudan are two of the scenarios. It was very clear in Libya that the Council wanted to get Qaddafi out. The recent crisis in South Sudan has been a bit of a shock for Western members in the Security Council because they're good friends with the SPLM, the movement that is now falling apart, and they themselves don't know who the good guys and the bad guys are and it's risky to send the ICC in.

OS: Sir Roberts told us that there is quite a big community of South Sudanese in London. In The Netherlands there is a practice of prosecuting asylum seekers when it turns out that they have committed international crimes. Is that also an option, that instead of the Sudanese exercising their criminal justice system the other States exercise universal jurisdiction?

If one's aim is to set a standard for international accountability then universal jurisdiction definitely is an option, if the country concerned has adopted universal jurisdiction in its domestic laws. If the aim is to make a contribution to a peace process, then it is not necessarily helpful or harmful. That said, it would again be an isolated step towards a particular type of justice rather than a holistic approach to resolve a crisis.

OS: Let's look at it in a more general way. In what way can and should international law impact recent developments in the Sudan? If we leave aside international criminal justice, what can international lawyers do?

We shouldn't forget that we don't need to come up with an activist agenda for international law. It already plays its role. For example, the question whether the Ugandan support for the government of South Sudan is legal or not is a question determined by international law. But I don't think that we need to find a solution for a political crisis essentially in international law.

The biggest role for international law in South Sudan is respect for the principle of self-determination. The secession of South Sudan was based on the right to external self-determination, not on the basis of customary international law, but on the basis of a grant of that right to the South Sudanese by the Sudanese government. As a result of that right, the South Sudanese were allowed to say what they don't want to be, and they don't want to be part of Sudan. But it also means that they should be allowed to say who they do want to be, and that means that space should be made for domestic political processes towards a peace agreement, as opposed to imposing the conditions of that peace agreement from abroad, which is in a way a denial of the principle of internal self-determination.

AdJ: During the conference in October 2013 you were the only one who asked about the meaning of the word "peace." What kind of peace are we talking about? What is our definition of peace? Do you consider it important that, when you have a peace agreement, both parties share the same concept of peace? Or could you imagine a situation in which different parties have different conceptions of peace, and manage to conclude a peace agreement anyway?

I don't want to be too idealistic about it, because the ideal can become an enemy of the good. Very often, people at the negotiating table don't even have peace as their ideal. Their aim is rather to avoid being defeated by the other party, and to try and get the most out of it. I think the key lesson from this is that the negotiators and the international actors around that table should be fully aware of the stakes of the parties. And then they ought to see how they can ensure that the peace process actually contributes to peace in the future, rather than becoming an incentive for more violence.

AdJ: One of the criticisms of the Treaty of Versailles was that it was far too idealistic. It was argued that it was only 30 years later that the world was ready for some of the ideas proposed there. Should peace agreements take the situation as it is, or can they also be a little idealistic?

It is really important that they are realistic, because if they are not, then they become irrelevant, which is the least bad option. The worst option is that they become an incentive for more violence, and this is what we have seen in Sudan, where a lot of peace agreements were seen as dividing the cake among two parties, leading a third party to take up arms in order to get itself also involved in the peace agreements, so you get a chain of peace agreements. Peace negotiations should be realistic in the sense of seeing what the stakes are, but they should be idealistic in terms of opening up processes and allowing domestic political processes to take place for a better future. The problem with a lot of peace agreements is that they close off the space for such a political process, because this is spoiled by the parties that are at the table.

OS: What always fascinates me is the obsession lawyers have with texts. All these international lawyers come from all over the world to the South Sudan to sit at the negotiating table, and as soon as there is a peace agreement, they think: "We have produced our text, our job is done, and now we fly back home." You pointed out at the conference in October 2013 that this is a bit of a naïve way of judging the importance of such a piece of paper. The peace agreement is only part of the process, it is not the beginning nor the end.

Absolutely, there are several dimensions to this. First, in order to get to the text, you need a process to get people to the table, which is a very important political process. Secondly, the parties themselves should in a way be actively involved in claiming ownership of the text. That doesn't prohibit other people from writing the text, because the parties themselves might not be interested in writing, so the lawyers may have to come up with drafts which the parties can then discuss. But they have to feel they own the process. This is another example for what I think is going wrong in Darfur. The most beautiful draft peace agreements were written in the West, but not by the parties to the conflict. Finally, it's also about what happens afterwards, and then I think we have an obsession with checking boxes: this element of the peace agreement has been fulfilled, that element of the peace agreement has been fulfilled, etc. But there's very little attention to what is actually taking place. I think the current South Sudan crisis is a good example of that, where all the boxes were checked, but a civil war was in the making.

OS: So what would be some of these boxes that we want to check? Elections, rule of law?

Indeed. Many peace agreements look very similar these days. Many of the "comprehensive" peace agreements all have the same elements, many of which have very little to do with the actual conflict. Of course, they all have very noble aspirations, but it's not to say that by checking those boxes you resolve the crisis.

AdJ: One could say that every situation is very different from the other, but do you still think it will be useful to do further research to identify certain general criteria that ought to be considered when drafting a peace agreement? Would it be useful to identify some lessons learned from all the peace agreements written down in the last fifty years or so?

It depends on what the basis is for these criteria/rules/lessons. You see a lot of analysis of ongoing peace negotiations at the moment, and then they search for common factors, and try to derive the rules for peacemaking therefrom. But that intensifies the problem rather than resolves it, because then you get the general provisions on rule of law, human rights, etc being inserted in agreements even if they have nothing to do with what is happening on the ground. The key question for me is: what is the starting point for this analysis, is it the actual politics of the peace process? Then I'll say, yes, that's definitely a very useful way for future research. If it is analysing existing peace agreements, purely on what type of text they contain, then that may be very useful research for identifying certain trends in peace-making, but I don't see what it tells us about the success of a peace process.

OS: It might be important to place the present peace negotiations in the larger history of the Sudan, which goes back centuries. And those people that are presently engaged in the negotiations should be aware of this larger history, and aware that what they are doing is just a tiny part of that big story of the Sudanese people.

I think in a way that *they* are extremely aware of that, but some outsiders portray this as a unique moment in Sudanese history. The current South Sudan crisis is a good example of this. We were all shocked in December to see Ministers and Presidents returning to their military outfits. But that is what they have been doing for 20-30 years, and that's only the history of their own lives. For them, there was just a temporary peace and they are not afraid of going back to arms, as part of the new negotiation. For them, peace negotiations are not an end; it's just the continuation of the war on a different battlefield.

AdJ: You said earlier that if we adopt a holistic approach, cultural differences and cultural awareness plays an important role. Would you see that as part of the research that you'd like to continue with?

I think it is necessary to approach a peace process more bottom-up. The starting point should be: what is the current crisis all about? Take South Sudan. The political crisis is obvious to all. At the same time there is an institutional crisis: the lack of a national army and other national institutions. There are militia embedded in patronage systems. Thirdly, there is a society in crisis, a society with centuries of animosities but also friendships among particular groups, and these are now being exacerbated by the other two types of crises. If you start thinking about how those crises can be resolved and what have been the mechanisms in the past through which they have been resolved, you can get much further than by copypasting from peace agreements used in neighbouring countries in the past. Peace agreements built on an ideal state fail to recognise that current model states, to the extent they exist, were not created by peace agreements (alone).

AdJ: So maybe the solution could be found in the pre-colonial, cultural ways of dealing with each other, i.e. more traditional ways of defining peace or justice?

Perhaps. But one can't think away the impact of colonialism or the independence period after colonialism, so all these crises have to be addressed. I would focus on how people in a situation of conflict define as injustice. Mareike Schomerus, a colleague at the LSE, has conducted some very insightful research in South Sudan. All interviewees wanted justice, but if you asked them what injustices they were confronted with, many pointed to the failure of the political leaders to build up a stable South Sudan. It wasn't about human rights violations, it wasn't about particular crimes committed. They wanted a kind of political accountability of their leaders. What you then need is a political process rather than a criminal accountability process. Not to say that law doesn't play a role, because the South Sudanese have great expectations of their new constitution. But they don't have the hope that a legal text can resolve all problems. Others felt as injustice the lack of basic services. In South Sudan, women have a higher chance to die in pregnancy or in childbirth than to finish primary education.

OS: This morning I saw in the New York Times an article about how a lot of refugees were fleeing from the South of the Sudan to the North. This is interesting, as they seem to prefer an oppressive order in the North over the present chaos in South Sudan, which is very tragic if you think about how they fought for their independence from the North.

It's only so much part of the story of South Sudan's independence. Even during the North-South War, there were 2 million out of about 8-10 million South Sudanese in Khartoum. Similarly, a lot of Darfuri refugees have gone to Khartoum. This also shows you that the criminal frame of genocidal intent doesn't capture the entire story.

OS: Earlier you spoke of self-determination. It's quite fascinating that in almost all these peace negotiations self-determination plays a role. Are there some general lessons that we can learn from the negotiations at Dayton, at Kosovo, or here in Sudan? It's always about self-determination and how to give that a proper place in a new constitutional framework. Do we give them independence or autonomy? What are they entitled to? These are the questions that continuously emerge.

I think it matters a lot how you define self-determination, because there is a bit of a risk that people have political aspirations and in order to bolster their political aspirations, they refer to concepts of international law because these concepts seem to support their case. Self-determination is one of those. I think in a way that, apart from the colonial context, self-determination as a right to secession, seldom resolves the crisis at the core. It may be an intermediate, and necessary step, but it is a negative way of dealing with problems.

OS: But increasingly often secession is the result, like in Kosovo and now in Sudan; that does indicate a trend.

Yes, but I think on different grounds. The interesting thing about the Sudan case is that Garang didn't want self-determination – he wanted a united Sudan. The insertion of self-determination in the Machakos protocol was a coup against him.

OS: South Sudan as a State owes its existence to this right to self-determination. Doesn't that oblige them to give the same rights to the minorities that are now in South Sudan?

They don't owe their existence to self-determination as an independent right under customary international law; they owe their existence to a political right of self-determination that they forced the government of Sudan to grant to them in a peace agreement. The current crisis in South Sudan is not one of self-determination; it is, at least in part, a political crisis. The political leaders have always been split about the future of South Sudan – that's expressing it optimistically. The more pessimistic view of the crisis is that it's about who gets the best jobs and the money that comes with it.

OS: It's always a bit tricky to predict the future, but since you've been in the Sudan many times, both in the North and also in the South, I wanted to ask you this question: everybody is very pessimistic about the future of South Sudan. Could you give us some reasons for hope or optimism?

I think the many disappointments that have been expressed since the crisis broke out in December have a lot to do with our own expectations. In the West we saw South Sudan as our little project of building an independent State overnight. The first lesson is that you can't build somebody else's State. Secondly, this is going to take time, and years. I mean, very strong States in the West have over centuries and decades been built on many bloody political crises, and this may happen as well in South Sudan. The key challenge is to create a space that the South Sudanese are allowed to have these political processes, while of course protecting civilians as much as possible. I am not saying: "Put a gate around South Sudan and fence it off and let them kill each other." But we shouldn't turn South Sudan into a kind of new international protectorate.

In terms of the future of the peace negotiations more generally, I there are two types of scenarios. In one type of scenario you really see peace negotiations being conducted in accordance with the particular international norms and expectations. In the other type of scenario, those norms and expectations are almost forgotten, simply because a practical solution to a conflict *must* be found, and such an approach is much more pragmatic. Which scenario is used often depends on the views of the big international players, and the stakes of the international players in those negotiations. I'm concerned about the increasing divergence between these two tracks. Some countries are allowed to have all kinds of peace agreements, simply because the big powers really want peace there. But other countries are supposed to comply with all kinds of putative international norms of peace agreements and UN best practices etc., because they have become a playground for peace negotiations and for these types of processes.

AdJ: Maybe different interest groups from civil society could also play a role in peace negotiations, and not only States.

Absolutely. With a lot of negotiations that space is entirely closed off, and that's a very bad indication for the future. Earlier, I spoke about creating space for political processes. If the negotiations themselves closed off that space, it may be really difficult to open it up later on. That said, we've also talked about the need to be realistic. Very often the negotiating parties refuse to allow other parties, including civil society, to participate, because they fear it might undermine their position. But there are peace processes that are more inclusive. In the peace talks concerning the Lord's Resistance Army that were conducted in Juba in South Sudan, there were extensive consultations of the people in Northern Uganda about how they envisaged peace, what they wanted their leaders to agree upon and they sent delegates to the negotiating table who really helped their leaders to account for what they were negotiating. I think this could be an important model for the future.

AdJ: And the UN should take part of the responsibility to promote such a new approach to peace negotiations?

Yes.

CHAPTER 3.6

Interview with Barney Afako

Otto Spijkers and Anneleen de Jong

Barney Afako is a lawyer from Uganda. He is an expert on peace negotiations, with much hands-on experience in that field, especially in Africa. Most importantly for present purposes, he was the chief legal advisor to the Southern Sudanese mediation in the Juba Peace Talks between the Government of Uganda and the Lord's Resistance Army, in the years 2006 to 2008.

With Barney Afako, we discussed the strategy of a peace negotiator. We asked him to reflect on his personal experience as a peace negotiator in the Sudan and elsewhere. What is the role of (international) law in peace talks? What is the role of other types of considerations, such as cultural connections or shared histories? We asked him to share some best practices of a peace negotiator. What are the necessary characteristics of an effective and successful peace negotiator? We also asked him to reflect on developments in South Sudan that had occurred after he gave his keynote speech at the Peace Palace in the Fall of 2013.

OS: You are a peace negotiator. And once you are assigned that role, you have to start somewhere. How do you choose your strategy? And what is your role in deciding on the strategy? How do you approach the negotiations? Do you start with a plan in mind?

I think it very much depends on the negotiations because with some negotiations the mediator is given the free hand to devise the strategy after the parties have given their input. Then there are other negotiations where at least one of the parties is stronger and wants to give strong input to set the agenda. So it very much depends on the situation. But of course always the role of the mediator is to make sure that there is equality of arms. Even in developing the strategy it is important to make sure it does not advantage one side unfairly and disadvantage the other. In situations where there is ongoing violence, the priority in my experience is on bringing the hostilities to some kind of pause, if not to an end. There is an immediate need to secure a cessation of hostili-

Van Hoogstraten, Schrijver et al. (eds.), The Art of Making Peace: Lessons Learned from Peace Treaties
 ISBN 978-90-04-32123-6. pp. 111-122.

ties or any other precursor to a ceasefire. You will then find that a lot of time is taken up by those details and during that stage the negotiator can have the time to identify the issues on which the different parties disagree. In my experience these issues often come down to power or its misuse, and in order to prevent the abuse of power it is important to include participation by each side and thereby to respect their interests and demands. So an easy way is to ask each side for their issues and then having received these in written form, one should wrap those issues up in groups and into agenda items. Then it will be for the parties to expand their positions with respect to each agenda item. This makes some kind of framework. The mediation should then decide how it proposes to approach the negotiations, the form of the negotiations and the order in which the issues are addressed. Remember that the parties would very often straight away set up their highest demands; so you may have to take matters as the parties present them, or be prepared to persuade them of the merits of a different approach.

OS: Do you sometimes have to convince the parties that there is no alternative to peace negotiations because sometimes the balance of power may shift and one of the parties may decide that they might actually win the conflict on the battlefield, so why negotiate...?

Absolutely, nobody negotiates if they can win on the battlefield – that is the hard reality. Everyone who negotiates has calculated that there is some advantage in negotiating. The advantage may be simply that they will get political or other dividends because they have agreed to the talks. This may be in the form of economic or other advantage from a third party. It may not be because they are so keen on the negotiations, but because tactically talks are a useful thing to do. They may also be under pressure; not everybody comes voluntarily to the talks. However, everyone around the negotiation table would usually rather have won in the battlefield. But, of course, the weaker party sometimes fights in order to be taken seriously and to have the chance to negotiate afterwards. For some parties, the negotiations are their highest political aspiration, but the militarily stronger party is normally not interested in negotiations, and may stall them, negotiate half-heartedly, or try to create maximum advantage in the field before the talks begin. That is why we often see hostilities escalating around talks rather than de-escalating. Everybody wants to be in an as strong a position as possible, even if they are not winning the way, they want to strengthen their hand in the negotiations by military activity such as capturing territory.

OS: I want to ask you about framing the negotiations. I am a lawyer and look at peace negotiations as a legal process, the making of an agreement. But if you were a historian, you would look at peace negotiations in a very different way. I was wondering if the background of the mediator plays a role in how the person frames the process, taking into account that if you have a background as a lawyer, you may look at the role of the mediator differently than if you were a political scientist, to give an example.

It is correct that the background experience and training of the mediator will affect the way that he or she conceives of what is an appropriate process. My own view is that all negotiation processes are apparently political, and that within that political process a mediator must have a maximum of flexibility in the search for solutions. But on the other hand, there is increasingly a resort to this idea of normativity, which insists that there are particular legal principles by which various problems are to be resolved, whether these are territorial issues or political issues. Therefore, increasingly mediators are pressured to uphold "international standards", which is a shorthand for positions that the broader international community and activists for various causes might want to see reflected in law. So negotiations are never just about drafting the consensus. You can have a brilliant draft but two or three months or years down the line it will look increasingly less brilliant and may simply become problematic because it has not gone into sufficient detail on some issues or has closed off avenues. So if the mediator is coming from one particular professional background it is important to strengthen the mediator's team to have a balanced outlook. So when the issues are predominantly political, they also need good legal people, analysts and historians. The historical perspective is actually extremely important. Mediators themselves need not be historians, but it is critical that they have a grasp of where the conflict has come from. The danger with history, however, is that history is the vision of the person writing it. But to have a grasp of the key events and the various parties involved in those events, and their different interpretations of those events, is crucial for understanding the positions that will be brought to the table and the other issues a stake today. So as a mediator you need to be multi-faceted. You cannot afford to be only one thing because you cannot produce a good agreement in that way.

AdJ: In the interview we had with Sarah Nouwen of Cambridge University, she mentioned that this holistic approach is necessary to improve the area of international law in order to better assist in the process of making peace. However, this also complicates matters on the negotiating table because that would probably mean that not one concept of peace could be used, but divergent concepts of peace should be integrated in the negotiation. Do you have experience with this or is the experience more tending towards discussions leading to everyone agreeing on the same concept?

I think it is possible to overcomplicate the notion of peace. We should agree that there is no perfect peace and that every peace will be imperfect because society is always evolving. And there are certain things that will be lacking in any given process or agreement. And there will always be groups, social groups, whose interests are not fully acknowledged. This is a dynamic process, and a dynamic process means that the number of people who are left behind in the progress of the society is decreased. The danger I see now is that people take the occasion of a peace process, which sets out to achieve the cessation of violence, to be the opportunity to design the perfect society. Whereas very often the answers to societal problems are not yet available, and not all of the parties who ought legitimately to construct a new society are, or can be, around the table. Because some of the grievances which lead to conflict will be recent and regionally specific, the analyses may fall short because the emphasis is on correcting specific grievances. On that basis, it would not be appropriate for the negotiators to attempt to reconstruct the whole of society, as the process is not genuinely inclusive in themes and participants. I am sceptical about the notion that international law should construct the content of a perfect peace, and thereby shape the content of peace processes. I would lean towards the approach that you give each country and the population of that country the opportunity to craft for themselves a blueprint of what they perceive their future to be. I think of it as an extension of the notion of self-determination, which is the right to make those decisions, including the mistakes, for yourself. So I would consider it problematic if international law were to decide what the ultimate peace should look like and to require negotiators to conform to that ideal. There ought to be liberty to design what is appropriate for a country, or part of a country, at a particular time, acknowledging that the pursuit of peace is a continuous process, which will have to be revisited, but within the internal politics rather than through external mediators and negotiators.

AdJ: So the peace concept that you are looking for, or the peace you are looking for is a compromise?

It has to be a compromise. Politics is a compromise. That is why you vote for a party and not another because you are not satisfied with the politics they adopt, the direction in which they are taking the country. The danger of translating peace into a legal paradigm that it becomes normative, whereas peace is politics and it should be treated as such. This implies that the peace in East Africa will be different from the peace in Latin America, but that hopefully both societies will be developing themselves and be respectful to the different constituencies within. I am sceptical of a law on what peace should look like, as it is most likely that the content of that international law will be designed from particular countries and points of views and will reflect the aspirations and the legal values that dominate international law at the moment. That is why I am sceptical of the legalisation of what peace negotiations should be aiming for.

AdJ: Considering what you just said, looking for this situation-specific kind of negotiation, this means that the negotiator needs very specific characteristics. He needs to have knowledge of the situation, stakeholders involved, what is realistic and not, in order to make the peace negotiations possible. Could you tell us what you experienced as key characteristics of your function as a negotiator?

I think you put your hand on it to say that the negotiator needs to understand the context in which the parties are operating, and of course also the broader context of the region and the international context. But critically, what is the history of the country, what are the challenges it has faced, what has caused the conflict that gave rise to the negotiations? That is background research and correct analysis is important, but is not a fixed text, it changes, and it is crucial that the mediation should be able to adjust its position and abandon beliefs that turn out not to be incorrect from the analysis. So the analysis is continuous and you have to be ready to change your mind all of the time, adjust your position, responding to the facts and making new analyses. It means that you have to be able to listen at very many different levels to the parties, not only to those that are negotiating, but also those outside of the negotiating room who are also stakeholders of the peace that you and the parties are trying to construct. You need that listening ear, but you also need the analytical capability to read the situation and to look for possible solutions. The whole problem is not just information for its own sake, analysis for its own sake: you are moving the parties from a position of conflict towards a minimum level of consensus beyond which they can continue the efforts to solve their own problems. So that is one. The other function is, I suppose, more intuitive. It is a learned intuition, to be able to detect and identify when the moment in a process is right for decision. When you are negotiating you go back and forth over the issues, the parties rehearse their positions; you explore common ground and so forth. There comes a moment when the time is right to push either one or both parties to reach an agreement and to accept a reasonable consensus. You can miss that opportunity, and if you let the parties sleep on an issue, the next day the mood might have changed and the issues might also change. You need to be able to detect when the time is right for particular concessions that may not resolve the whole conflict but can advance elements of it. The mediator always needs to be alert to know when the moment is right or ripe for compromise. The mediator least therefore has to be decisive as well as constantly adapting his analysis, listen well and trust his or her instinct.

AdJ: You have to be at the same time listening and a bit in the background and taking decisions at the right moment?

Absolutely. It is not an inert listening. It is listening for the purpose of being ready to act, you are always very high on the alert. Listening to make sure that nothing is changed, looking for the ultimate opportunity to make consensus. I think that is quite critical. Therefore you need to be good at reading people. You are dealing with individuals. It is not enough to simply recite normative values to the parties. You are to persuade them to make the compromise at the right time. If you are bad with people you cannot be a good mediator. You will miss opportunities to influence them.

AdJ: They have to understand that you are neutral to the case. That must be difficult to convince them that you have no gains in the process yourself.

Absolutely. That is not so much a skill, but actually a matter of hard work. You always have to be mathematical in the way that you spend time with the parties; in the way you come across to them; in how you talk to them in private, as well as in meetings, so that nobody can say that they have a reason to suspect that you are not utterly impartial. That means that you may have to hold meetings that you did not want to hold, but which are important to maintain the perception of your neutrality. It is important to be seen to be even-handed. You must also be willing to be blamed by each side and sometimes when both sides attack the mediator, then you know that the mediator is doing something right, as both sides are equally disaffected.

OS: It is clear that a lot is expected of a mediator. That brings up another issue. It is an enormous responsibility that you have to handle. Just one or two people, the mediators, have all this responsibility on their shoulders. And then one might ask: is there something that you might need from the international community? How could the international community assist you and your colleagues in being a successful mediator?

In many ways, the international community in contemporary mediations and negotiations is very much a part of the process, as in fact often its representatives are in the room as observers. They are almost always outside the room as well, having direct access to the parties. Now this cuts two ways. It can be a useful intervention if they understand the mediation strategy and want to support it. As a mediator, sometimes instead of going yourself to engage the parties, it is easier to ask representatives of the international community to talk to the parties they are more close to in order to tray and persuade them on a particular issue. This is because a party may be able to take certain suggestions from their friends which they will certainly not take from the other party and perhaps not from the mediator. This can therefore be a constructive role for the international community to play. The international community also acts through its institutional decision-making processes. Think of the EU, AU and the UN. Sometimes these institutions might impose the structure and even the deadline for the negotiations. You can't nowadays wish away the international community, and it very rare indeed to have a mediation process that is isolated from international influence. This can also come at a cost if external actors do not see things in the same way that the mediator is trying to develop. In that case, you might get outright sabotage of the process. Sometimes this might come in the form of parallel initiatives and unhelpful suggestions, which complicate the attitudes and responses of the parties. Yes, international intervention is quite significant and can be decisive in a process. It is a fact of life that one has to manage. That is one of the other skills that the mediator needs to have: to manage all the people who become involved in a process along with the different perspectives and influences they bring.

Another area where the international community plays a role is of course in the funding of processes. Once you have a big and cost intensive process, you will need money, and money often comes from various sources from the international community. With money comes influence. Nobody pays for these things without exerting a certain degree of influence. So the mediation needs to manage that aspect as well. With the funding comes the problem that very quickly the money issue begins to dictate the time frames for the negotiations. If you run out of money, you need to reach decisions quickly. That might be helpful to some parties in some processes, but quick decisions might not be so helpful in other processes. The parties and the mediation have to deal with the constraints and other negative aspects of external funding.

OS: How do you see the role of academia and research institutes? Some provide entire peace plans and agreements, and others might come up with general principles, such as the principles formulated by the Hague Institute for Global Justice recently. They came up with principles on the rule of law and successful peace-building. Are they in any way helpful to the day-to-day work of the mediator?

Yes and no. I think I need to go back and say that we are now in a world of proliferation of information and advocacy. The ease with which information can be transmitted can be overwhelming for negotiators and mediators. Some of these research institutes work on abstract and academic principles and frameworks and their proposals can be extremely confusing for parties who are perhaps not schooled in these issues. To be told that these are principles and concerns to be taken into account can be overwhelming, when all they wanted perhaps was simply to secure a demobilisation deal or participation in government, and were ready to resolve the other details in the future. If you demand of the parties that they craft the perfect peace, this might leave them out of their depth, and has the effect of removing the process from the parties and into the hands of experts. And so the parties become dependent on these experts who have an answer for everything. The agreement that you produce at the end might not be recognised as owned and originated by the parties themselves. That is the danger of external inputs.

On the other hand, the advantage is that there is now the possibility for specialised analysis and input. When historical political analysis of the situation is done, it means that as a mediator you have various sources to draw from outside of the parties who are likely to give you a partial perspective of a conflict; of what is happening on the ground or of the historical realities. So the analysis of the politics is helpful and very educative for the mediator. So if you have well-written pieces about various recent conflicts or other forms of identity conflicts, that can be useful. An analysis by someone who knows what he or she is talking about is often far more valuable than the narratives that come from the parties, which are almost by definition partial, although that is legitimate from their perspective. I think the role of academia is quite important, especially if academic reports are dispassionate, and simply set out what they see as the range of options without bias. In that case, they are highly valuable.

OS: Can you also say a few words about how you as a mediator can make use of the international media?

The media is problematic, firstly because the parties are also making use of the media. Everyone is trying to win the propaganda war. You will have no control of what the media purports you have said. So you have to adapt to and manage the media. It is important of course that you directly speak to the media about the mediation process, the difficulties it might be facing, its hopes and its aspirations. At the same time you should be very careful to try and avoid the possibility of being misrepresented, because a headline which is inaccurate can set you back for days, weeks, even months as it can affect that perception of impartiality that is so important to protect. I would say that by all means the international media should be managed, sometimes by keeping it at bay, or regulating the parties' use of the media during the talks. Sometimes you have to take the parties away to a place where the media cannot come, although you cannot prevent the parties from talking to the media by modern means of communication. The media has limitations to what it can contribute, and will focus on the news angle. It is others such as historians who might be better able to bring the analysis that might be missing. The media serve publicity purposes. I am not sure that every negotiation would benefit from publicity. The point of the negotiations is not to seek publicity as an end in itself but to achieve consensus between the key entities.

AdJ: Could you mention something about the impact that you had in the Sudan negotiation? Was there a difficulty in controlling the media? Did you come up with limits of your capacity as a mediator? What was your impact as Barney Afako in the processes that you managed?

That is a difficult one to talk about because I am not yet done with that situation. Maybe it is too early because I still have to go back and try to finish the work. Let me make a general remark instead. In a situation of conflict where the parties are trying to resolve difficult issues, it doesn't help to have a mediator whose diary is very full, and who wants to be somewhere else in a couple of months' time. It is important that we design forms of mediation that are akin to politically supporting the parties to solve the problems over an extended period. What the African Union has been trying to do in Sudan is along that model. That model of course can of course be frustrating. If you are in a hurry the solutions will not come as fast as you want to see them. It is necessary to have the endurance to act as long-term facilitators, so that we keep coming back until the parties reach a stage where they can resolve these matters for themselves. We have to be tenacious and patient with the parties knowing that the goal of resolving these issues will improve the fate of the people of both countries – Sudan and South Sudan – and of the region. It is important that we stick to that model of mediation rather than focus on our own frustrations with the parties or the lack of success. The focus must never be on the individual facilitator. If we can put in place an institutional framework, which makes appropriate facilitation available to the parties, it doesn't matter who is providing this facilitation, the process must go ahead.

OS: Do you see a role for international institutions like the ICC or the UN?

The ICC has become very controversial on the African continent. This controversy I happen to think is a good thing because it is forcing us to go back to first principles to look at the Rome Statute and our own response to serious crimes. What sort of instrument was the Statute; who takes priority in dealing with situations where crimes may have been committed? And how do we develop appropriate responses, in situ, wherever these types of crimes might have happened; what solutions should be crafted and what processes of justice and accountability should be developed and adopted? I think that having this standoff with the ICC makes all of us reflect more deeply. Many countries will now have to approach this matter of accountability which might not otherwise have been given priority. Every situation needs to own the agenda of accountability, reconciliation and peace, and to find a formula for advancing all three in situations of conflicts. True, the ICC is now a part of the justice architecture, but it is not the only element, and should not use up all the oxygen. The Rome Statute says the Court plays a complementary and not a primary role. We need to rediscover this key principle of complementarity because there is a danger that it has been interpreted out of existence.

As for the UN: almost all countries of the world are members of the UN, and therefore are subject to the Charter and have obligations flowing from the Charter. The Charter's key obligation is the promotion of peace; the prevention and ending hostilities. When hostilities break out it is inevitable that the UN will become involved; sometimes at the highest level of the Security Council. Consequences for mediation follow from the decisions that the UN makes about how to respond to situations of conflict. The same is true for responses of regional bodies like the African Union and decisions its Peace and Security Council. But in terms of resolving the issues of conflict within a State, it cannot be assumed that external solutions, even those from the UN will work. Sometimes regional bodies and neighbouring states might be better placed to assist in the search for solutions.

OS: What do you think of the UN Security Council imposing economic sanctions?

That is one of the interventions available to the Council, and it is possible to make a judgement about the impact of sanctions in each situation. Imposition of sanctions is normally an expression of frustration with the lack of progress, and is intended to signal international concern and ultimately to serve the purpose of peace.

Going back to the point where we began, when we think about peace, we must accept that there is a baseline of standards of what a State can and cannot do particularly to its population. The international community must be concerned about what conditions the population of each state is subjected to. Beyond that, in order to achieve lasting solutions, you need the people for each State to reach their own accommodations that are workable. External actors, such as the UN and others, can of course help the parties to reach the necessary accommodations with each other. But it cannot be stressed enough that the development and content of a peace must come from within and must be internalized by the affected communities and parties, otherwise all efforts will be built on sand.

FIGURE 10 *Juba, South Sudan, 29 April 2016. A new Unity Government is sworn in.*

PART 4

The Absence of Peace Agreements

FIGURE 11 *First sign of UN peacekeeping in Iran after the ceasefire in Iran-Iraq war, August 1988.*

FIGURE 12 *Political prisoners making clothing for the war effort, Evin Prison in Tehran, 1986.*

Introduction to and Texts of Security Council Resolutions 598 (1987) and 687 (1991) Concerning Iran and Iraq

Since its founding in 1945, the United Nations Security Council has adopted dozens of resolutions with the aim of bringing about an immediate cessation of armed hostilities between two or more belligerent parties. Although the UN Charter does not explicitly mention this particular function of the Security Council, practice has proven that the role of the Security Council can be very effective in peacemaking processes. Through the development of the Security Council as a political body, warring parties no longer are the sole players in matters of international peace and security. In this chapter, various Security Council resolutions are discussed as instruments in peace making, notably Resolutions 598 (1987) and 687 (1991), as well as the role of the highest judicial body of the United Nations, the International Court of Justice.

United Nations Security Council Resolution 598 (1987) called for an immediate ceasefire between Iran and Iraq and the repatriation of prisoners of war, and for both sides to withdraw to the internationally recognized boundaries. The Resolution requested the Secretary-General to dispatch a team of UN observers to monitor the cease-fire while a permanent settlement was reached to end the conflict. It became effective on 8 August 1988. While the war (now also known as the first Gulf war) was over, Iraq spent the rest of August and early September clearing the Kurdish resistance, in which 400 Iraqi soldiers and 50.000 Kurdish civilians and soldiers were killed.

United Nations Security Council Resolution 687 (1991), the longest resolution adopted in the history of the Security Council, set the terms with which Iraq was to comply after losing the second Gulf War. Resolution 687 was passed by 12 votes to one against (Cuba), with two abstentions (Ecuador and Yemen). The Resolution urged Iraq and Kuwait to respect the boundary between the two countries, calling on the Secretary-General Javier Pérez de Cuéllar to assist both in demarcating the border and setting up a plan for the immediate deployment of the United Nations Iraq-Kuwait Observation Mission (UNIKOM) in a demilitarized zone. The Resolution stated that Iraq is liable for any loss, damage, and injury inflicted upon Kuwait, further demanding that Iraq repatriate all Kuwaiti and third country nationals in cooperation with the ICRC and

Van Hoogstraten, Schrijver et al. (eds.), The Art of Making Peace: Lessons Learned from Peace Treaties
© 2017 The Editors. Printed in The Netherlands. ISBN 978-90-04-32123-6. pp. 125-138.

hand over any remaining property seized from Kuwait. It also includes liability under international law for any direct loss, damage, including environmental damage and the depletion of natural resources, or injury to foreign governments, nationals and corporations. Furthermore, Resolution 687 stipulated that Iraq destroy all its biological and chemical weapons under international supervision and accept inspection of all nuclear weapons. In order to keep Iraq under pressure the sanctions regime established under previous resolutions was continued, with exceptions for medical supplies, foodstuffs, supplies for "essential civilian needs" and payments related thereto. Lastly, the Security Council demanded that Iraq would not engage in acts of or support for international terrorism. During the debate preceding the adoption of this Resolution on 3 April 1991, the Iraqi government expressed a series of objections and reservations with respect to its contents and submitted a seven-page letter dated 6 April 1991. In the penultimate paragraph the Minister of Foreign Affairs wrote, however, that Iraq "has no choice but to accept this resolution" (see UN doc. S/22456). While Iraq thus accepted this mandatory and comprehensive peace package, it is obvious that it did not do so voluntarily and that Resoltion 687 (1991) cannot be viewed as a peace agreement.

UN Security Council, Resolution 598 (1987)

Adopted by the Security Council at its 2750th meeting, on 20 July 1987, 20 July 1987, S/RES/598 (1987), adopted unanimously.

The Security Council,

Reaffirming its resolution 582 (1986)

Deeply concerned that, despite its calls for a cease-fire, the conflict between Iran and Iraq continues unabated, with further heavy loss of human life and material destruction,

Deploring the initiation and continuation of the conflict,

Deploring also the bombing of purely civilian population centers, attacks on neutral shipping or civilian aircraft, the violation of international humanitarian law and other laws of armed conflict, and, in particular, the use of chemical weapons contrary to obligations under the 1925 Geneva Protocol,

Deeply concerned that further escalation and widening of the conflict may take place,

Determined to bring to an end all military actions between Iran and Iraq,

Convinced that a comprehensive, just, honourable and durable settlement should be achieved between Iran and Iraq,

Recalling the provisions of the Charter of the United Nations and in particular the obligation of all member states to settle their international disputes by peaceful means in such a manner that international peace and security and justice are not endangered,

Determining that there exists a breach of the peace as regards the conflict between Iran and Iraq,

Acting under Articles 39 and 40 of the Charter of the United Nations,

1. *Demands* that, as a first step towards a negotiated settlement, Iran and Iraq observe an immediate cease-fire, discontinue all military actions on land, at sea and in the air, and withdraw all forces to the internationally recognized boundaries without delay;
2. *Requests* the Secretary-General to dispatch a team of United Nations Observers to verify, confirm and supervise the cease-fire and withdrawal and further requests the Secretary-General to make the necessary arrangements in consultation with the Parties and to submit a report thereon to the Security Council;

3. *Urges* that prisoners of war be released and repatriated without delay after the cessation of active hostilities in accordance with the Third Geneva Convention of 12 August 1949;
4. *Calls upon* Iran and Iraq to cooperate with the Secretary- General in implementing this resolution and in mediation efforts to achieve a comprehensive, just and honourable settlement, acceptable to both sides, of all outstanding issues in accordance with the principles contained in the Charter of the United Nations;
5. *Calls upon* all other States to exercise the utmost restraint and to refrain from any act which may lead to further escalation and widening of the conflict and thus to facilitate the implementation of the present resolution;
6. *Requests* the Secretary-General to explore, in consultation with Iran and Iraq, the question of entrusting an impartial body with inquiring into responsibility for the conflict and to report to the Security Council as soon as possible;
7. *Recognizes* the magnitude of the damage inflicted during the conflict and the need for reconstruction efforts, with appropriate international assistance, once the conflict is ended and, in this regard, requests the Secretary-General to assign a team of experts to study the question of reconstruction and to report to the Security Council;
8. *Further requests* the Secretary-General to examine in consultation with Iran and Iraq and with other states of the region measures to enhance the security and stability of the region;
9. *Requests* the Secretary-General to keep the Security Council informed on the implementation of this resolution;
10. *Decides* to meet again as necessary to consider further steps to insure compliance with this resolution.

United Nations Security Council Resolution 687 (1991)

Adopted by the United Nations Security Council at its 2981st meeting, on 3 Apri 1991

The Security Council,

Recalling its resolutions 660 (1990) of 2 August 1990, 661 (1990) of 6 August 1990, 662 (1990) of 9 August 1990, 664 (1990) of 18 August 1990, 665 (1990) of 25 August 1990, 666 (1990) of 13 September 1990, 667 (1990) of 16 September 1990, 669 (1990) of 24 September 1990, 670 (1990) of 25 September 1990, 674 (1990) of 29 October 1990, 677 (1990) of 28 November 1990, 678 (1990) of 29 November 1990 and 686 (1991) of 2 March 1991,

Welcoming the restoration to Kuwait of its sovereignty, independence and territorial integrity and the return of its legitimate Government,

Affirming the commitment of all Member States to the sovereignty, territorial integrity and political independence of Kuwait and Iraq, and noting the intention expressed by the Member States cooperating with Kuwait under paragraph 2 of resolution 678 (1990) to bring their military presence in Iraq to an end as soon as possible consistent with paragraph 8 of resolution 686 (1991),

Reaffirming the need to be assured of Iraq's peaceful intentions in the light of its unlawful invasion and occupation of Kuwait,

Taking note of the letter sent by the Minister for Foreign Affairs of Iraq on 27 February 1991 and those sent pursuant to resolution 686 (1991),

Noting that Iraq and Kuwait, as independent sovereign States, signed at Baghdad on 4 October 1963 "Agreed Minutes Between the State of Kuwait and the Republic of Iraq Regarding the Restoration of Friendly Relations, Recognition and Related Matters", thereby recognizing formally the boundary between Iraq and Kuwait and the allocation of islands, which were registered with the United Nations in accordance with Article 102 of the Charter of the United Nations and in which Iraq recognized the independence and complete sovereignty of the State of Kuwait within its borders as specified and accepted in the letter of the Prime Minister of Iraq dated 21 July 1932, and as accepted by the Ruler of Kuwait in his letter dated 10 August 1932,

Conscious of the need for demarcation of the said boundary,

Conscious also of the statements by Iraq threatening to use weapons in violation of its obligations under the Geneva Protocol for the Prohibition of the Use in War of Asphyxiating, Poisonous or Other Gases, and of Bacteriological Methods of Warfare, signed at Geneva on 17 June 1925, and of its prior use of chemical weapons and affirming that grave consequences would follow any further use by Iraq of such weapons,

Recalling that Iraq has subscribed to the Declaration adopted by all States participating in the Conference of States Parties to the 1925 Geneva Protocol and Other Interested States, held in Paris from 7 to 11 January 1989, establishing the objective of universal elimination of chemical and biological weapons,

Recalling also that Iraq has signed the Convention on the Prohibition of the Development, Production and Stockpiling of Bacteriological (Biological) and Toxin Weapons and on Their Destruction, of 10 April 1972,

Noting the importance of Iraq ratifying this Convention,

Noting moreover the importance of all States adhering to this Convention and encouraging its forthcoming Review Conference to reinforce the authority, efficiency and universal scope of the convention,

Stressing the importance of an early conclusion by the Conference on Disarmament of its work on a Convention on the Universal Prohibition of Chemical Weapons and of universal adherence thereto,

Aware of the use by Iraq of ballistic missiles in unprovoked attacks and therefore of the need to take specific measures in regard to such missiles located in Iraq,

Concerned by the reports in the hands of Member States that Iraq has attempted to acquire materials for a nuclear-weapons programme contrary to its obligations under the Treaty on the Non-Proliferation of Nuclear Weapons of 1 July 1968,

Recalling the objective of the establishment of a nuclear-weapons-free zone in the region of the Middle East,

Conscious of the threat that all weapons of mass destruction pose to peace and security in the area and of the need to work towards the establishment in the Middle East of a zone free of such weapons,

Conscious also of the objective of achieving balanced and comprehensive control of armaments in the region,

Conscious further of the importance of achieving the objectives noted above using all available means, including a dialogue among the States of the region,

Noting that resolution 686 (1991) marked the lifting of the measures imposed by resolution 661 (1990) in so far as they applied to Kuwait,

Noting also that despite the progress being made in fulfilling the obligations of resolution 686 (1991), many Kuwaiti and third country nationals are still not accounted for and property remains unreturned,

Recalling the International Convention against the Taking of Hostages, opened for signature at New York on 18 December 1979, which categorizes all acts of taking hostages as manifestations of international terrorism,

Deploring threats made by Iraq during the recent conflict to make use of terrorism against targets outside Iraq and the taking of hostages by Iraq,

Taking note with grave concern of the reports of the Secretary-General of 20 March 1991 and 28 March 1991, and conscious of the necessity to meet urgently the humanitarian needs in Kuwait and Iraq,

Bearing in mind its objective of restoring international peace and security in the area as set out in recent resolutions of the Security Council,

Conscious of the need to take the following measures acting under Chapter VII of the Charter,

1. *Affirms* all thirteen resolutions noted above, except as expressly changed below to achieve the goals of this resolution, including a formal cease-fire;

A

2. *Demands* that Iraq and Kuwait respect the inviolability of the international boundary and the allocation of islands set out in the "Agreed Minutes Between the State of Kuwait and the Republic of Iraq Regarding the Restoration of Friendly Relations, Recognition and Related Matters", signed by them in the exercise of their sovereignty at Baghdad on 4 October 1963 and registered with the United Nations and published by the United Nations in document 7063, United Nations, Treaty Series, 1964;

3. *Calls upon* the Secretary-General to lend his assistance to make arrangements with Iraq and Kuwait to demarcate the boundary between Iraq and Kuwait, drawing on appropriate material, including the map transmitted by Security Council document S/22412 and to report back to the Security Council within one month;

4. *Decides* to guarantee the inviolability of the above-mentioned international boundary and to take as appropriate all necessary measures to that end in accordance with the Charter of the United Nations;

B

5. *Requests* the Secretary-General, after consulting with Iraq and Kuwait, to submit within three days to the Security Council for its approval a plan for the immediate deployment of a United Nations observer unit to monitor the Khor Abdullah and a demilitarized zone, which is hereby

established, extending ten kilometres into Iraq and five kilometres into Kuwait from the boundary referred to in the "Agreed Minutes Between the State of Kuwait and the Republic of Iraq Regarding the Restoration of Friendly Relations, Recognition and Related Matters" of 4 October 1963; to deter violations of the boundary through its presence in and surveillance of the demilitarized zone; to observe any hostile or potentially hostile action mounted from the territory of one State to the other; and for the Secretary-General to report regularly to the Security Council on the operations of the unit, and immediately if there are serious violations of the zone or potential threats to peace;

6. *Notes* that as soon as the Secretary-General notifies the Security Council of the completion of the deployment of the United Nations observer unit, the conditions will be established for the Member States cooperating with Kuwait in accordance with resolution 678 (1990) to bring their military presence in Iraq to an end consistent with resolution 686 (1991);

C

7. *Invites* Iraq to reaffirm unconditionally its obligations under the Geneva Protocol for the Prohibition of the Use in War of Asphyxiating, Poisonous or Other Gases, and of Bacteriological Methods of Warfare, signed at Geneva on 17 June 1925, and to ratify the Convention on the Prohibition of the Development, Production and Stockpiling of Bacteriological (Biological) and Toxin Weapons and on Their Destruction, of 10 April 1972;

8. *Decides* that Iraq shall unconditionally accept the destruction, removal, or rendering harmless, under international supervision, of:

(a) All chemical and biological weapons and all stocks of agents and all related subsystems and components and all research, development, support and manufacturing facilities;

(b) All ballistic missiles with a range greater than 150 kilometres and related major parts, and repair and production facilities;

9. *Decides*, for the implementation of paragraph 8 above, the following:

(a) Iraq shall submit to the Secretary-General, within fifteen days of the adoption of the present resolution, a declaration of the locations, amounts and types of all items specified in paragraph 8 and agree to urgent, on-site inspection as specified below;

(b) The Secretary-General, in consultation with the appropriate Governments and, where appropriate, with the Director-General of the

World Health Organization, within forty-five days of the passage of the present resolution, shall develop, and submit to the Council for approval, a plan calling for the completion of the following acts within forty-five days of such approval:

(i) The forming of a Special Commission, which shall carry out immediate on-site inspection of Iraq's biological, chemical and missile capabilities, based on Iraq's declarations and the designation of any additional locations by the Special Commission itself;

(ii) The yielding by Iraq of possession to the Special Commission for destruction, removal or rendering harmless, taking into account the requirements of public safety, of all items specified under paragraph 8 (a) above, including items at the additional locations designated by the Special Commission under paragraph 9 (b) (i) above and the destruction by Iraq, under the supervision of the Special Commission, of all its missile capabilities, including launchers, as specified under paragraph 8 (b) above;

(iii) The provision by the Special Commission of the assistance and cooperation to the Director-General of the International Atomic Energy Agency required in paragraphs 12 and 13 below;

10. *Decides further* that Iraq shall unconditionally undertake not to use, develop, construct or acquire any of the items specified in paragraphs 8 and 9 above and requests the Secretary-General, in consultation with the Special Commission, to develop a plan for the future ongoing monitoring and verification of Iraq's compliance with this paragraph, to be submitted to the Security Council for approval within one hundred and twenty days of the passage of this resolution;

11. *Invites* Iraq to reaffirm unconditionally its obligations under the Treaty on the Non-Proliferation of Nuclear Weapons of 1 July 1968;

12. *Decides* that Iraq shall unconditionally agree not to acquire or develop nuclear weapons or nuclear-weapons-usable material or any subsystems or components or any research, development, support or manufacturing facilities related to the above; to submit to the Secretary-General and the Director-General of the International Atomic Energy Agency within fifteen days of the adoption of the present resolution a declaration of the locations, amounts, and types of all items specified above; to place all of its nuclear-weapons-usable materials under the exclusive control, for custody and removal, of the International Atomic Energy Agency, with the assistance and cooperation of the Special Commission as provided for in the plan of the Secretary-General discussed in paragraph 9 (b) above; to accept, in accordance with the arrangements

provided for in paragraph 13 below, urgent on-site inspection and the destruction, removal or rendering harmless as appropriate of all items specified above; and to accept the plan discussed in paragraph 13 below for the future ongoing monitoring and verification of its compliance with these undertakings;

13. *Requests* the Director-General of the International Atomic Energy Agency, through the Secretary-General, with the assistance and cooperation of the Special Commission as provided for in the plan of the Secretary-General in paragraph 9 (b) above, to carry out immediate on-site inspection of Iraq's nuclear capabilities based on Iraq's declarations and the designation of any additional locations by the Special Commission; to develop a plan for submission to the Security Council within forty-five days calling for the destruction, removal, or rendering harmless as appropriate of all items listed in paragraph 12 above; to carry out the plan within forty-five days following approval by the Security Council; and to develop a plan, taking into account the rights and obligations of Iraq under the Treaty on the Non-Proliferation of Nuclear Weapons of 1 July 1968, for the future ongoing monitoring and verification of Iraq's compliance with paragraph 12 above, including an inventory of all nuclear material in Iraq subject to the Agency's verification and inspections to confirm that Agency safeguards cover all relevant nuclear activities in Iraq, to be submitted to the Security Council for approval within one hundred and twenty days of the passage of the present resolution;

14. *Takes note* that the actions to be taken by Iraq in paragraphs 8, 9, 10, 11, 12 and 13 of the present resolution represent steps towards the goal of establishing in the Middle East a zone free from weapons of mass destruction and all missiles for their delivery and the objective of a global ban on chemical weapons;

D

15. *Requests* the Secretary-General to report to the Security Council on the steps taken to facilitate the return of all Kuwaiti property seized by Iraq, including a list of any property that Kuwait claims has not been returned or which has not been returned intact;

E

16. *Reaffirms* that Iraq, without prejudice to the debts and obligations of Iraq arising prior to 2 August 1990, which will be addressed through the normal mechanisms, is liable under international law for any direct loss, damage, including environmental damage and the depletion

of natural resources, or injury to foreign Governments, nationals and corporations, as a result of Iraq's unlawful invasion and occupation of Kuwait;

17. *Decides* that all Iraqi statements made since 2 August 1990 repudiating its foreign debt are null and void, and demands that Iraq adhere scrupulously to all of its obligations concerning servicing and repayment of its foreign debt;

18. *Decides also* to create a fund to pay compensation for claims that fall within paragraph 16 above and to establish a Commission that will administer the fund;

19. *Directs* the Secretary-General to develop and present to the Security Council for decision, no later than thirty days following the adoption of the present resolution, recommendations for the fund to meet the requirement for the payment of claims established in accordance with paragraph 18 above and for a programme to implement the decisions in paragraphs 16, 17 and 18 above, including: administration of the fund; mechanisms for determining the appropriate level of Iraq's contribution to the fund based on a percentage of the value of the exports of petroleum and petroleum products from Iraq not to exceed a figure to be suggested to the Council by the Secretary-General, taking into account the requirements of the people of Iraq, Iraq's payment capacity as assessed in conjunction with the international financial institutions taking into consideration external debt service, and the needs of the Iraqi economy; arrangements for ensuring that payments are made to the fund; the process by which funds will be allocated and claims paid; appropriate procedures for evaluating losses, listing claims and verifying their validity and resolving disputed claims in respect of Iraq's liability as specified in paragraph 16 above; and the composition of the Commission designated above;

F

20. *Decides*, effective immediately, that the prohibitions against the sale or supply to Iraq of commodities or products, other than medicine and health supplies, and prohibitions against financial transactions related thereto contained in resolution 661 (1990) shall not apply to foodstuffs notified to the Security Council Committee established by resolution 661 (1990) concerning the situation between Iraq and Kuwait or, with the approval of that Committee, under the simplified and accelerated "no-objection" procedure, to materials and supplies for essential civilian needs as identified in the report of the Secretary-General dated

20 March 1991, and in any further findings of humanitarian need by the Committee;

21. *Decides* that the Security Council shall review the provisions of paragraph 20 above every sixty days in the light of the policies and practices of the Government of Iraq, including the implementation of all relevant resolutions of the Security Council, for the purpose of determining whether to reduce or lift the prohibitions referred to therein;

22. *Decides also* that upon the approval by the Security Council of the programme called for in paragraph 19 above and upon Council agreement that Iraq has completed all actions contemplated in paragraphs 8, 9, 10, 11, 12 and 13 above, the prohibitions against the import of commodities and products originating in Iraq and the prohibitions against financial transactions related thereto contained in resolution 661 (1990) shall have no further force or effect;

23. *Decides further* that, pending action by the Security Council under paragraph 22 above, the Security Council Committee established by resolution 661 (1990) shall be empowered to approve, when required to assure adequate financial resources on the part of Iraq to carry out the activities under paragraph 20 above, exceptions to the prohibition against the import of commodities and products originating in Iraq;

24. *Decides* that, in accordance with resolution 661 (1990) and subsequent related resolutions and until a further decision is taken by the Security Council, all States shall continue to prevent the sale or supply, or the promotion or facilitation of such sale or supply, to Iraq by their nationals, or from their territories or using their flag vessels or aircraft, of:

(a) Arms and related materiel of all types, specifically including the sale or transfer through other means of all forms of conventional military equipment, including for paramilitary forces, and spare parts and components and their means of production, for such equipment;

(b) Items specified and defined in paragraphs 8 and 12 above not otherwise covered above;

(c) Technology under licensing or other transfer arrangements used in the production, utilization or stockpiling of items specified in subparagraphs (a) and (b) above;

(d) Personnel or materials for training or technical support services relating to the design, development, manufacture, use, maintenance or support of items specified in subparagraphs (a) and (b) above;

25. *Calls upon* all States and international organizations to act strictly in accordance with paragraph 24 above, notwithstanding the existence of any contracts, agreements, licences or any other arrangements;

26. *Requests* the Secretary-General, in consultation with appropriate Governments, to develop within sixty days, for the approval of the Security Council, guidelines to facilitate full international implementation of paragraphs 24 and 25 above and paragraph 27 below, and to make them available to all States and to establish a procedure for updating these guidelines periodically;

27. *Calls upon* all States to maintain such national controls and procedures and to take such other actions consistent with the guidelines to be established by the Security Council under paragraph 26 above as may be necessary to ensure compliance with the terms of paragraph 24 above, and calls upon international organizations to take all appropriate steps to assist in ensuring such full compliance;

28. *Agrees* to review its decisions in paragraphs 22, 23, 24 and 25 above, except for the items specified and defined in paragraphs 8 and 12 above, on a regular basis and in any case one hundred and twenty days following passage of the present resolution, taking into account Iraq's compliance with the resolution and general progress towards the control of armaments in the region;

29. *Decides* that all States, including Iraq, shall take the necessary measures to ensure that no claim shall lie at the instance of the Government of Iraq, or of any person or body in Iraq, or of any person claiming through or for the benefit of any such person or body, in connection with any contract or other transaction where its performance was affected by reason of the measures taken by the Security Council in resolution 661 (1990) and related resolutions;

G

30. *Decides* that, in furtherance of its commitment to facilitate the repatriation of all Kuwaiti and third country nationals, Iraq shall extend all necessary cooperation to the International Committee of the Red Cross, providing lists of such persons, facilitating the access of the International Committee of the Red Cross to all such persons wherever located or detained and facilitating the search by the International Committee of the Red Cross for those Kuwaiti and third country nationals still unaccounted for;

31. *Invites* the International Committee of the Red Cross to keep the Secretary-General apprised as appropriate of all activities undertaken in connection with facilitating the repatriation or return of all Kuwaiti and third country nationals or their remains present in Iraq on or after 2 August 1990;

H

32. *Requires* Iraq to inform the Security Council that it will not commit or support any act of international terrorism or allow any organization directed towards commission of such acts to operate within its territory and to condemn unequivocally and renounce all acts, methods and practices of terrorism;

I

33. *Declares* that, upon official notification by Iraq to the Secretary-General and to the Security Council of its acceptance of the provisions above, a formal cease-fire is effective between Iraq and Kuwait and the Member States cooperating with Kuwait in accordance with resolution 678 (1990);

34. *Decides* to remain seized of the matter and to take such further steps as may be required for the implementation of the present resolution and to secure peace and security in the area.

FIGURE 13 *Mausoleum of the Unknown Soldier in Baghdad, Iraq. Ceremony marking the end of the war against Iran, 2000.*

CHAPTER 4.1

Keynote, Djamchid Momtaz, University of Tehran

Excellences, mesdames, mademoiselles, messieurs,

Nombreuses sont les résolutions adoptées par le Conseil de Sécurité à l'issue de conflits armés par lesquelles cet organe, auquel la Charte des Nations Unies a conféré la responsabilité du maintien de la paix et de la sécurité, a contribué au rétablissement de la paix et à sa consolidation.

Cette étude se limite aux résolutions adoptées dans le cadre du chapitre VII de la Charte par lesquelles le Conseil de Sécurité a été amené à constater la rupture de la paix ou la perpétration d'un acte d'agression dans le cadre d'un conflit armé international.

Dans les deux cas, le Conseil de Sécurité peut, en vertu des attributions que la Charte lui confère, prendre les mesures qu'il estime nécessaires pour le rétablissement de la paix. Mesures qui se limitent généralement à exiger un cessez-le-feu entre les belligérants ainsi qu'un retrait des forces armées aux frontières internationales, ceci en vue de faciliter, le cas échéant, des pourparlers de paix par les bons offices ou la médiation du Secrétaire Général.

Toutefois, dans certains cas dont le nombre reste très limité, ces mesures peuvent aller au-delà et comprendre :

- l'ébauche d'un plan de paix ou
- un véritable plan de paix

Relèvent de la première catégorie les mesures adoptées par le Conseil de Sécurité dans le cadre de la Résolution 598 du 20 juillet 1987 lors du conflit armé opposant l'Irak à l'Iran, alors que la Résolution 687 du 3 avril 1991 mettant fin au conflit armé opposant l'Irak aux Etats coopérant avec le Koweït adoptait des mesures relevant de la seconde catégorie.

Dans les deux cas, l'approche adoptée par le Conseil s'inscrit dans le contexte de la fin de la guerre froide, caractérisée par l'entente entre ses Etats membres permanents, cette approche ambitionnant de consolider la paix entre les belligérants dans la région, avec le concours des Etats tiers dominants.

Van Hoogstraten, Schrijver et al. (eds.), The Art of Making Peace: Lessons Learned from Peace Treaties
 ISBN 978-90-04-32123-6. pp. 139-143.

Le Conseil de Sécurité se porte donc garant du plan de paix qu'il a élaboré, quitte à en assurer le respect par l'adoption d'autres mesures coercitives en cas de non respect de ses dispositions (I).

De surcroit, l'évolution de la situation peut amener le Conseil à appliquer le plan de paix avec souplesse en modifiant ses dispositions ou en renonçant à les mettre en œuvre pour l'adapter à des circonstances nouvelles (II).

I – Le Conseil de Sécurité garant de l'application du plan de paix

Dans le cadre des deux résolutions précitées, les plans de paix n'ont pas été imposés aux belligérants. Il est vrai que, s'agissant du conflit Irak-Iran, le Secrétaire Général avait menacé d'imposer le cessez-le-feu en cas de refus des belligérants alors que, lors du second conflit, l'Irak exsangue n'avait d'autre choix que d'accepter les dispositions du plan de paix, condition sine qua non à l'acceptation du cessez-le-feu par les Etats coopérant avec le Koweït.

Le consentement ainsi extirpé présente pour le Conseil de Sécurité l'avantage de :

- produire un effet d'estoppel interdisant aux belligérants de remettre en cause les dispositions du plan de paix et
- conférer aux résolutions, actes unilatéraux par excellence, la nature d'un accord international.

Les deux résolutions garantissent le cessez le-feu par le déploiement de groupes d'observateurs des Nations Unies chargés de vérifier son respect et de rapporter au Conseil les cas de violations par les belligérants.

Dans le cas du conflit Irak-Iran, ils seront chargés de vérifier le retrait des forces armées aux frontières internationales reconnues, alors que dans le cas du conflit Irak-Koweït, la tâche qui leur était assignée était plus délicate, en l'occurrence surveiller la zone démilitarisée tant terrestre que marine.

Le Conseil de Sécurité se préoccupe dans les deux cas de la responsabilité du conflit armé.

- Dans le cas du conflit Irak-Iran, il demande au Secrétaire Général d'explorer, en consultation avec les deux belligérants, la possibilité de charger un organe impartial d'enquêter sur la responsabilité du conflit et de faire rapport au Conseil de Sécurité.

- La condamnation par le Conseil de Sécurité (Rés. 660 – 2 août 1990) de l'invasion du Koweït par l'Irak le dispense d'enquêter sur les faits. Il constate en conséquence que l'Irak est responsable en vertu du droit international de toute perte, de tout dommage, y compris les atteintes à l'environnement et la destruction des ressources naturelles, et de tout autre préjudice subi par les Etats étrangers et des personnes physiques et sociales étrangères du fait de son invasion et de son occupation illicite du Koweït. L'approche adoptée par le Conseil de Sécurité reste fondée sur le droit de la responsabilité classique ne tenant pas compte du fait que la violation de la norme sur laquelle la responsabilité de l'Irak est fondée est de nature impérative (*jus cogens*).

Le Conseil crée un fonds d'indemnisation financé par une partie des revenus tirés de l'exportation du pétrole irakien et chargé d'indemniser les victimes (plus de 50 milliards de $ alloués à ce titre).

La responsabilité de l'Irak dans le déclenchement du conflit armé constitue le fondement des mesures que le Conseil de Sécurité sera amené à adopter en vue d'enlever aux forces armées de cet Etat toute capacité offensive, notamment :

- la destruction des fusées ayant une portée supérieure à 250 km
- l'interdiction d'importer des armes conventionnelles, et
- la destruction de ses armes de destruction massive et de ses capacités d'en acquérir ainsi que la mise en place à cette fin d'un système d'inspection sous l'égide des Nations Unies.

Allaient s'ensuivre de nombreuses mises en demeure du Conseil de Sécurité en raison du refus de l'Irak de coopérer avec les inspecteurs, allant jusqu'à mettre cet Etat en garde contre les « graves conséquences » qui pourraient en résulter.

II – L'adaptation du plan de paix par le Conseil de Sécurité

Cette mise en demeure sera le principal argument invoqué par la coalition menée par les Etats-Unis et le Royaume-Uni pour rompre le cessez-le-feu et recourir à la force contre l'Irak en mars 2003. Le Conseil de Sécurité n'aura alors d'autre choix que de reconnaître implicitement le fait accompli et d'adapter en conséquence, par l'adoption de nouvelles résolutions, le plan de paix initial aux nouvelles circonstances.

- La Résolution 1483 du 22 mars 2003 exige que les Etats-Unis et le Royaume-Uni respectent, en tant que puissances occupantes, les dispositions pertinentes du droit international humanitaire, tout en prévoyant des exceptions, et qu'ils assurent la transition vers un régime représentatif en Irak.
- La Résolution 1511 du 16 octobre 2003 apporte un assouplissement implicite sur les armes conventionnelles dans la mesure où elle souligne qu'il importe de constituer une force irakienne de police et de sécurité tout en demandant aux Etats de concourir à son équipement.
- La Résolution 1957 du 15 décembre 2010 autorise l'Irak à prendre les mesures nécessaires afin de reconstruire ses installations nucléaires utilisées à des fins exclusivement pacifiques. Le Conseil décide par la même occasion de lever les restrictions relatives aux missiles édictées par la Résolution 687.

Les mesures prévues par la Résolution 687 pour l'éradication des armes de destruction massives et des missiles vecteurs, considérée pourtant comme l'une des « étapes » sur la voie de la création d'une zone exempte de telles armes au Moyen-Orient, ne furent malheureusement suivies d'aucune initiative concrète. L'initiative du Secrétaire Général de réunir en 2012 une conférence internationale à cette fin aurait pu consolider la paix dans cette région et éviter la tension qui résulta de l'utilisation, en 2012 et 2013, d'armes chimiques en Syrie.

Dans le cas de la Résolution 598, le Secrétaire Général, chargé de son suivi, fut amené, compte tenu de l'évolution des circonstances, à prendre certaines initiatives dont les effets positifs pour la consolidation de la paix ne firent pas l'unanimité.

Pour ce qui est de la responsabilité du conflit, le Secrétaire Général parvient à cette conclusion qu'il serait vain de vouloir appliquer la disposition de cette Résolution lui demandant d'explorer la possibilité de charger un « organe impartial » d'enquêter à cet effet. Prenant l'initiative de consulter certains experts indépendants, il parvient à cette conclusion que c'est l'Irak qui a agressé l'Iran en violation de l'interdiction de l'usage de la force, qu'il considère comme étant une norme de *jus cogens*. Il n'en demeure pas moins, dans le rapport qu'il soumet au Conseil de Sécurité le 9 décembre 1991, que, « dans l'intérêt de la paix », il ne sera pas donné suite à cette conclusion, ce que le Conseil de Sécurité entérine par son silence, alors même que l'Irak venait de récidiver en envahissant le territoire du Koweït.

De même, le Secrétaire Général ne donnera pas suite à la demande que le Conseil de Sécurité lui avait faite d'examiner les mesures susceptibles de renforcer la sécurité et la stabilité dans la région. Mission sans doute délicate et difficile que le Conseil aurait du soutenir avec fermeté et dont l'accomplissement aurait pu éviter deux nouvelles ruptures de paix (1990 et 2003) dans la région au cours des deux décennies qui suivirent la fin des hostilités Irak-Iran.

Conclusion

La vision élargie du concept de paix adoptée par le Conseil de Sécurité (dans les deux cas précités), qui ne se limite pas à un cessez-le-feu et un retrait des forces armées aux frontières internationales, est conforme à la dimension multilatérale de la paix. De surcroit, l'intérêt porté par le Conseil à la responsabilité des belligérants dans un conflit armé international doit être considéré comme l'une des manifestations précoces de la nouvelle théorie de la responsabilité telle que conçue par la Commission du droit international dans son projet de 2001, laquelle va au-delà du bilatéralisme. De plus, la substitution du Conseil de Sécurité aux belligérants pour entreprendre l'ébauche d'un plan de paix ou le fixer en détails présente l'avantage de

– ne plus soumettre la construction de la paix aux aléas de négociations longues et fastidieuses et
– empêcher que le belligérant en situation de force n'impose sa volonté au risque de rendre la paix contestée et donc fragile.

CHAPTER 4.2

Commentary: Nico Schrijver, Leiden University

I would like to make some supplementary comments on the roles to be played by the Security Council and the International Court of Justice in the absence of peace treaties. The Security Council obviously has the legal powers to engage in peace-making. In practice, the limelight is often on Chapter VII of the Charter, which describes the activities of the Security Council. However, the legal basis for peace-making activities by the Security Council can also be found in Chapter VI, which is on the pacific settlement of international disputes. Perhaps the threshold to employ Chapter VI is often somewhat lower than to take the high threshold of the mandatory Chapter VII. Moreover, also the general Article 24 of the UN Charter, by which Member States confer on the Security Council the primary responsibility for the maintenance of international peace and security, can also be invoked. It occurs to me that the facilities under Chapter VI are often somewhat underutilized, while they can be very useful and also be employed in an active interplay with the UN General Assembly and the Secretary-General. In my paper I examine some cases of moderate successes as well as failures of Security Council engagements in peace-making. As to what could be seen as achievements, I refer to two cases, the case of Namibia and the case of Cambodia.

As to Namibia: in 1966, the General Assembly terminated the mandate of South Africa to administer South West Africa, later on called Namibia. Only from the 1970s on did the Security Council adopt some resolutions on the Namibian question. The two most important ones are Resolution 276 of 1970 and Resolution 435 of 1978. In the first resolution the Council declared the continued presence of South Africa in Namibia to be unlawful and imposed the duty on South Africa to withdraw, as well as a duty upon the entire community of States not to cooperate with South Africa in regard of its administration over Namibia.

It took eight years and a very interesting Advisory Opinion by the International Court of Justice (ICJ) to finally adopt a kind of peace agreement in the form of an independence plan for Namibia after free and fair elections under UN supervision and control. From that point of view the comprehensive Resolution 435 could be called a peace agreement, or for that matter the Namibian charter for independence. After many years

Van Hoogstraten, Schrijver et al. (eds.), The Art of Making Peace: Lessons Learned from Peace Treaties

ISBN 978-90-04-32123-6. pp. 144-148.

of negotiations and stalemates it finally worked out, although it took the end of the Cold War for Namibia to acquire its independence in 1990.

As to Cambodia: no need to recall here the very sad post-1945 history of Cambodia, which to a certain extent is also a decolonization issue. I recall the horrible Khmer Rouge regime in the 1970s and the Vietnamese invasion to bring that horrible regime to an end, followed by the occupation of Cambodia for 10 years while establishing the Communist regime in the newly established People's Republic of Kampuchea. Only in 1980, and not at the level of the Security Council but in the context of the UN General Assembly, did a Cambodian peace process start. Like in the case of Namibia, it was only after 1989, after the end of the Cold War, that a comprehensive peace agreement came on the horizon. Especially France and Indonesia have been instrumental by co-organising the Peace Conference on Cambodia. It led to the adoption of a number of agreements, the so-called Paris Peace Agreements, and they were endorsed unanimously by the Security Council in Resolution 668 in 1990. These agreements provided for a broad and comprehensive settlement of the Cambodian conflict. It consisted of four separate agreements signed by 19 States that participated in the Paris Conference, and were finally unanimously adopted by the UN Security Council. These agreements provided for a Supreme National Council of Cambodia that took care of human rights protection, repatriation of refugees, arms control for disarmament, mine clearing and free and fair elections under international supervision. The Council also worked on the constitution writing on the basis of principles that had been included in the Paris peace agreement and in the UN Security Council resolution for a UN Transitional Authority in Cambodia (UNTAC). In spite of the many comments, I do believe that the role of the UN in bringing peace to Cambodia has been a significant achievement.

Now as to failures, I could mention many examples. It is a bit of a boulevard of broken dreams. Once again I mention only two. First of all, the Arab-Israeli conflict, or the Question of Palestine as it is known in the United Nations. From the start there have been many resolutions adopted by both the UN General Assembly, Resolutions 181 of 1948 on the future government of Palestine, and by the Security Council, well-known Resolutions 242, 338, 1515 on the two States solution, as well as the findings by the ICJ in the Israeli wall opinion. *But all of this proved not to work.*

My second example is Cyprus. 50 years of engagement with the Cyprus question has resulted in no more than conflict-freezing on the divided island. Time and again UN efforts to achieve a negotiated settlement and an overall peace agreement failed. Probably it is still very useful to have UNFICYP controlling the buffer zone between the two communities while the Council continues to call in vain for the establishment of a bi-communal and bi-zonal federation and requests the Secretary-General to continue his mission of good offices.

When discussing some achievements and some failures, the current situation in Syria is very much on our mind. So far the Security Council has failed to adopt substantive comprehensive resolutions on the question of Syria. Although the initial resolutions on establishing the peace monitors and providing the envoys with a mandate are not to be underestimated. There is a window of hope and hopefully also a window of opportunities that this may change in the weeks to come, now that there is an agreement between Russia and the United States to bring the chemical and biological weapons of the regime under international control. Could this trigger a wider peace agreement? Could such a new initiative be integrated for example in a previous draft resolution tabled by Morocco as a member of the UN Security Council in February 2012? The Moroccan resolution was based on a substantive plan set out by the League of Arab States. It was endorsed by at least 13 Members of the 15 in February 2012 in the UN Security Council, but rejected by Russia and China. Perhaps this peace plan with many interesting elements can be revitalized. Then there is still the Geneva process towards the organisation of a peace conference on Syria. A potential peace agreement may well be submitted for adoption by the UN Security Council. It may also well be that certain tasks will be allocated to the Council in a way similar to the resolutions concerning Cambodia and Yugoslavia, as well as to that of the The Hague-based OPCW. In itself this possibility raises interesting legal questions on the relationship between a peace agreement and the sovereign powers of the UN Security Council and the OPCW.

Since we are here hosted in what is sometimes called the *Temple of Justice,* I believe it is appropriate to pay some attention to the role of the ICJ in settling international disputes and preserving peace. As one of the principal organs of the UN and its principal judicial organ, the ICJ often addresses issues of war and peace, either in legal proceedings between States or in the context of advisory opinions. Through its decisions the Court on various occasions has made a contribution to the maintenance or restoration of peace and security. Furthermore, it has also clarified and further developed the international law on the use of force, on self-defense and on non-intervention. For the purpose of my presentation I would like to distinguish three particular categories of contributions by the ICJ:

1. Boundary disputes
2. Military interventions
3. Advisory opinions

As to my first category, boundary disputes, the Court really has settled a number of potentially explosive boundary disputes between States. To mention a few: the land boundary disputes between Burkina Faso and Mali, between Libya and Chad, between Cameroon and Nigeria, between Cambodia and Thailand. In all these cases I believe that the Court has been instrumental in keeping the peace and avoiding war. This also applies in a similar way to maritime boundary disputes like the ones between Cameroon and Nigeria, between Nicaragua and Colombia and recently between Peru and Chile. Once again here the Court has been instrumental in keeping the peace at least.

My second category relates to cases concerned with military interventions. Reference can be made to cases in which the Court was called upon to declare whether alleged intervention of one State into the territory of another State involving the use of military means was unlawful or lawful. We have a landmark judgment of Nicaragua versus the United States in 1986, but also to be mentioned are the Iranian oil platform case (2003), the 10 use of force cases instituted by Serbia against NATO countries (1998), the Congo versus Uganda case of 2005 and more recently Georgia versus Russia (2009). Of course, each case is different but the common thread appears to be that the ICJ was called upon by one of the parties to contribute to the efforts of restoring peace in the absence of peace treaties.

Lastly, I would like to mention the third category, the instrument of advisory opinions. The Court often provides clarifications of a specific situation from an international law point of view through advisory opinions. Occasionally, these involved issues of conflict and peace such as in the cases of South West Africa, Namibia, the Western Sahara and the Israeli wall. These advisory opinions contain statements as to the unlawful nature of the continued presence of occupying powers, for instance by South Africa and Israel. Or they concern the validity of the people's right to self-determination, and, also very importantly, the applicability of the international human rights law and international humanitarian law to the situations under review.

Mr. Chairman, let me conclude with four points. First: under the UN Charter both the Security Council and the ICJ serve as principal organs for, as it is written down in the Preamble: *to maintain international peace and security and to ensure by the acceptance of principles and the institution of methods that armed force shall not be used, save in the common interest.* Secondly, I recall that under Article 24 of the Charter, the Council has primary responsibility for the maintenance of international peace and security. The end of the Cold War, as we could note in some of my case studies, has contributed significantly to the possibility of the Council to assume its Charter-indicated role. As the two case studies on Namibia and Cambodia demonstrate, the Council can engage in useful peace-making, peace-keeping and nation-making roles in the absence of peace treaties. Peace agreements can thus be brokered by the UN and in principle a wide arsenal of peace tools, including under Chapter VI, can be employed to supervise the implementation of such peace agreements.

Thirdly, all too often the United Nations fails in its peace-making role in the absence of peace treaties. Reasons for this include the extreme complexity of the situation concerned or the lack of agreements among the Permanent Members of the Security Council due to a direct interest of a Permanent Member as a party to the dispute. We should really recall that the Council has a primary responsibility to act in the absence of peace or in the absence of peace treaties. Lastly, as regards the role of the ICJ in view of its function and powers, I would like to state that obviously the Court can only play a limited role since it is only competent to deal with a dispute if the states concerned have accepted its jurisdiction. Nonetheless, through the settlement of a) boundary disputes, b) its case law with respect to military interventions and c) through its advisory opinions, the ICJ has made a significant contribution to preserving or restoring peace in the absence of peace treaties.

CHAPTER 4.3

Roundtable Debate

Ambassador Hans Corell, Sweden: For 10 years I observed the Security Council in the UN. We are discussing the art of peace-making and lessons learned from peace treaties. It is in the absence of peace treaties where the Security Council has a role to play. Having been a legal counsel at the UN for 10 years, it is mind-boggling to me that this Council doesn't realize the potential it has, and in particular its 5 permanent members. I observed them for 10 years and after I left I observed them again. Everybody is looking at Syria, to me Syria is the symptom of what is wrong, the inability of the Council to join hands and make decisions when we have situations like this. I am already looking for the next Syria. It could be anywhere in the world where democracy and the rule of law is missing, and then the next Syria, and the Syria after that. Do they not understand that when they behave in this manner, they actually invite conflicts like the one we see in Syria?

I wrote a letter to the members of the UN in 2008, and the title of the letter is: *Security Council reform. Rule of law more important than additional members.* What's the point of having additional members in the Council if they continue behaving the way they do? I suggested that instead of adding members to the Council, because they have the veto to prevent that, they should give as a gift to the Organisation an agreement among themselves, binding under international law, with 4 elements:

1. From now on we are actually going to bow to the law that we are said to supervise. Is that too much to ask? Look at Iraq, look at Georgia, attacked by Permanent Members of the Council in violation of the Charter.
2. From now on we are not going to use our veto unless our innermost concerns are at hand, and if we do we will explain why.
3. From now on we are not going to use force unless in the two situations allowed by the Charter: self-defense (Article 51) and after a clear and unambiguous resolution by the Security Council. Resolution 1441 from November 2002 in Iraq was not an approval of using force.
4. Responsibility to protect. If Heads of State or warlords start killing their own people, we will intervene.

Van Hoogstraten, Schrijver et al. (eds.), The Art of Making Peace: Lessons Learned from Peace Treaties
 ISBN 978-90-04-32123-6. pp. 149-156.

They should have done so in Syria. I am not suggesting that they should have used force from the beginning, but a united signal from a united Council to the parties here would have made a great difference. I am going to reiterate this proposal for as long as I can speak up. Because it is appalling that they do not realise that if they continue in this manner they might undermine the UN Charter. And we should respect that Charter negotiated by a generation that had experienced two World Wars. Don't talk about a new UN and new Organisation. These 5 States will never, ever have the legal power they have under the Charter today to decide about the use of force, legally deciding that force should be used, they will never be given that again. Don't they realise that they have a privilege they should be careful to protect? And that protection can only be done if they bow their heads and join hands.

Professor Jan Pronk, The Netherlands: I would like to follow up on Professor Corell, I agree with him, especially on two points:

1. You need some changes in the system.
2. There are many more countries to follow Syria. There are already 10 countries at the moment which after a number of years will be in a similar situation as Syria, take Pakistan, take Nigeria, for instance.

So what can be done? This session is on peace-making, the role of the system when there are no peace agreements. Most of the examples mentioned by the two speakers are about conflicts between States and not conflicts within States. But the future will see particular conflicts within States. Which brings me to preventive diplomacy, as something which has to precede peace-making, peace-keeping, peace-building, as was explained in the Agenda for Peace by Boutros Boutros Ghali. We are discussing and working in the UN system on the other 3 chapters: peace-making, peace-keeping, peace-building. Preventive diplomacy, which is essential, is not being discussed. The Security Council is not involved in preventive diplomacy because of, amongst others, the reasons mentioned by Professor Schrijver, the extreme complexity of the situation and the lack of agreement between the members and the special interest of the Permanent Members. Not all domestic conflicts are so complex from the beginning, they become complex after a long period. If the international community would step in early with preventive diplomacy, there might be a chance. Perhaps the Security Council is not that interested because of that specific role of the Permanent Members and their specific interests.

But there are other options, and Professor Schrijver could have mentioned the Secretary-General, but the Secretary-General after Hammarskjöld is not playing that role any more. Like one of the Ambassadors in the UN used to say, he is more of a secretary and not a general anymore, he is just following the major powers. His role, his possibilities in terms of preventive diplomacy are very limited. The General Assembly is another example. They did do preventive diplomacy once, in Cambodia, but you can hardly call that an example of moderate success because you have 2 million people being killed and then the General Assembly came in. So that is a success in the very, very, very end. The 3rd possibility is indeed the ICJ, but it is always on judicial matters and always on matters between States. There is hardly a role of political, economic, social, cultural diplomacy, preventive diplomacy for that body.

Let me suggest: We have in the system of the UN a committee, a special chamber, set up by the Security Council and the General Assembly, on peace-building, which the UN calls post-conflict. The Security Council could also establish itself a special chamber dealing with preventive diplomacy, in order for it not to be left only to the Secretary-General nor to be hammered by vetoes. This chamber could come in in a very early stage of a specific conflict and only deal with diplomacy, non-military issues, economic diplomacy, political, mediation, and cultural diplomacy. Maybe this is very difficult without a very important reform procedure to the system of powers within the UN. May I recall that many of my suggestions and those of Professor Corell were mentioned in the report on Global Governance by Ingvar Carlsson and Secretary-General Shridath Ramphal of 1995.

Professor Paul de Waart, The Netherlands: I ask myself what lessons I have learned today and I wonder whether one of the lessons is that the last topic, dealt with by Professor Momtaz and Professor Schrijver, is not so much the absence of peace agreements but another way to conclude peace, namely to make peace by the resolutions of international or regional organisations. In that respect, I ask myself whether international organisations have really learned the lessons of the former peace agreements between States. For instance, in the case of Iraq-Kuwait it was said at the time that the content of the resolution had more in common with the Versailles Treaty than with later peace treaties, so that it was not an effective way to make peace between these two countries, between Iraq and the region, and between Iraq and Iran.

You mentioned rightly that making peace through the UN Security Council resolution has the profit of avoiding lengthy negotiations, but that it is a matter of peace between mostly unequal parties. Is that not an asset for international organisations interfering, for instance, in a situation like Syria, where you have by definition unequal parties? One party is a State and all the other are non-State actors, either people, or religious bodies or so-called terrorist movements. My question is whether these international organisations have learned the lesson from the past that it doesn't make sense to put Heads of State or others on trial before peace has been made? As has been done now in Syria, where there are accusations against the President while he is one of the main players in getting peace or not.

Then there is the question of fact-finding, which is not a special talent of States. Should fact-finding not be more a specialty of international organisations? In the past the Netherlands have proposed in vain a fact-finding center within the UN, Professor Tammes did that at the moment as one of the delegates in the UN. Mediation – it struck me that both you and Professor Schrijver didn't mention mediation by the General Assembly. In the case that the Security Council is not in the position to deal with, for instance, Syria, why doesn't it call upon the General Assembly under the Uniting for Peace Resolution? This Resolution was made for those situations in which the Security Council failed by lack of agreement.

An interesting question for the ICJ is: Is it excluded for an individual State, particularly a permanent member, to use military force without the approval of the Security Council? It is not sure that under present international law this is the case. When Professor Schrijver referred to the Preamble, and said that armed force shall not be used save in the common interest, would it be thinkable that in the case of Syria, when it is proved that the government has used chemical weapons, it would be in the common interest to take punitive action with armed force?

Sir Adam Roberts, United Kingdom: Just two points. First of all this relates to Professor Momtaz's very interesting paper. I have to confess that it reinforces me in my belief that the UN system at best can offer what I would call selective security. It is not a complete system of collective security, even in the Charter it isn't, for various reasons, and that's a rather sobering conclusion. But I think it is one that follows from the fact that one reason why the UN has not been successful in some peace negotiations is because there are issues on which the UN has very strong preconceived positions that make it difficult for it act as an intermediary. And of course it is difficult to bring along so many members that negotiations become cumbersome. There are times when the UN doesn't work very well.

That brings me to my second point which relates particularly to Nico Schrijver's very interesting remarks. I think, if I may say so, he has simplified the presentation of Namibia, no doubt because of the interest of brevity. The settlement in Namibia arose not only because of Security Council involvement, but also because of United States' led negotiations over Angola and Namibia, which were led among others by Chester Crocker. And that seems to me to be an interesting example of a more general truth that the UN exists in a world of States and has to collaborate with States. One of my favourite UN resolutions is General Assembly resolution 38/39 of 5 December 1983 denouncing the US policy of so-called 'constructive engagement' in southern Africa as assisting racism, repression, aggression and destabilization. And yet later the same General Assembly passed a resolution appreciating the outcome of that, which of course helped pave the way for the Namibian outcome. All I am saying is that I think, and I am sure you will agree, that the picture is quite a complex one in which States have a part as well as international bodies.

Dr. Abiodun Williams, The Netherlands: Well, I enjoyed both presentations, but I share Corell's heartfelt plea that the Security Council should do a better job and fulfill its responsibilities more effectively. But my first point takes up what Sir Adam just mentioned, that I think it is important just to underline that the Security Council is fundamentally a political body and it cannot be divorced from the wider political climate. That is certainly my own experience. When you talk about the P5 and the P5 acting together or not acting, you talk about whether the foreign policy interests of 5 Permanent Members come together or whether they don't come together, and that's the reality.

The second point is that certainly in the UN, in the Security Council, in the General Assembly, some States believe in an effective United Nations some of the time, some States believe in an effective UN all of the time, but you never have all the States who want an effective UN all of the time. And that's the reality you have to work with. And the 3rd point is about what Mr. Pronk mentioned about the role of the Secretary-General. Yes, of course, it is a position which has no real political power in the strict sense, but it has great opportunities for exercising influence. Even in the area of preventive diplomacy there have been some examples, even since Hammarskjöld. I think of what Kofi Annan tried to do with the Bakassi peninsula and the withdrawal of troops from Lebanon and so on, and you can point to examples where the Secretary-General has managed to play a role. The relation between the Secretary-General and the Security Council is a very delicate one based on all the time-honoured principles of diplomacy. It works best, from my experience, when the Secretary-General recognises that the Security Council has primary responsibility for the maintenance of international peace and security, that is what the Charter says, and when the Security Council, especially the P5, recognises that the Secretary-General is more than a Chief Executive Officer, which is the term used in the Charter.

Response by Djamchid Momtaz:

Concernant la remarque faite par M. Adams, j'aimerais préciser que ce que j'ai tenté de mettre en évidence dans mon exposé est l'approche sélective que le Conseil de sécurité avait adoptée dans les deux conflits. Il n'était en effet nullement question de « la sécurité collective » au sens large. Il n'était absolument pas dans mon intention de discréditer le Conseil de sécurité en soulignant son incapacité d'assumer le mandat qui lui a été confié. Bien au contraire, j'ai voulu démontrer que l'accord unanime des membres permanents du Conseil de sécurité lui ouvre de grandes perspectives, allant jusqu'à lui permettre d'entreprendre l'ébauche d'un traité de paix entre les belligérant ou d'élaborer et imposer un véritable traité de paix. Il reste que cet organe n'utilise pas toujours les possibilités que le chapitre VII de la Charte lui offre.

Le problème qui se pose est de savoir dans quelle mesure on pourra faire face aux défaillances du Conseil de sécurité résultant de l'absence de consensus entre ses cinq membres permanents. L'Assemblée générale a la possibilité de s'y substituer dans le cadre de la Résolution « Union pour la paix » qu'elle a adoptée mais, pour des raisons politiques, elle n'y a pas eu recours au cours des deux dernières décennies.

La Cour internationale de Justice pourrait également se substituer au Conseil de sécurité. Je rejoins ici ce que M. Schriver soulignait, à savoir le rôle consultatif de cette juridiction. L'exemple de l'avis consultatif qu'elle a rendu sur les conséquences juridiques de l'édification du mur dans les territoires palestiniens occupés est à cet égard très significatif. A cette occasion, la Cour ne s'est pas contentée de répondre à la question que l'Assemblée générale lui avait posée mais est allée plus loin. Elle a condamné Israël pour la construction du mur en violation de ses obligations internationales, ce que le Conseil de sécurité n'avait pu faire. La Cour a mis l'accent sur toutes les dispositions de la quatrième Convention de Genève de 1949 qui avaient été ignorées par Israël. Elle a mis en exergue la responsabilité, non seulement des Nations Unies mais aussi des Etats, à faire respecter par Israël les dispositions pertinentes de cet instrument. Cet avis n'a d'ailleurs manqué d'être critiqué sur ce point.

Response by Nico Schrijver:

Let me start by paying my respect and tribute to the *filippica* by Ambassador Corell against the Permanent Members. I can well imagine his level of frustration, having worked for 10 years as the Legal Counsel of the UN. At the same time, it also has considerable merit for the UN to keep the Permanent Five within the system. If you stimulate their disassociation from the UN there will be more operations beyond if not in contravention against the UN Charter. And this provides us with a dilemma.

On the inspiring comments by Professor Pronk, I would like to respond that indeed we have a host of very good ideas on the reform of the UN, very good that you also refer to the Carlsson Ramphal Report of 1995 entitled *Our Global Neighbourhood*. At the same time, we are confronted with the reality of reform fatigue. Therefore it is very useful that you refer to a number of small steps that could be taken within the UN system. We should still have hope that the Peacebuilding Commission will be allowed to deal with peace-building and not only post-conflict peace-building.

I believe there are also other elements within the UN system which could be better integrated into the entire effort of preserving peace or restoring peace. For example, in the recent decade the Office of the High Commissioner for Human Rights has become much stronger than in the past. It has also undertaken many interesting rule of law projects, sometimes in cooperation with UNDP and the World Bank. I believe this can all be expanded and should indeed be taken up with your plea to have more room for preventive diplomacy. An interesting idea is to have a special chamber, a special committee of the Security Council, which should focus on preventive diplomacy. Once again I advertise Chapter VI of the UN Charter on the pacific settlement of international disputes under which more could be done.

And fortunately, and in response to Professor Pronk and Professor de Waart, we have the Secretary-General of the Permanent Court of Arbitration (PCA) back on the table. I do believe there are untapped opportunities in the Hague Convention on the Pacific Settlement of International Disputes. The institutional name is Permanent Court of Arbitration, but the tasks allocated to the PCA are of a wider nature and also include fact-finding, mediation and conciliation. It may well be that if it doesn't march very well within the UN proper it may be interesting to see to what extent the facilities of the PCA can be employed in a more active way in this regard.

Professor de Waart referred to the Uniting for Peace Resolution, and so did Professor Momtaz. It is interesting to recall that the last time this resolution was applied by the General Assembly was in the case of the Israeli Wall Advisory Opinion, a request tabled in the UN Security Council. It got 14 votes in favour, but a veto from the United States, and then it was taken up by the General Assembly and led to this very interesting advisory opinion. The General Assembly endorsed it in the context of a special session, admittedly without much result so far.

As to the issue of punitive action by military means, I really believe that such an approach would have had disastrous consequences in the current situation in Syria. Perhaps if military action is used to prevent the launching of a new attack with chemical weapons, which is about to take place tomorrow, then we are in a different situation. But to launch a military attack by way of punishment, I believe that this is very much against the spirit of the responsibility to protect and I believe that we are on one line with that.

Sir Adam raised the very interesting and long history of the settlement of the Namibia issues. It was one of my first international jobs to serve as an election observer in 1989 in Namibia and I vividly recall the role by the United States in these crucial days. But we should also give some credit to former President Gorbatchev of the Soviet Union. Once again, it was very interesting that the United States and the USSR found a common interest. The Soviet Union was very instrumental in telling the Cubans to leave Angola and Mozambique and so the United States was instrumental at last in telling South Africa that they had to leave Namibia and to dismantle the apartheid regime.

I am very happy with the remarks by my colleague Dr. Williams. It was very good that you brought us back with two feet on the ground that we have to cope with the P5 as they are and occasionally when they are on relative good terms, like in the early 1990s. Thereupon one can witness immediately some result, despite the absence of peace treaties.

PART 5

Roundtable Debate: Mediation versus Adjudication Peace Palace, 16 September 2014

FIGURE 14 *Great Hall of Justice, Peace Palace, during a hearing before the International Court of Justice in The Hague, The Netherlands.*

FIGURE 15 *Front view of the Peace Palace, The Hague, The Netherlands.*

Roundtable Debate: Mediation versus Adjudication

Introduction

Words of welcome by *Steven van Hoogstraten*, explaining that as Moderator he will speak on behalf of the Carnegie Foundation, and *Otto Spijkers* will represent the academics in this conversation.

The idea for this roundtable debate started with the conference that we held in September 2013, in which a number of high-level scholars and experts discussed the art of making peace and the lessons learned from the different historic peace treaties of the 20th century. We felt that it was useful to take a closer look at the field in which both mediation and adjudication are being executed and play a role. We thus invited a known mediator, Barney Afako, to contribute with experiences from his world, and we invited a number of judges, as well a representative of the Permanent Court of Arbitration (PCA), to elaborate from theirs. Interesting topics of discussion were how these two instruments interrelate and if there is a certain logic to choosing one and not the other.

Present:

His Excellency Judge Owada, International Court of Justice

His Excellency Judge Keith, International Court of Justice

Her Excellency Judge Donoghue, International Court of Justice

Mr. Barney Afako, Lawyer, Mediator in several conflicts in East African region, mainly Sudan

Dr. Aloysius Llamzon, Senior Legal Counsel at the Permanent Court of Arbitration

Mr. Steven van Hoogstraten, General Director of the Carnegie Foundation, Moderator

Van Hoogstraten, Schrijver et al. (eds.), The Art of Making Peace: Lessons Learned from Peace Treaties
 ISBN 978-90-04-32123-6. pp. 159-189.

Dr. Otto Spijkers, Assistant Professor in Public International Law, University of Utrecht, Editor

Mrs. Anneleen de Jong, Policy Advisor at the Carnegie Foundation, Editor

Question 1

Could you share with us your ideas and experiences with similarities or differences between mediation and adjudication? When should one choose for one or the other? Is there a certain logic to it? What considerations will be central to governments when they make the decisions and how should they be put into perspective?

Steven van Hoogstraten as Moderator invited Barney Afako to start the conversation.

Barney Afako stated that it very much depends on the type of dispute. Governments will tend to begin with some form of negotiation if the matter can be settled amicably. The reason for that is that you have much more control over the process and over the outcome. Even if in the negotiation you have to make concessions, there is some flexibility in negotiation that is attractive to governments.

The problem comes when the subject matter is technical, it may be a dispute of a commercial or environmental nature, and for which you need expertise to identify the issues and work out what might be viable solutions. It may not be possible to do that exclusively between the parties or even with a mediator. Adjudication then becomes attractive as it brings the expertise of the adjudicators to the problem and the possible solution. Adjudication often tends to come in when there is an impasse or where the parties conceded that they may not make the progress that they would make through negotiation.

Adjudication is also attractive where one party thinks that the merits are on its side and wants to go to the law to have this announced in their favour. This often occurs in boundary disputes where the parties may feel from their own reading that they stand a high chance. They would then be hostile to any attempt to negotiate that process, although sometimes the result of the adjudication isn't very conclusive either or doesn't lead to a satisfactory conclusion. This has tended to affect how States view adjudication right now across the continent in Africa. There is much more investment in exploring options for mediated settlements of various disputes, including boundary disputes rather than referring them automatically to the Court for adjudication. There is always a calculation by each party as to where it may get returns in its favour whether to go for mediation or adjudication.

Steven van Hoogstraten then asked Judge Keith to present his view.

Judge Keith confirmed that there is a calculation to be made, with many elements to it. Sometimes there is the question of how the issues should be defined, and sometimes it is suggested that more issues are brought into the mix, instead of fewer. Maintaining control is very important as well as considering the costs involved. Litigation is expensive and risky as you are in a win or lose situation.

To give an example. When in 1973 New Zealand and Australia came to the Court to dispute the legality of France's nuclear testing, the anecdote goes that the Prime Minister of New Zealand said that he had no faith in lawyers "because they lose half their cases". The point is that when you litigate you are in the hands of the court or tribunal and you do lose control. Besides, it may not be possible to get the right kind of outcome. There is obviously a lot to be said, looking carefully at all the means of dispute resolution. Sometimes it is not a matter of finding solutions, but a matter of managing an ongoing situation. At the ICJ we are looking at countries that continue to live and work together and it is important to envisage the maintenance of good relations in the future. It is not like national litigation where the parties may never see one another again.

Steven van Hoogstraten asked Judge Keith whether he would say that the relation between two States is more affected by adjudication of a dispute than by mediation? Or is it a sort of healthy new start if the adjudication is taking place?

Judge Keith stated that States that have an ongoing good relationship might be very reluctant to litigate because it may influence the relationship in a negative way. But it may be the case that they decide to leave the matter to the lawyers to argue the case and to the court and tribunal to make the binding decision. For instance, for many years Australia refused to allow the import of New Zealand apples for claimed phytosanitary reasons. Negotiations failed and in the end New Zealand considered that it had no choice but to invoke the WTO dispute settlement procedure involving expert assessment and binding decision. That process led to a decision in New Zealand's favour.

Steven van Hoogstraten then invited Judge Owada to give his comments.

Judge Owada stated that in considering the issue of similarities and differences between mediation and adjudication there were psychological elements as well as other more technical aspects that have to be taken into account. In choosing either mediation or arbitration the intention of the parties is the primary factor.

In the case of mediation, it is important to note that mediation is in essence a continuation of the direct negotiations. If the parties get stuck in the course of their negotiations, they often look for a third party for help in this process. Adjudication is different in this respect as it has a more definitive character to it as a method for the resolution of a dispute. The decision would be final and settle the matter once and for all. That is an important difference which the parties to the dispute should take into account. Article 33 of the UN Charter mentions that parties may seek a solution to their dispute by a variety of different methods, including negotiation, enquiry, mediation, conciliation, arbitration, judicial settlement, resort to regional agencies or arrangements, or other peaceful means of their own choice.

As for the technical aspects of the means for the settlement of disputes, mediation and adjudication can be regarded as, in a sense, complementary to each other. They can be employed in a mutually exclusive manner; they can be consecutive, one following the other; or they can also be alternative. Adjudication in this sense is a method to bring a definitive end to the dispute, rather than a process towards an end. In the end, once the decision is given in an adjudication, it is final and closes the situation unless there is a request for interpretation of the judgment. By comparison, mediation, though not necessarily, can be a process in the sense that it is something which can be employed as a step in the course of settling the dispute, while the parties may change their mind even after the mediation effort has been successful or has failed. It does not give the same degree of finality to the outcome. Because of this indeterminate character of the institution of mediation, some countries prefer to seek a final settlement of the matter through adjudication. This is illustrated in a recent case before the ICJ concerning Pedra Branca (Singapore v. Malaysia).

There is an extremely interesting book on the background of the case written by the Singaporean side (see S. Jayakumar and Tommy Koh, *Pedra Branca: The Road to the World Court* (NUS Press, 2009)) . The book explains the background as to why Malaysia and Singapore had decided to come to the ICJ in a territorial dispute which had for a long time been a bone of contention between the two States. After many years of difficult negotiations and after trying various means of settling the dispute by negotiation, mediation, and other means, they finally came to the conclusion that after all this was a technical issue which should be settled once and for all. From a broader perspective, they considered it important to get rid of that issue as a basis for starting to build good relations between the two countries, so that the fundamental relations between the two countries would become much more stable and much more satisfactory, rather than seeking a settlement which could only be a temporary solution but could not provide the final resolution of the issue. So this aspect of the issue is one relevant factor that we have to take into account in considering the issue of choice.

Another factor which in Judge Owada's view is important to bear in mind is the point referred to in Article 2, paragraph 3 of the UN Charter which states that the parties have to resort to the peaceful settlement of disputes "in such a manner that international peace and security, *and justice*, are not endangered" (emphasis added). This last underlined element is an important one in a dispute resolution, because if you seek peace and security as the sole goal to be pursued in the process then you might be able to arrive at a solution of a dispute which could be acceptable to the parties, but not necessarily a "just solution" of the dispute. If one includes justice in the approach then a different element emerges to be added to the situation. The whole purpose of the resolution of a dispute may not be simply to achieve a peaceful settlement whatever the content of that settlement may be, but to achieve a peaceful settlement that is based on, or in line with, a sense of justice that would prevail in the resolution in the eyes of the disputing parties. Adjudication contains that element, and this undoubtedly is one significant advantage of adjudication as compared to other methods for the settlement of disputes.

By contrast, the disadvantage of adjudication is that there could be a situation in which one of the parties may prefer adjudication as a method for the settlement of a concrete dispute because it would settle the dispute on the basis of the law. Once the appropriate law is identified and applied, then that is the end of the adjudication. By comparison, however, that could necessarily be the reason why the other party might prefer to have recourse to other methods than adjudication, including mediation, so that some element of equity could be brought into a balanced equation. This outcome cannot be achieved by adjudication in the strict sense of the word. The cases before the Permanent Court of Arbitration may be different from either mediation or adjudication before the ICJ to the extent that the procedure is that of arbitration and not of mediation. You resort to the special procedure by arbitration to settle disputes, which may not only be by the strict application of the law but also *ex aequo et bono*, but not as opened-ended as by mediation. Though such a specific procedure based on a decision *ex aequo et bono* is envisaged also under the Statute of the ICJ, this is possible only with the agreement of the parties. Such agreement of the parties will not be easy to come by, since one party may prefer a settlement strictly by law while the other party may think such a solution wouldn't be appropriate. These are the objective factors that have to be taken into account when deciding on the choice between mediation and adjudication.

Mr. van Hoogstraten mentioned that if there is this difference between the Court following the law and the PCA having the right to go wider in this sort of equitable solution, not necessarily in conformity with the law, it may be interesting to now hear the view of the PCA. He invites Aloysius Llamzon to step into the discussion.

Dr. Llamzon stated that arbitration through the PCA is really far more akin to a formal dispute settlement process as international law has been employed since 1899. It is true that there is a perception out in the world that when you go to arbitration, arbitrators are far more willing to look at the law but then also try to balance the scales through equitable considerations. But strictly speaking that cannot be done. Arbitration is a formal process that is bound by international law and as with the Statute of the ICJ, arbitrators are only empowered to decide *ex aequo et bono* if the parties empower them to do so.

Judge Owada wished to add in this context that in their origins there was a difference in this sense even between adjudication in the strict sense and arbitration. However, the practice has developed in such a way that the PCA is nowadays more likely to act on the strict application of the law. In that sense arbitration should be regarded as a type of adjudication, classifying mediation in a totally different category. However, the choice of the PCA, rather than the ICJ by the Parties to a recent dispute between Croatia and Slovenia demonstrates this difference (or rather the nuances) between the two institutions.

Dr. Llamzon continued. One aspect in which arbitration differs from both mediation and adjudication is the fact that parties are able to choose the specific arbitrator for a dispute. Sometimes they will choose them for technical reasons, sometimes because they feel there is a political acceptability to a decision that is rendered by particular decision-makers based on their background and experiences. So States do have choices. When they look at the various choices they have, sometimes they prefer the most formal mode of settlement in the form of adjudication with pre-chosen judges. What we are starting to see more often again is the desire of States to actually choose the individual third-party decision-makers. That seems to be of increasing importance to them. In a sense the loss of control that occurs when a binding decision is rendered by a third party not chosen by the parties can be a reason why States hesitate to go to adjudication in international courts instead of arbitration. When existential, highly political issues, or sovereignty issues are involved, no State wants to be seen in a negotiating situation as having given something away. We have seen time and time again arbitration where there were years of negotiations without success, and finally a decision was made to go to arbitration with the knowledge that that even if we lose the arbitration, the outcome of loss is better than what the status quo was. Arbitration becomes a way to externalize the possibility of loss, as no State official wants to be seen as giving something important away; so you have a third party make that binding decision.

Mr. van Hoogstraten then asked Judge Donoghue to give her comments on this first point of discussion.

Judge Donoghue thanked Judge Owada for his reminder that there are mechanisms for the peaceful settlement of disputes beside adjudication and mediation. Arbitration fits closely with adjudication, although it is distinct. Focusing here on mediation in contrast to adjudication, we can look at three key variables relevant for the peaceful settlement of disputes. First, it is up to disputing States to decide whether to involve a mediator. On the other hand, adjudication of a dispute can be compulsory if the parties have agreed in advance to adjudication of that dispute. Second, to what extent do the disputing parties retain control over the outcome? In adjudication, a Court decides the result. In mediation, ultimately it is up to the parties to accept or not to accept a particular result. Third, the final result of adjudication is binding on the disputing parties. In mediation, the result can be reflected in a binding legal agreement, but it can also take other forms.

As to the question of party control over the outcome, a point addressed by Judge Owada, this is a variable about which party views will depend on the particular dispute. Sometimes one or both disputing States wishes to be in a position to reject a solution presented by a third party. But that is not always the case. One example that comes to mind is the decision of the United States and Canada to submit to the ICJ their dispute over the Gulf of Maine. The dispute was important to both States, both in terms of resources and domestic politics. In this kind of case, if leaders have been making statements such as "these are our fish"or "that is our island," a decision to compromise can be criticised as a decision to give "our" fish or "our" island to the other side.The two States may be in a better position to arrive at a durable solution if it is imposed by a court.

More generally, we have to acknowledge that we often have very incomplete information about why States choose one form of dispute settlement over another. Among the factors that are often identified are the cost and the speed of the proceedings. No State wants to spend more money than is needed to settle a dispute. However, it is not always the case that a party that initiates dispute settlement seeks a speedy resolution. We see this in the way that parties to ICJ cases approach the pace of cases. Sometimes channeling a dispute into a particular mechanism, taking it out of a bilateral relationship, achieves important objectives.

When we look at the Iran-US Claims Tribunal, which is still settling disputes after many decades, one has to wonder why these two States preserve that institution for so long. One has to presume that it is in their interest to keep that tribunal operating, rather than settling the outstanding disputes quickly.

Another consideration in the selection of a dispute settlement mechanism is confidentiality. In our Court, proceedings are normally public. This provides a forum for each party to make public the details of its case. However, for some disputes, one or both parties may favour confidential proceedings.

An additional factor affecting a State's choice of a dispute settlement mechanism is the way that a particular dispute fits within the overall relationship of the parties. What precedents will be set within that relationship for the settlement of other disputes?

Finally, as has been discussed, there are variations in the ability of the parties to control and tailor the procedures governing settlement of a dispute. The parties have complete flexibility in mediation. Our Court does have some procedural flexibility, but we are limited by our Statute and Rules, and we have less flexibility than do ad hoc arbitrators.

Question 2

Otto Spijkers introduced the second question of the roundtable, by raising the following issue.

He stated that he wanted to address the topic of the two processes of mediation and adjudication running simultaneously. For instance, when a case is pending before the ICJ and in the meantime the parties continue to negotiate to reach an agreed settlement. Is that appropriate? He mentioned the Ecuador v. Colombia case which was settled just before the Court was starting its oral proceedings to hear the case.

There is a second aspect to this. If in a legal dispute adjudication is chosen, it becomes detached from the more comprehensive peace process. As happened in the Abyei case, the limitation of one particular boundary became a legal issue whilst at the same time, through the Machakos Protocol, the Comprehensive Peace Agreement was being negotiated. Could one state that the Abyei issue became detached from its context because of the different choice of settlement?

Judge Keith wished to intervene, and stated that it is certainly possible for the parties to continue to negotiate as happened in the Ecuador Colombia case. It happened in the past too, in the Nauru case and and in the Great Belts case, where the court made rulings on provisional matters in one case and jurisdiction in the other. Those rulings led to negotiations with the results that the disputes were settled and the cases withdrawn.

In the Ecuador v. Colombia case the Court had issued to the parties a long list of questions. In their letters recording their agreement and the discontinuance of the case thanked the Court for its critical role in prompting settlement. Returning to the Rainbow Warrior, the New Zealand and French governments engaged in lengthy negotiations over a wide range of issues following the blowing up of the Greenpeace vessel in Auckland Harbour by agents of the French secret service. The issues related to the two agents who had been sentenced to 10 years imprisonment for manslaughter of the photographer, a Dutch national, on the vessel, the compensation and other remedies for New Zealand, the compensation to be paid to the family of the photographer, the compensation to be paid to Greenpeace in respect of its ship which was British flagged and trade issues. The detailed story has still to be told but some things are clear on the public record. The Dutch Prime Minister offered his good offices with the consequence that the UN Secretary General, Perez de Cuellar, was given the task of making a principled and equitable mediation which would be binding on the two States. It did that in a very short time, which, with other evidence, indicates that much of the ruling had already been agreed, and the ruling was quickly incorporated into agreements between the two Governments. The political position in both countries made it impossible for them to have agreed to those terms in a direct way without that third party intervention. So the Secretary-General was in fact a one-man arbiter, endorsing, however, what had largely been agreed between the parties.

Later, after the two agents were returned to Paris by France from the Pacific atoll to which they had been sent in terms of the ruling and agreements in apparent breach of them, a regular arbitration tribunal consisting of three members was set up, again in terms of one of the agreements. It followed a standard written and oral proceeding, found that France was in breach, but that there would be no order for their return to the Island, and, in addition to ruling that the declarations of breaches were themselves remedies for New Zealand, recommended that the two States set up a friendship fund, with France making the first substantial contribution, to facilitate contact between the young people of the two countries. In this way the long friendly relations between the two countries would be reinforced. Such an action is much more likely to come from a small specially composed tribunal than from a regular court.

One of the things that the tribunal did was to bridge in various ways. As it was a small size tribunal, many things were settled that would have been more difficult when a large institution would have been involved. One particular positive outcome was the setting up of a friendship fund to facilitate the movement of young people between the two countries. This way the long peaceful relation between the two countries would be reinforced.

Mr. van Hoogstraten commented that he is intrigued by the word principled, and equitable.

When would you say that a decision by the Secretary-General is principled? It sounds as if it was based on principles, not necessarily on the law. After a short discussion on the translation of the word equitable in French and English, the Moderator then invited the panel to return to the idea of a simultaneous application of adjudication and mediation. He asked Judge Owada for his comments.

Judge Owada stated that as a matter of the framework for dispute settlement both instruments are compatible and an approach to work with both procedures simultaneously can be done and has been done. Judge Owada does not think there is anything wrong with such a dual approach. In fact in some jurisdictions, such as in many domestic jurisdictions, Judges often have the power to make a recommendation leading to a settlement of the dispute outside the Court while the dispute is still pending before the Court. If the ultimate goal is to reach a peaceful settlement of the dispute, then it is natural that the Court could cooperate in achieving this goal. It goes without saying that the discontinuance of a case in the middle of its adjudication process can create an embarrassing situation for the Judges who have been involved in the case and have spent so much time on it. But if you focus on the outcome, you have to accept the best way that the parties have chosen to achieve the peaceful settlement of the dispute.

In general, if you compare the two solutions, there is no incompatibility between the two; though the outcome may not be exactly what the Court will have reached if it had pursued its own course of adjudication. Such a situation happens particularly in relation to a political settlement of a dispute in which a body like the Security Council gets involved, as against mediation by the Secretary-General. Under the Charter, parallel with the Security Council, the Secretary-General has its own power to take the initiative for the settlement of a dispute and to get into this exercise of mediation role. However, the outcome of such mediation has to be accepted by the Security Council in order to become a part of the political settlement. Sometimes the Secretary-General may work hard to try to work out a settlement that in its mind and in the minds of many of the members of the Security Council would be an acceptable solution. This may not always be a "just" solution in the eyes of all members of the Security Council. How this justice aspect of the settlement comes into play in the political process could become a delicate issue.

It might be important to remind ourselves of the situation created by a mediation effort tried in Munich in 1938. An interesting recent example took place in 1997 when the Security Council handled the Iraqi crisis relating to the allegedly secret development of weapons of mass destruction by Saddam Hussein's regime. The negotiations between the UN inspection team and the Iraqi regime went into an impasse. The Secretary-General decided to intervene to mediate between the two and negotiate a workable solution. Some of the members of the Security Council considered it unwise to negotiate with the Iraqi regime as it was obvious to them that the Iraqi regime had been trying to forestall the efforts of the Security Council through secretly developing weapons of mass destruction. The Secretary-General, however, thought otherwise and tried to test whether this suspicion on the part of members of the Security Council was legitimate or not. He decided to try his hand by going to Iraq on his own initiative. He in fact worked out a solution which to many members of the Security Council was a reasonable way out of this impasse while to others this solution was not acceptable.

As some members of the Council tried to work out a draft resolution which would endorse what the Secretary-General had achieved, a permanent member of the Council who was opposed threatened to exercise a veto if the majority would go ahead with the draft resolution. In fact, the veto was not exercised and the Council eventually unanimously endorsed the mediation efforts of the Secretary-General. As this episode illustrates, there could arise a kind of tension between the dominant participants in the dispute settlement process who stick to what they thought to be an important point of principle on the one hand and the effective functioning of the mediator on the other.

Mr van Hoogstraten invited Barney Afako to present his views.

Mr. Afako stated that he sees compatibility between adjudication and mediation because a lot of disputes have legal elements which may well be beyond the capacity of a negotiation to settle, as negotiations tend to be highly politically charged. And they are not always the conducive environment for the objective analysis of legal principles and seeking an answer arising from those principles. So the parties have a difficult task to reach that kind of legally sound conclusion because the facts are contested and this contestation may extend to questions of law because it is part of the game of negotiations not to concede even on the legal principles. Sometimes it is more appropriate if a matter is a legal point that requires to be settled, that one goes to a third party who can then make a pronouncement on the basis of which the negotiation could continue. For instance in the Ecuador v. Colombia litigation before the ICJ the process of framing the issues for the Court to determine may well have clarified issues for the parties, allowing them then to reach a consensus on the legal points. This then allowed the whole mediation or negotiation process to move on to a resolution. So Mr Afako thinks they can be compatible, even when the matters do not come to the Court. Increasingly we see the parties tend not to refer the legal questions to the system for adjudication, but call in experts to answer the narrow points in order for the matters to cease being a point of contention so that the process can move on.

Mr. van Hoogstraten wished to make an analogy to the domestic legal system which in the practice of mediation is veiled with an aura of confidentiality, whereas if the case comes in front of official tribunals and Courts it will be dealt with in its fullness. Mr. van Hoogstraten wondered if in the international legal system, there is a sort of coming together of mediation and adjudication in a way that the Judges can take into account what happened in the mediation, or is the mediation also secluded from public hearing? To take one example, in the recent case about whaling, a lot of negotiations had taken place outside the framework of the Court before the case ever came to the Court. Is it the case that the Court can take into consideration what happened in the mediation or is that a matter that is as it were out of balance? Mr van Hoogstraten invited Judge Donoghue to present her views on this matter.

Judge Donoghue offered two comments about situations in which the distinction between adjudication and mediation can be blurred. First, building on Mr. van Hoogstraten's reference to the use of mediation in domestic legal proceedings, she noted that within the US there are some circumstances in which parties to a court case are required to mediate before the court will decide the case. This is quite different from the inter-State dispute resolution system, in which we think of mediation as an entire voluntary process. She also noted that compulsory mediation has been controversial within the United States. Some proponents say that it reduces costs and leads to the more efficient settlement of disptues. Others say, no, it is just another step that parties must take before a court can decide a case, and that it is a waste of time and money in cases in which there is no appetite to settle.

Second, we have seen some greater interest in mediation in the context of investor-State dispute settlement. In particular, the International Bar Association has developed a set of rules that could be used for mediation of investor-State disputes. Those rules are a template for the possible use of mediation in this contest. They do not make mediation mandatory. However, the way those rules would operate, as I understand them, once the parties consent to mediation they have to stay in the mediation at least as far as a mediation conference. As with the compulsory mediation that we see in the US system, such rules can blur the distinction between adjudication and mediation. The blending of these two kinds of dispute settlement can give rise to opportunities for creative lawyers and policy-makers to design mechanisms that they think work best to advance either their particular interests or the shared interest of the two States.

Mr. van Hoogstraten invited the representative of the PCA, very familiar with investor-State relations, Aloysius Llamzon, to present his view.

Dr. Llamzon, responding to the comments made by Judge Donoghue, stated that it is very true there has been a little bit of disenchantment at least in the public-oriented NGO sectors, as they believe that there is a fundamental unfairness in investor-State arbitration and therefore they support a certain intention to move away from arbitration or at least try mediation and conciliation more often. At the PCA we are all for conciliation except that it has never really been used by parties and States. The PCA has had conciliation rules from the very beginning in 1899. We had our latest set of conciliation rules in the 1990s. It hasn't been used a single time. We see similar tendencies elsewhere. You might say that conciliation is in a way a more formal sort of mediation and that is why it is uninteresting to many people. Our experience really has been that when parties decide that they want third party resolution, they tend to want something that is binding. So I do not know if more mediation and conciliation will in fact occur in the coming years, including at the PCA.

Just two more points. Mediation within adjudication is a very important and interesting question. In many of our arbitration cases, at the last minute, you have a cancellation of the hearing. It is either rescheduled for six months from now and then is terminated, or the case is resumed, and suddenly everything continues as before. This might occur 50% of the time. I would ascribe it to the nature of the dispute. If it is an investment arbitration and it is about money, the parties can deal with money. If it is about high forms of principles, sovereignty, interstate disputes, there never really are cancellations for those kind of cases, as the potential for compromise is much more difficult at the point where such disputes have already gone into arbitration.

Sometimes these comprehensive settlements appear in an interstate context, like as Judge Owada mentioned when talking about the Malaysia versus Singapore case. Then they ask the arbitral tribunal to endorse their negotiated settlement, and when you have an arbitral award that confirms the agreement, you have the best of both worlds. Another example was what Judge Keith was saying with respect to the Rainbow Warrior case.

It is also interesting to discuss mediation within an adjudicatory context, like in arbitration. You often see that in arbitrations at distinct phases, third parties are brought in and that might be akin to mediators. Often this involves complex issues of evidence that parties do not agree mediation versus adjudication with and want to keep confidential from the tribunal because it might colour their decision-making. Then often a third party is introduced. I think of President Van Houtte in the Iran-USA Claims Tribunal who was in the past an expert in the Guyana versus Suriname case. He went to the Dutch archives and took a look at very important material related to that dispute on behalf of the Tribunal. Similarly, arbitrators are very good in the law, but when it comes to the financial implications parties suddenly do not trust them anymore and ask an economist to come in. That you see very often.

The last point I would like to make here is about *Abyei*. That case has been really made to bear a lot of weight that it wasn't meant to. The parties never gave the arbitral tribunal the authority to settle the most important political questions like who will be a voter in the Abyei region for purposes of the referendum, which has become the key stumbling block on the resolution of that region's fate. However, the parties were the ones that defined the Tribunal's mandate. I understand the frustration that many have with that arbitration when they say it didn't settle the dispute definitively, but my answer has always been: it was never asked to and never meant to. They only asked the tribunal to answer that first question which is what are the specific boundaries and then they left to the political process the decision on who would then be a voter. Which of course the political process was unable to come into a consensus on. That shows you the sort of discrete legal questions that can be brought to arbitration, and those questions that could be but are not brought to arbitration because of political sensitivities. Some questions will be brought to arbitration as a way of passing the political "football" to a third party and thus minimize the political fallout for one or both parties. But parties are often not willing to hand over control on the most sensitive issues to independent arbitrators. Certainly, if you give a panel of arbitrators or the ICJ *carte blanche* to decide something, they will decide it. But often parties will not give them that power.

Mr. van Hoogstraten asked Barney Afako the question: how important have legal questions often been in the cases that he dealt with as a mediator or an advisor or were the questions predominantly political?

Mr. Afako answered that most of the time the questions are political. The area where you tend to have legal questions often has to do with boundaries. The process of the secession of South Sudan, where it was necessary to have in place all sorts of arrangements, from dividing of resources, pensions, citizenship issues, and others as a consequence of the creation of a new state also generated significant legal elements which needed technical input. But the generally, the broad issues in negotiations are political, although the outcomes will need to be framed in a legal text. Once political issues are settled, then it is easier for the parties to tackle even the technical issues in an environment of trust. But where there is political difficulty, then the legal issues are accentuated, as for example in the matter of Abyei. Although the PCA clarified the international boundary, and because the political question remained unanswered, even that clarification is now back on the table.

That is the interplay between the politics and the legal question. If they don't resolve the pending political question, then the legal answer will always come under strain. The other quick example, going back to Sudan, is that of the demarcation of the international boundary between the two States. That is being settled through negotiations. The principle is that the international boundary is the line of 1st January 1956, but the process of the delimitation and demarcation of that line is a matter for the two States to negotiate. In the disputed areas—because there are disputes about five places—the parties have now called for experts' input. The African Union had to set up a team of experts to produce a non-binding opinion, but the terms of reference require the experts to take a legal approach and so in that way the Parties look to have the best of both worlds. To have a good quality legal opinion, there are eminent lawyers including an ex-Judge of the ICJ involved, but the opinion will not be binding, so the Parties can go back and negotiate on it. The parties, however, will recognise that even if the opinion is non-binding, it is going to help to shape the terms of the negotiation. Such an opinion removes the political implication of an outright referral to the

ICJ or other adjudication, and it allows the Parties to maintain control of the process.

Judge Keith stated that it is important to keep in mind that litigation quite often does not settle disputes definitively. We tend to be trapped by the words in the Charter stating the "peaceful settlement of disputes", where it is quite often the case that litigation and other methods of handling disputes do not bring a final result. Judge Keith was thinking in this context of two recent cases: Bolivia seeking a ruling that Chile is in breach of its obligation to negotiate in good faith concerning Bolivia's access to the Pacific Ocean; and the Marshall Islands similarly requesting a finding that the nuclear powers are in breach of their obligation to negotiate nuclear disarmament in good faith. The end-game in both cases is way beyond litigation. Litigation in those cases is designed to get processes moving rather than to produce a substantive outcome. Consider too the case between Peru and Chile before the ICJ. The Court took a long time to settle their boundary and we left it to the parties to fix the coordinates in the spirit of good, which they did. While on the Peruvian side there may have been questions of historic justice, the only present day practical issues were about fisheries. And that case had nothing directly to do with fisheries.

Fisheries is now being dealt with by the South Pacific Fishery Management Commission, which is a management system. It is not a final resolution system as quotas cannot be fixed for a long period, but rather year by year. And if a State complains about the year by year quota, you can then initiate a process which happened through the assistance of the PCA. There was a hearing on Monday and the decision was given on Friday, as that was the timing required. Partly this was due to the fact that you have to fix these quotas each year and you cannot have the more than twelve months that we took to fix that boundary. Whatever the Court said was not going to solve the fisheries issues, that practical issue, which was going to be dealt with by the other management system and by the PCA as registry.

Question 3

In the second half of the roundtable debate, Steven van Hoogstraten introduced the question of the role of non-State actors. He pointed out that there are many different types, with different roles to play. It would thus be helpful if the participants could clearly state which type they were referring in their remarks. Clearly, the adjudication process at the ICJ does not allow for intervention by non-State actors, unless invited to do so by the Court. In the mediation process, there are no such strict rules about their participation, their role being determined by the parties and the mediators in each specific case.

Mr. Van Hoogstraten asked Mr Barney Afako to start on this issue by explaining the role of non-State actors in the mediation work that he is currently involved with.

Mr. Afako explained that, the non-State actors he encountered in his work as mediator were mostly international non-governmental organisations. Their involvement was motivated either by an interest in the mediation process itself, or an aspect of the situation that needed to be resolved through the mediation. For example, these international NGOs might have a particular interest in a cease-fire – if it is an ongoing conflict – or in a particular resolution of natural resource issues. The negotiations usually take place between States, and States generally want to limit the issues under discussion and the number of participants involved. Very few States are very enthusiastic about inviting observers or NGO participation. State representatives prefer to lock all that out, and to proceed on the understanding that they come to the table with a clear and specific mandate from their government. Even the non-State actors involved in the mediation – such as rebel groups – do not want to take on board other considerations when they negotiate with the State. However, increasingly, and especially in situations where the mediation has been facilitated by regional bodies (e.g. African Union, ECOWAS, SADC, or others), such bodies will encourage and even require that States or other parties involved in the mediation listen to civil society and others. In practice, civil society participation tends to be synonymous with NGO participation, because in many countries civil society itself is not particularly well organised. Local trade unions generally do not follow the negotiations closely. Instead you have NGOs, highly specialised and often working not only within that State where the dispute has arisen, which present themselves. They are in fact international actors. These NGOs tend to be sponsored one way or the other by members of the international community (either a State, the EU, or other entities). And often they are viewed as proxies for those sponsoring entities. They come fairly well-equipped to the table, but are perceived to act largely as lobbyists – unless the parties themselves have agreed formally to consult them, which is rare. The absence of such a formal invitation does not stop NGOs from distributing their position papers and influencing the talks in that way. Most of the time the NGOs have an informal role in the mediation. They bring international backing and expertise, which often even the parties themselves may not have. The NGOs bring the best lawyers, specialised in wealth-sharing or constitutional matters. They produce papers, and turn around issues very fast. Where delegations come with a single lawyer, NGOs are able to muster more support and draw from a much wider network. Although formally States are in control of the process, NGOs and other non-State actors actually shape the debate in the room. And increasingly now they are literally finding their way into the room because of the notion of "inclusive dialogue". This term refers to the need to incorporate all of the various constituent elements of a State into a settlement, the argument being that unless they are on the table, you will not have a sustainable peace. But the danger is that this facilitates activist NGOs, who do not necessarily bring to the fore a balanced picture of what is going on within the State, to indeed be very active and influential in the process. Some less experienced NGOs cede their seat to a more experienced and activist NGO representative sitting behind them, and so the process loses an authentic voice of the internal constituency of the State. This happens increasingly often. It has not been studied effectively what the role of NGOs exactly is in the negotiations, but they are powerful, and they are no less powerful when their involvement in the process is only informal and *ad hoc*.

Mr. Van Hoogstraten addressed the question to Judge Donoghue. He first pointed out that at the moment the role of non-State actors is basically non-existent at the ICJ. And so he asked Judge Donoghue whether an opening should be made in the future. Could a procedure be developed for States to have the assistance of NGOs if they want to?

Judge Donoghue noted that even nowadays, States that appear before the ICJ may have as much assistance from NGOs and other advisers as they wish. More generally, she noted that some small States rely heavily on NGOs to support them on some of the legal and policy issues that are priorities for those States, and there is no reason why that trend could not occur at the ICJ as well.

The question of direct NGO participation in ICJ proceedings is more complicated. The issue of "amicus curiae" briefs of NGOs and other non-parties to a dispute has received considerable attention in other bodies, such as the World Trade Organization and UNCITRAL. When looking at the disparate views of States on this issue, one often sees that there is a tendency for lawyers and specialists in international dispute settlement to revert instinctively to practices and procedures that are found in their own national legal systems.

Judge Donoghue explained that, as an American, she comes from a system where amicus curiae briefs are common. Such briefs might or might not present views that assist the Court, but she does not consider that they would pose a threat to the work of the Court. Nonetheless, she expressed the view that it would be quite surprising for the ICJ to decide to accept the filings of amicus briefs from non-States. The ICJ has been hestitant to permit third States to present views in a case as non-party intervenors, a form of participation that is contemplated by the Statute of the Court. It is likely that there would be greater scepticism about procedures to permit participation by non-States.

Mr. Van Hoogstraten asked whether it is a right of a third State to intervene, or whether it is a decision of the Court to allow them to intervene?

Judge Donoghue explained that the particular type of intervention that she described – the intervention by a State not a party to the proceedings – is not a right but something that the Court would weigh and decide in light of the ICJ Statute, and the recent requests for such intervention were denied.

Judge Keith added that there are various ways not generally recognised in which materials of an NGO can reach the Judges of the ICJ. He recalled that in the *Pulp Mills*-case (*Argentina v. Uruguay*), there was a very close cooperation between the Pulp Mills company and Uruguay. A representative of the company was present during the oral pleadings. Huge amounts of technical material were gathered by Argentina and Uruguay, and much of that was provided by the Pulp Mills company itself, because it was obliged to provide this information under local domestic law. So there are various ways in which non-State material comes to court, and from time to time it will be by way of an expert witness.

In the advisory jurisdiction, the practice is a bit more open. The practice varied down the years, but if you go way back to the beginning of the old Court – the Permanent Court of International Justice – you will see that in those advisory proceedings involving the International Labour Organisation, trade unions appeared and presented arguments both orally and in written form. So there are precedents at least when it comes to the Court's advisory jurisdiction. At the same time, there was a reaction by the ICJ against wide participation in the *Nuclear Weapons*-opinion proceedings, because the Court was absolutely deluged with thousands and thousands of pages of submissions from third parties or NGOs. Also in that case, some national delegations appearing before the ICJ actually included people who were affected by nuclear testing in the past. And they basically gave witness testimony. And so there are ways that States can bring material produced by non-State actors forward in the advisory proceedings. Clearly, in the Wall case, and the Kosovo case, entities not recognised as States appeared, so there is a bit of flexibility in that area. In contentious cases however, the situation is altogether different.

Judge Owada said that, in his opinion on the role of the NGOs, there is a basic difference between the process of mediation and the process of adjudication as practiced by the ICJ. Undoubtedly, a lot of variations exist in the adjudication processes of different courts, but as far as the ICJ is concerned, the situation is clear. From a procedural point of view, there is no room for NGOs formally to appear before the Court.

In contrast, in mediation, which is basically a negotiating process facilitated by the participation or the intervention of a third party, there is a lot of room for non-governmental entities generally to influence the decision-making process, in a more or less formal way. To him that is the basic difference between the two processes of adjudication and mediation.

By contrast, if you include the roles played by independent experts and witnesses who provide facts, etc. in your definition of non-State actors, then it must be noted that participation of such non-State actors is part of the formal process before the ICJ as well. For example, in the Whaling case before the ICJ between Australia and Japan, it is pointed out that the expert opinions of both sides had a considerable impact factually and psychologically upon the minds of the judges. Whether that has actually been so and whether this is a good thing or a bad thing is a different matter, non-State actor involvement of this nature is clearly integrated into the process of adjudication, though there is no reason *a priori* to cast doubt upon the integrity of such experts and witnesses. In any case, Judge Owada did not think that non-State actor involvement of this type was what we were really dealing with here and discussing in the framework of the roundtable today.

Mr. Van Hoogstraten asked whether there is in general any debate to open up proceedings of the International Court of Justice?

Judge Owada responded that there have been a lot of discussions on this problem of ensuring "transparency" of proceedings before the Court. For example, this issue was taken up by several Presidents of the ICJ in the past in their speeches before the Sixth Committee of the General Assembly, which deals with legal issues. But he did not believe that the majority in that Committee as a whole has taken a position in favour of opening up the procedure of the ICJ to NGOs. By comparison, if you look at the issues that fall within the competence of the Third Committee which deals with social and human rights, the situation can be quite different, because there the questions are approached from societal and humanitarian points of view, where the transparency of the process may be an important factor.

Judge Keith added that it is increasingly going to be a problem that only States may be involved in the ICJ's contentious proceedings. Think, for example, of the EU being a party to the Law of the Sea Convention. Judge Keith described a case between the Former Yugoslav Republic of Macedonia and Greece, which was about the name that should be used to refer to the former within NATO. In many ways, NATO itself was a party to the dispute, as it was NATO that made a formal decision that was being complained about. In the Whaling-case, an important role was played by the Whaling Commission. So we see that international organisations – not NGOs but international *governmental* organisations – are getting increasingly involved in international disputes. There is a real issue about how all of this can be handled in the future by the ICJ, since it only allows States to appear as parties in a contentious proceeding. Some of those disputes can be handled by the ICJ's advisory jurisdiction, provided that the parties involved agree beforehand that they consider the advisory opinion as binding on them. The kind of cases involving international organisations like the EU, that arise at the WTO, or under the Law of the Sea Convention, could not come to the ICJ at all easily at present, and that is a real problem right now.

Judge Owada added that the rules of the Court provide for some participation of international organisations. This is informal in the sense that while the judges can listen to the views of the international organisations relevant to the case, these organisations cannot be parties to contentious proceedings between the litigating States. The current position of the Court is that the term "international organisations" refers to inter-governmental organisations, and not to NGOs.

Dr. Llamzon began by saying that, in his view, when there was a certain unity of interest between States involved in adjudication or arbitration and third parties, the latter could always find a way to get into the process through those States. As example, one can think of the Abyei Arbitration between the Government of Sudan and the Sudan People's Liberation Movement, where representatives of tribes, like the Mysseriya, were allowed to give testimony during the arbitration proceedings. So when there is a unity of interest, this is not really a problem; in fact, this is probably not the issue we are really talking about today.

On the other hand, when you have a disunity of interest, when you actually have constituents within the State or international interests that are running against the parties, that is where the question gets really interesting. That is when you actually have a question of two parties that may not necessarily want the decision-makers to hear what these third parties have to say. At the same time, permitting them to get involved might enhance the legitimacy of the adjudication or arbitration process.

This debate has been going on especially in investment arbitration for a long time. Basically, the forces of transparency – those calling for third-party *amicus* briefs, for example – have already won that debate in a way. But there is a degree of artificiality to their victory. In arbitration proceedings, and in investment arbitration in particular, you will have NGOs, third parties, in the room, in the hearing room, but they are not in the deliberation room, which is really where the key points are decided. And when a decision comes out, it usually turns out that the influence of these third parties is very limited. In fact, there has never been a case, at least in investment arbitration and inter-State arbitration, where a third-party *amicus* brief has been cited as a determinant of any kind of outcome.

Mr. Van Hoogstraten asked Dr. Llamzon if, when he mentioned that the NGOs were "in the room," he referred to a right of NGOs to actually participate in the proceedings? Or were they just there to observe?

Dr. Llamzon responded that they were there to observe mostly. There is a certain element of transparency. Non-State actors have the ability in an orderly fashion to make their views known. That is normally not done in open Court, but they can file their own *amicus* brief or some other form of correspondence, and these documents will be accepted as part of the proceedings. But some are skeptical about what is actually done with these documents. One never knows. On the other hand, in the ere are many valid considerations that affect decisions but never make it to the actual text of an arbitral award.

Mr. Afako referred, as example, to the ongoing negotiations in the South Sudan conflict. He indicated that he was not involved in this personally – as a mediator or otherwise – so he could speak about it quite freely. Before the start of the mediation, the parties had agreed on a formula for the negotiations, which expanded the table beyond the government and the SPLM, to political parties in the country, NGOs, religious leaders, etc. So now instead of having an adversarial setting, there was a roundtable, with a place for lots of different actors.

Both the government and the opposition, between whom the dispute arose, were initially opposed to inviting all these other actors to the table. They held that it was going to complicate a resolution of the issue, because it would introduce all kinds of other issues they were presently not prepared to deal with. But the African Union and some of the other regional bodies are increasingly of the opinion that, in the mediation context, there is almost a duty to make sure the process is representative, and that nobody is left out. Otherwise you will have unresolved issues to deal with afterwards.

It sounds very nice on paper, but in practice you can ask questions about whether these NGOs really are representative of the interests of the community in South Sudan. Often you see that a local representative, who has never been to such negotiations before, is approached by an NGO offering to do all the paper work for him, which means that this NGO will have a disproportionate influence in the process.

Mr. Van Hoogstraten asked Mr. Afako whether he believed that the participation of non-State actors in mediation was positive or negative, perhaps even dangerous.

Mr. Afako responded that he thought it was still early days. There are two types of non-state actors, those that have specific and genuine expertise in mediation issues, and are, therefore, a big help to the parties. These groups are often invisible, or may champion issues that might otherwise be lost, such as children, minority or women's issues. Some may also be instrumental in getting the parties to the table and preparing the sides to talk in the first place. Because of their expertise, they may even assume the role of mediation. On the other hand, there are organisations whose involvement in a process is not primarily to assist the parties to reach consensus but to influence the outcomes of the negotiation in the direction of their own agenda. His own experience was that he had yet to come across an even-handed campaigning NGO. Especially on points of law, including international law, all sorts of claims were made by NGOs in the name of international law. They claim that international law requires so-and-so, and in substantiating that claim they omit reference to the cases and authority and principles that go against their advocacy position. That is why it is preferable to have a system where you can draw on genuine experts, who then weigh up both sides and give an opinion that everybody can use. In his experience in mediation, Mr. Afako had never encountered such NGOs admitting to being wrong or admitting that they needed to amend their position. And this shows they are actually not very good at mediation themselves, because they are not coming to the table with an open mind, ready to find a compromise. They are still advocates. And when they participate in the mediation process, they do not stop being advocates, they are not ready to say: "Let us concede that point, because we shouldn't push our own agenda at this stage." This phenomenon is here to stay, and is likely to increase. And until we have more NGOs who can play the role of a genuine expert – collecting all the arguments and facts for all sides, presenting them so that the negotiators are better informed about the context – Mr. Afako preferred to reserve his judgement.

Judge Keith commented that all this involvement of non-State actors and third parties in the mediation process might lead the parties to the dispute to discuss their issues elsewhere. And then the real mediation no longer takes place where it was supposed to take place.

Mr. Afako agreed, and added that in practice it means that the State representatives need to go outside the mediation room to propose to fix something before they go back into the room.

Mr. Van Hoogstraten spoke about his experiences working for the Ministry of Health of the Netherlands, where he was a Director for Food Legislation. In that capacity, he often had to go to meetings of an international committee called the Codex Alimentarius. They had a system where the delegations could be composed of both government officials and non-State actors – such as a representative of the national consumer union or the industry. The consumers also had an independent right to act as observers. They were extremely vocal, but they were also extremely good. And thus the meeting tended to listen carefully to the sometimes quite extreme views taken by the consumers.

Judge Keith added that there has been a massive growth of the role of NGOs in trade negotiations. Sometimes they manage to get things off the agenda too, when there exist strong reactions against the matter being handled by governments.

Question 4

Dr. Otto Spijkers introduced the final question of this roundtable meeting. He proposed to discuss what happens after an agreement is reached in a mediation process or a judgment is issued by a Court. A judgment by the Court is issued on a particular day. This is the day that is eagerly anticipated by everyone involved, and by the public at large. It is the day everyone is looking forward to. The next day, there might be some comments in the newspapers, and scholars might continue to study it, but that is basically it. In contrast, when it comes to mediation, the signing of the agreement is much more seen as an important stage in the process, but not the end of it. The process continues, and all those involved will continue to be involved in it. So the question is: what is the role of the mediator or the Court after the agreement is signed or the judgment has been issued? Is there a role for the Court to do more when it comes to outreach, explaining its decisions to the public? You can leave the explaining to NGOs or the local media, but they tend to have a particular interpretation of the Court's judgment. So perhaps it is better for the Court to do the explaining itself? And can the Court play a role in the implementation of its decisions?

Judge Donoghue responded that this is a topic about which she speaks quite frequently in her lectures in the United States and elsewhere. She has urged academics to study the implementation of the Court's judgments. Of course, the ICJ's jurisdiction ends when the judgment is delivered and the case goes off the Court's docket. The Court itself has no formal mechanism to evaluate what happens afterwards. It is not a monitoring body. It is a Court, and thus it settles the dispute before it. But in Judge Donoghue's view, it is quite artificial to think of the legal dispute, as decided by the Court, as the full dispute between the parties. The Whaling case (Australia v. Japan) is a good example. The Court was asked a specific legal question, which it answered. But the judges were of course very much aware that there were broader debates in the international community, about the future of whaling, about the role of the International Whaling Commission, and about whether the moratorium on commercial whaling should continue or not. This more general debate would not be framed in the same way as the precise legal dispute that was settled by the ICJ. It would be broader.

What happens after a judgment? How do the parties react? How does the prevailing party make use of its victory? How does the losing party respond? Does it implement the decision or not? And if not, what are the obstacles? The Court frequently has very little visibility into all these things. Sometimes the Court is fortunate that the parties state publicly what they have done to implement a judgment. This happened recently in the maritime boundary case between Peru and Chile. Sometimes, however, the judges of the ICJ simply do not know what has happened in the wake of a judgment.

Judge Donoghue considered that it would be worthwhile to find ways to create greater visibility into what does happen after the Court's judgments are issued. And there is also value in scholarly analysis of the way that the Court's judgments affect the broader disagreements on law and policy within which a dispute before the Court inevitably is nested, because the Judges of the ICJ are generally not confronted with cases that are hermetically sealed off from the rest of the world.

Judge Owada expressed the view that it is quite clear, as far as the ICJ is concerned, that the Court is exclusively asked to settle a specific legal question, though the Court's judgment could be only a part of the whole picture and may not in itself represent the entire picture of the issues involved in the dispute. On the other hand, the Court's function, in terms of its jurisdiction, is to confine itself to that particular aspect of the dispute referred to the Court, and to give judgment on that particular aspect.

The issue of implementation of the judgment can be interpreted more narrowly or more broadly, as the case may be. Faithful implementation of the judgment in a narrowly defined sense is clearly a concern of the Court. The Court does not have the power of enforcement of its judgments, but how its judgments are implemented in this sense is a matter of concern for the Court. If there is any problem arising with respect to the implementation of the Judgment in relation to the concrete manner of its implementation, a party can always bring the case within the context of interpretation of that judgment before the Court. It can seek an interpretation of that judgment, as happened recently in the Avena and Other Mexican Nationals case between Mexico and the United States, and in the Temple of Preah Vihear case between Cambodia and Thailand. The Court gives its view on the judgment in question, though limiting itself to what the earlier judgment had said. This is one aspect of interpretation and implementation in the narrow sense.

Implementation can also be defined in a broader sense. Then the question is whether the judgment has been implemented in the sense it was meant to be put into effect and in line with the spirit or according to the intention of the Court. But that is not something that the Court is formally competent to deal with. It is beyond what the Court can control.

Judge Keith said that it was more than thirty years ago when he was first acting as a judge in in Western Samoa. In a really difficult case, someone asked him, soon after the judgment was given: "Why did you decide the way you decided?" To which Judge Keith replied: "Read the judgment." The same could be suggested to those interested in what the ICJ decided and why. Now these days it is also possible to read the pleadings of the parties to any ICJ proceeding, because these are now made available on the Court's website. The Court and its judges will get into all sorts of difficulties if on top of all of this they start explaining what they have done. The judgment is the judgment. If you are writing an academic paper, you can keep revising and changing things, but a judgment stays as it is.

Mr. Van Hoogstraten explained that in the Netherlands, it has become customary for the judiciary to explain, through a Press Officer, to the public at large what the Court has decided and why. For some time, the International Court of Justice also gave a press briefing after each decision. He remembered Judge Guillaume doing that in the Small Courtroom.

Judge Owada said that this broad issue of implementation can be, and often is, a very controversial issue. One problem is the fact that the judgment is a majority judgment. In other words, it is a result of the divergent views of a number of judges with nuanced positions, and the basis of the judgment represents the lowest common denominator of the judges' views belonging to the majority. As a result, an official account of the

Judgment, even by the President, could prejudice its common denominator reflecting nuanced positions of judges. One typical example was the Kosovo Advisory Opinion, which could be liable to be misinterpreted. The Court took pains to elaborate what it wanted to clarify so that there would be no misunderstanding. But obviously there was a lot of misunderstanding of this Opinion when it was announced, as is obvious if you look at the newspaper comments about what the Court stated in the context of its Advisory Opinion. The Court anticipated that confusion and was concerned about the possible widening of the implications of the opinion of the Court in the Kosovo Advisory Opinion. In such a situation, one suggestion that can be made is to give a press briefing after the announcement of the Opinion in order to clarify the scope of the decision. But the prevailing view in the Court is against such an idea, because it could not be ensured that the briefing by the President could not jeopardise the carefully crafted language employed in the Opinion. The prevailing view has been that the Court should let the judgment speak for itself, rather than offering additional comments.

Judge Keith agreed with Judge Donoghue that it would be good if people paid greater attention to what happens after a judgment has been rendered. He referred to a really good, solid book on this topic published about 12-15 years ago, which did an excellent job at tracking what had happened to disputes after the judgment was issued, but he had not seen anything like that in recent times. Sometimes the Court leaves huge practical issues to be sorted out by the parties themselves. For example, in the case between Cameroon and Nigeria, the Court decided that the Bakassi Peninsula was Cameroonian and not Nigerian, and Nigeria said there was no way they would comply. But eventually they did comply. But then the States were confronted with highly complex questions about nationality and citizenship and landownership of the people on the peninsula, and whether foreigners could own land and so on.

In general, Judge Keith pointed out that there are always such important practical and ongoing issues to deal with. And in a number of cases decided by the Court in recent years, such ongoing issues were actually already identified in the judgment itself. For instance, in the Pulp Mills case, there was a reference in the judgment to the importance of the ongoing role of the Joint Commission, which was established by the two countries to administer the river.

Another case, which was significant in that way, was the Southern Blue Fin Tuna case before the International Tribunal for the Law of the

Sea, in which Australia and New Zealand brought a case against Japan. The special Tribunal decided it had no jurisdiction, but before it reached that conclusion, ITLOS had already prescribed provisional measures, reminding the parties that it was critical that they actually made the Commission for the Conservation of Southern Blue Fin Tuna work properly. The special Tribunal reinforced that point. Because it had just got stuck; it got bogged down on political and scientific arguments. Sometimes a Court or Tribunal can issue such reminders to promote the ongoing management of the situation.

Mr. Afako added that in the issue between Nigeria and Cameroon referred to by Judge Keith, the UN Secretary-General actually came in and set up a Joint Commission, and that it was in that Commission where Nigeria's initial resistance to the ICJ's decision was addressed. They were able to work out how to make sense of the implications of the Court's decision. That is not something that the Court could have become involved in.

Judge Donoghue added that another interesting aspect of the case between Cameroon and Nigeria was that, in her recollection, the Secretary-General got involved before the decision of the Court was issued. And similarly, Peru and Chile were talking to each other, at high levels, about ways to implement the Court's judgment, even before the judgment was issued. This is important, because prior to a judgment, each side is equally interested in having an effective mechanism for implementation of the judgment. At that time, the parties are as yet unsure of the outcome of the adjudication process. There is real value in laying some of the groundwork for implementation before the judgment, because as soon as the judgment is made public, one party or the other might find it difficult to implement the judgment enthusiastically.

Judge Keith mentioned that, in the Rainbow Warrior case, the parties were actually given the award a week before it was released, and that was on the basis that it might be easier that way for the parties to implement the award.

Dr. Llamzon described how, when the decision in the Abyei Arbitration was forthcoming, the Permanent Court of Arbitration was inundated by calls from the UN mission in Sudan, as well as from New York, wanting to know what the decision would be in advance – an understandable request given the acute security concerns on the ground arising from whatever the Tribunal's decision might be. This put the PCA in an awkward situation, as it realised how it could be really helpful to the people on the ground to know the decision beforehand: it would allow them to prepare for possible reactions in the region. But the PCA's greater duty to the parties and the Tribunal was to keep the Tribunal's deliberations and decision confidential and the process as untainted by political considerations as possible.

At the PCA, participants in the process are always thinking about implementation and enforcement of the eventual arbitral award. It is also the first question that the outside world asks them when they want to know something about the work of the PCA. Research shows that compliance is actually above 90%. Of course it is always difficult to say definitively, for example in the ICJ's Cameroon versus Nigeria case, whether the parties complied with the Court's judgment or not. In that case, there was no real compliance for at least 8 years, but then ultimately the Court's decision was the basis of the final settlement concluded a decade later. So this might be considered an example of "delayed but ultimate compliance."

Unlike the ICJ, arbitral tribunals do not have a life beyond the common consent of the parties. They become *functus officio* thirty days after a decision has been rendered. Because it is difficult for the judges or arbitrators themselves to monitor compliance with their decisions, the PCA is trying to fill in at least some part of that void by offering a reporting mechanism where parties report on their progress of implementation. That is something the PCA is trying to build into its latest arbitration rules. But it is true that at present this is not an automatic part of the PCA's mandate. In the face of rare instances of non-compliance, diplomacy, international moral consensus, and even shaming are the most effective ways to bring parties into compliance. The Cameroon/Nigeria case shows that international decisions create a political reality of their own that States have to deal with, and eventually comply with, even if it sometimes takes years and States will not acknowledge that they are acting out of a sense of legal obligation to that award or decision.

FIGURE 16 *Syria Peace Talks, UN Mediator Staffan de Mistura at a news conference in Geneva, Switzerland, 2016.*

PART 6

Concluding Remarks on Lessons Learned

FIGURE 17 *Soldier of SPLA (South Sudan) reads comprehensive peace agreement, 23 January 2005.*

CHAPTER 6.1

Concluding Remarks on the Conference by the Chairman of the Carnegie Foundation, Bernard Bot

On the 19th and 20th September 2013, a Conference with the title "The Art of Peace-Making" was organised to commemorate 100 years Peace Palace and 300 years Peace of Utrecht.

The principal question before the participants was which lessons can be learned from peace treaties. Two days of intensive discussions did not always lead to consensual opinions but at least clarified many of the topics under review. In these concluding remarks, I have tried to summarise the various issues raised without claiming completeness.

When talking about the art of peace-making one of the first questions asked was: 'What do we mean by peace?' Several definitions of this notion were submitted during the debates, but none of them were deemed entirely satisfactory. Some said it should be the preservation of order. Others, it should imply a new balance of stability. Most participants felt it should at least comprise two elements: 1. It should bring conflicts to an end and 2. It should contain the promise of long-term stability.

Many scholars and philosophers, such as the Abbé de Saint Pierre or Kant, have dreamt throughout the ages of creating a situation of Eternal Peace. Meanwhile, it is common knowledge that eternal peace is unattainable, although its pursuit, certainly, remains a worthwhile endeavour. However, just as peace is not eternal, so peace treaties are almost by definition finite. But for as long as they last, it is necessary and useful to find out what works and what does not in drafting them, which are useful techniques of peace-making and which are not. And should international institutions increasingly play a role? Furthermore, how do we safeguard the implementation of peace arrangements? These questions are not easy to answer, because every conflict has different origins, a different history and a different outcome. Consequently, general rules for solving conflicts are hard to formulate, but certain useful guidelines can certainly be drawn.

To start with, a holistic approach is desirable. Often studies concentrate and comment only on separate elements of the peace-making pro-

Van Hoogstraten, Schrijver et al. (eds.), The Art of Making Peace: Lessons Learned from Peace Treaties
 ISBN 978-90-04-32123-6. pp. 193-195.

cess. When dealing with peace-making, it may be useful to distinguish between three separate stages.

The *first* one comprises the stage of negotiations: the intense efforts to formulate and put down on paper a mutual consensus by all parties involved to bring to an end a conflict and to clarify the conditions under which a new order may be created. Preferably, negotiations should not take place in an atmosphere of "winners and losers". Furthermore, the importance of the role of key negotiators or trusted facilitators and mediators merit further study. And ideally, negotiations should take place on the basis of a clear set of principles, which command a solid international consensus. Recent experience also shows that regional organisations may increasingly fulfil a role as facilitators.

The *second* stage comprises the implementation in practice of the agreement reached by the warring factions. A new truce, a mere breathing space before the next stage of a conflict will erupt, is to be avoided. Here again, Versailles may serve as a warning post. On the other hand, a transition stage in the process of nation-building may in many instances be unavoidable. A lot can be learned in this respect from the Sudan Peace Agreement of 2005.

The *third* aspect deals with monitoring once a settlement has been reached so that one can truly speak of the emergence of a new order or a new form of stability permitting economic growth, good governance and respect of human rights. Here again, the UN and regional organisations may play an important role as monitoring authorities or as guardians of the peace treaty.

Can we only draw lessons from successful peace negotiations and treaties? The Treaty of Versailles, extensively discussed during this conference, demonstrates that often one can learn more from failure than from success. Versailles taught future negotiators, among other things, that peace-making requires the participation of all parties and not only of the victors; that a peace arrangement should not be tantamount to a capitulation; that imposing unreasonable burdens on the vanquished may lead to new hostilities, sow the seeds of future conflicts rather than create a new and stable international order.

In this context, the question of justice was brought to the fore. Is peace possible without justice, was a topic raised frequently during the discussions. In other words: how to deal with the punitive aspects of peace-making? Should retribution, punitive actions and sanctions be an integral part of any peace settlement? Or should we learn from the Versailles Treaty and find other ways and means to meet the often justified desire for punishment and the wish to be compensated for the suffering and hardship caused by the culprits? In the past, writers on the subject thought that a punitive peace answered to the logic of a just peace, ending a just war. Fortunately, this concept has been relinquished. Nowadays, much seems to depend on the degree of acceptance of the claims to punishment by the "punished" power. But the question certainly remains relevant. For example, the introduction of reconciliation commissions as we know them from, *inter alia*, South Africa and Colombia should be further examined.

Further attention should also be paid to the role of the UN and the International Court of Justice. As laid down in the UN Charter, they should serve as the principal organs to maintain international peace and security. But the practice of the past years demonstrates that they fail all too often in exercising these powers. As was noted, the reasons can be found in the complexity of the situation, and more often than not in the failure to reach agreement among the Permanent Members of the Security Council. The role of the International Court of Justice is almost by definition limited because it is only competent to deal with a dispute once the States involved in conflict have accepted its jurisdiction.

From the foregoing it will be clear that many issues raised during the debates merit further elaboration. Certainly, many lessons were learned from peace treaties, but many other issues remained unexplored. All participants felt, however, that it had been useful to broach this somewhat neglected subject in international law and that nonetheless some preliminary conclusions could be drawn. Given the success of this meeting and its outcome, it was suggested that it deserved a follow-up. Perhaps in another two years another gathering could be organised. It would certainly meet the wishes of all the participants to this successful two-day conference in Utrecht and the Peace Palace in The Hague.

CHAPTER 6.2

Personal Experiences with Peace Mediation: An Interview with Bernard Bot, Former Minister of Foreign Affairs of The Netherlands

Otto Spijkers and Anneleen de Jong

Our first question is a very broad one: at the conference, different ways of approaching peace treaties were proposed. Some considered peace treaties to be most successful when there is an external third party involved, primarily an international actor such as the United Nations, the European Union, or some powerful State. Others considered that many conflicts are regional, and that it is better for the implementation of the peace agreement if local actors play the first role. We would like to ask you what your experience has been with this.

Well, my experience in this respect is that you need a mix of both. But I think that the presence of directly involved parties is essential. If you only try to broker peace, let's say by means of a mediator or an outside organisation like the United Nations, or a regional organisation, you run the risk that once the peace agreement has been concluded and you have a text, that a few of the parties that were not directly involved in the negotiations will not observe the terms of the treaty or the agreement. So my experience is that you always should try to get the directly involved parties around the table. If you take for example Afghanistan or the Sudan, or even the conflict in Indonesia at the time, it was in the end only successful once we had managed to get everybody assembled, and once everybody had the feeling that they had made a meaningful contribution to the negotiations. Otherwise you can say: "this is a peace agreement, this is the right solution to the problem", but if one of the warring parties says: "I wasn't involved in the negotiations, so I will continue the fight", the whole agreement falls apart.

The Indonesian question is interesting, although it's been a long time ago. The UN played a big role in putting the Netherlands under pressure. In a

Van Hoogstraten, Schrijver et al. (eds.), The Art of Making Peace: Lessons Learned from Peace Treaties
© 2017 The Editors. Printed in The Netherlands. ISBN *978-90-04-32123-6. pp. 196-207.*

way, without the UN, *maybe an agreement would not have been possible; or it would have been a very different kind of agreement form the one we ultimately got.*

I think it wasn't so much the UN. Perhaps the UN played a major role in the later stage around the issue with Papua New Guinea. I think the war of 1949 was finished because we were simply tired of fighting it. Of course there was outside pressure, especially by the United States. But there was also the recognition by the parties directly involved that the moment had arrived to come to terms.

The Netherlands argued that it was a purely internal question and that the UN said: "no, it's a question between Indonesia and the Netherlands". In that sense, the UN very much framed the issue.

That was of course the first step, the Linggadjati Agreement of 1946. At that moment, we still had the feeling it was an internal settlement. We would retain a certain say in matters and only later on we conceded to Indonesia that a transfer of sovereignty was necessary. But let us focus on the issues we are facing today. Nowadays, a third party like the United States, the United Nations or the African Union can play a very useful role. Let's look at Syria, for example. I know Syria very well. President Bashar al-Assad of Syria and I had several discussions, and even today I am discussing the situation with a few of our people who are at this moment negotiating a kind of peace deal. They say that the problem is that you cannot broker a peace or even come to a ceasefire unless you have all the involved factions around the table. If you only focus on concluding a truce or agreement with Assad, it is not enough. Assad still dominates a smaller portion of Syria, but it is the part where the vast majority of the population is living. This is what people often forget when they look at the map and see that there is only so much territory left that remains under the control of Assad. But a fact is that he has the most important part of Syria in his hands and let's say 80% of the population lives in his area. But even so it wouldn't help to conclude an agreement with Assad unless you also come to terms with two or three of the factions that are battling each other or are battling Assad. So I think we should not aim for an overall peace process or treaty, but begin very carefully by setting up some confidence building measures based on relatively apolitical issues, such as transportation, food questions and so on. And basic security, of course. Every peace agreement is different, every approach is different. I find it very dangerous to generalise, because the big wars as we used to know them in the past centuries are over. Increasingly, we see regional conflicts, thus you have to place yourself in a regional context, and think in regional terms of ways to get all these factions around the table. At the time I was living in Belgium, I was very much involved with the Congolese negotiations. My neighbour was one of the negotiators and he told me often enough about the problems, and the need to get the tribes to agree and to accept any outcome of the negotiations. Today the country is divided into two parts, French and Belgian Congo, Congo Brazzaville and Congo Kinshasa. Fighting goes on in certain parts of the Congo, and there you see how difficult it is to have a final agreement unless everybody involved also accept the terms.

When you invite representations of a certain faction or rebel group to the table, you sort of give them some legitimacy. Would you invite representatives of IS, if they can be identified, to join in the negotiations?

Eventually I think you cannot do otherwise. If IS really dominates a certain area and is in steady control of the situation, and you want to broker a sort of cease-fire, or truce in order to bring a certain amount of stability in the country, you will have to sit around the table with them. I remember when I was dealing with problems in Afghanistan, that I discussed this often with American generals. They would ask the question: “Do we have to involve the Taliban now already or not?” They had just beaten the Taliban, and won the battle, but wondered whether or not to accept them as parties in the negotiations. I said: “yes”, and the American generals agreed. They said they were not ready yet but understood that if they eventually wanted to come to terms with the situation, they could not eliminate or ignore the Taliban. They're still everywhere, and although they don't demonstrate that power now, we know that in all these tribes you have quite a few Taliban elements, or rather a Taliban philosophy. So we have to deal with Taliban, and we did, and we are doing it at the moment.

When it comes to selecting the third party capable of bringing the warring sides to the table, a big institution like the UN or the EU, or a big State like the US, might not always be the best option. Maybe it could also be simply one individual?

Martti Ahtisaari is an interesting example. I met him quite often, especially when he was negotiating the Atjeh-deal, and later of course I met him again in Kosovo. There you see that there is one individual making a difference. But they are very rare, and how do you find them? It's often quite by coincidence that somebody pops up who is trustworthy, who has the knowledge, who is willing to engage in such a lengthy process, and to live in inhospitable areas. I always told him: "I admire you very much for the sacrifice that you're willing to make: to live there and discuss with all these difficult persons". When negotiating with rebels, you have to keep your cool and they have to continue to respect you. That is also very important. Yes, every peace process is different, but every party intervention is also different. I think these huge organisations, UN, EU, etc. are often too powerful to soften a particular problem. Better to have one person. Many of these conflicts cannot be resolved in one or two years, so you also have to be patient.

As a third party, you must have a clear idea of what you want to realise, what your aim or objective is. I think you have to be very clear about that. Take Syria again as an example. Somebody in Geneva said that since there was at the moment no other way to get the people around the table, the idea was to establish these small working groups. I think this is a very prudent and careful step without disturbing the equilibrium, or without giving the parties the feeling that you're trying to encroach upon their territory. I reread the whole story about the Sudan in our book, which is of course fascinating because you see that in the end they're still fighting with each other, North and South, and there is enormous distress. when I was talking to the government in Sudan, the Sudanese President Omar al-Bashir – who should appear here in The Hague before in the International Criminal Court – each time said: " you don't know the situation in my country, you and the rest of the world are judging us from your point of view, but you should see it from our point of view." We have to understand that the situation isn't going to be solved that way.

Sudan is again a very actual topic that we wanted to address. In the newspapers yesterday, it said that they agreed to sign a peace agreement, but only because they were threatened with sanctions. Sanctions are a direct form of external influence. What is your experience with sanctions as an instrument to influence peace negotiations?

Sanctions may be helpful in the short-term, but if there isn't something behind it like a durable solution that is equitable and fair, the parties will only accept an agreement because they have to. With the first and best opportunity, they will just start fighting again, in spite of the sanctions. So I'm always wary of sanctions. I remember the discussions I had at the time about Myanmar and the sanctions. All my Asian friends said: "Sanctions against Myanmar don't work because China and India are helping Myanmar. These countries will not comply with the sanctions. You try to isolate Myanmar, and so do we". That made it clear to me that what is most important in these situations is to continue the dialogue. In the end that is what worked.

What do you think of the opposite of sanctions: positive incentives? States might promise to provide official development assistance if the warring sides cooperate. The EU's strongest incentive is perhaps membership; it doesn't always work, but in the former Yugoslavia it worked. At least to promise Serbia the possibility of becoming EU-member worked out well. Although this is also kind of pressure, like sanctions, it is a more positive type of pressure. What are your thoughts about this?

Everything in life is a mix of carrots and sticks. Serbia got both: American bombs, exhaustion, sanctions, the carrot of eventual membership.

In that order?

It was first the bombing, etcetera, then, finally, they came to terms. If you look at most of the world, you see that, always, the first start of a settlement is still the stick. People don't start moving unless they actually experience the negative impact of sanctions, bombing, fighting, attacks, whatever. I think that Syria eventually also will come to terms with the situation because no war faction can continue for a very long period in these circumstances. A simple exhaustion of financial resources, and a certain sense of exhaustion will kick in. That is why at the moment I have accepted those four working groups as a first step towards a settlement. I don't know whether IS is represented in these groups, which I doubt because IS itself does not want to participate. To have a number of the most important factions around the table, is always a good way to start.

IS rejects almost everything we believe in so if they would sign an agreement, what is it worth?

That is the basic problem we are discussing now, how do you manage to impose, let's say, a peace settlement on a country where three or four factions are fighting each other formally. In the past, we had one State or group of States fighting another, and then it was over. But now it's very difficult, it's never over. You see that in Afghanistan it sort of was over and you see everywhere, everything we tried to accomplish disappears because the Taliban pops up again. The Taliban feels that it has never been party to any agreement, that it was excluded and it wants revenge. Whether they will succeed, nobody knows, but we have to be very careful. So there is a process one should respect, and the process is what we are discussing now: how many parties do we need to get around the table to be successful. And then the second thing to decide is the content: How far can you make concessions with yourself and with two or three of the parties in order to get a reasonable treaty, agreement or cease-fire on the table? What is it you can live with for a couple of years, because no peace treaty has eternal life. They are practically all broken after a while, sometimes already after a few years. That makes it such a complex issue and therefore worthwhile to discuss. Especially important is to further investigate the role of non-state actors because nowadays every conflict practically involves non-state actors.

When we interviewed Sir Adam Roberts he spoke about Prague in the 60's and he said, talking about the different steps towards a peace treaty, that peace processes often commence with public revolt.

This is true. Take Syria, take Afghanistan etcetera, everywhere you see people escape from their country. Let's say half of the population in Syria lives outside of the warzone of Syria and these are the people who aren't mentioned in those agreements with Assad and those warring factions. That makes it extremely difficult because you're trying to impose something on people who aren't directly involved. I lived in the DDR for 4 years, and I always say in the end, a little bit the same way, blood is thicker than ideology. So the willingness to come together again to reunite is always stronger than any ideology. I'm still firmly convinced that that is true. Nevertheless, for now one has to question how to tackle the problem, and what kind of instruments that are at our disposal. Happily, there are many instruments: mediation, negotiation, arbitration, local organisations and in Geneva a couple of people on a lower level, not the big bosses, who are experts in the field of transportation, food, agriculture, reconstruction. They sit around the table and try to get things going. This is very different from the high level ministers trying to broker a peace.

What do you think about the role of academics, so-called experts? At the conference Marc Weller had some interesting remarks about peace negotiations becoming an academic discipline. This means there are people with technical expertise and a bag full of model peace agreements. But when they are sent to these regions to negotiate the peace and apply what they've learnt at school, they often impose an ideal blueprint on a volatile situation. They insist that it's not enough to end the hostilities, we need democratic elections, we need rule of law, we need references to human rights, we need protection of minorities, we need this, we need that. What do you think of such so-called expert involvement?

It is very useful to analyse situations and try to build frameworks that can be used by the negotiators as a starting point. We distilled from these discussions what is the right procedure and how to distinguish between the different phases of the process. There are three phases: the negotiation process, the implementation period, and the monitoring phase. To start off with the right mindset, one needs a framework. Therefore I think it is very useful for a negotiator to have a sort of handbook with analyses of lessons learned that we have distilled from the past. It would read what we learned from Versailles, Sudan, Afghanistan, Indonesia, Vietnam, etc. Why several of these negotiations were successful, or just temporarily successful; why and in what circumstances one should start to include all the parties involved in the conflict. Perhaps you have a peace treaty that is no more than a truce or cease-fire, it lasts as long as it lasts. Of course, many parties use it – cease-fires – to restock their arms and build up their strengths. A lesson could then be not to agree to such a deal if basically this is going to lead to even greater fights in the long run. So I'd say, in the theoretical discussion in the end you aren't going to solve these conflicts, but a catalogue of lessons learned can serve the negotiators, the actors in a very useful way. If every new negotiator has to start from scratch, so to speak, in this field, it is very difficult. Let's be frank, if you look at who have brokered peace agreements, they are often people who have learned to trade in different areas: trade disputes, or in simple country negotiations. A lot of them are thrown into this complex environment and do need a sort of a guideline. With our Peace Palace conference therefore, we have provided insights not only in what we can do but also unveiled the issues on which we are ignorant. It's very popular in the United States at the moment, to teach courses in lessons of ignorance: "this is what I know, and this is what I do not know."

That is exactly what I was thinking about, if there is a relation between the limited success of peace treaties and a possible lack of knowledge. Humanity repeats the same mistakes over and over again, but shouldn't we be making progress? So I am curious: do you think that this lack of knowledge is dominant now, but that maybe 100 years from now our intelligence will be more developed so we'll be able to prevent these recurring conflicts in society?

I think we will be more experienced, each time we get confronted with these new situations which we haven't seen before. We are baffled in the beginning because we don't know what to do. Our international law is supposed to tell us what to do, but often it doesn't apply anymore. Each situation is completely different from what we have dealt with in the past. How are we going to tackle it? There are always people who say we should do this and that, and I think that is the moment when you should be frank to yourself and say: "this is what I know, this is my framework, but here I'm confronted with a new situation, this is my ignorance. Where am I ignorant?" Of course, we should admit that obviously we are still lacking insights and understanding. And we do not know how are we going to deal with it the next time.

But do you think we are making progress? That's sort of underlying this question, are we going somewhere?

I think so, because it's of course a very difficult art; negotiations and especially in these situations where we see a cruelty and we turn to medieval or pre-medieval measures and situations. The question is how do you cope with it? Can you intervene or can you not intervene? Then you get into different military issues, can chemical weapons be used or is that the red line, yes or no? Where can you intervene militarily or where do you ethically abstain? Our experience shows that, where we abstained we were often better off than where we intervened, because our intervention came back like a boomerang, and we paid heavily for it, despite our good intensions by the way. That also is part of a negotiation process; to decide: "do we first use the stick or rather should we put a frame around it, or a fence, and let them fight it out amongst themselves, and then we clean up the mess afterwards?" That is of course a very inhuman approach; you can't regard this as a serious option. And you cannot propose this in the newspapers either, as they will kill you, so to speak. The problem is that we are confronted with new situations which require new approaches. We cannot always rely on what we know from our past experiences, on how we responded to situations of war and peace from the past. Today we are dealing with parties we don't even know, with whom we have no contact but who are fiercely fighting. So the first question is: how do we make contact? How do we get them around the table? Do we do it at the high level or low level? Do we start with the working groups, or do we say,: "well, we first try to eliminate one or two of these warring factions, because they are such bandits"? Is it useful talking to them? That for me is the fascinating thing of this whole subject: we work from a certain framework, which is useful and we try to clearly clarify what we know. Who had expected 5 years ago that this situation in Syria with IS would happen, and in this particular medieval way? We are stuck. We work with very old-fashioned approaches and we are learning. Ukraine will be another very interesting case. We study and we analyse it. What kind of stance we have taken, where did we go, why did we make these mistakes, was Putin a better negotiator than we were? Should we have seen it coming? Etc.

So you think that the stuff we know is increasing and the stuff we don't know is decreasing and we are really making progress?

Of course, we should be aware, especially discussing this topic, that we know already a lot, that we perhaps know more than we realise, because we have never taken the trouble of clearly stating everything we do know. In other words, creating a framework. Nowadays, if you talk about war and peace, if you talk about trying to broker a peace agreement, these are the steps, which have served us well in the past. But we also see that, being faced with completely new situations and areas, that we should enlarge our knowledge. We should discuss this as scholars, but also as practitioners, and try to identify a number of issues where we see that we are in a minefield, and think of how are we going to solve them. Let's discuss them at least.

Like the role of the media. Social media. Traditional media. If you look at the situation in Syria, it is remarkable to see how professionally and effectively IS uses social media. On the other hand, we spoke to a musician who is a refugee from Syria, and he told me how difficult it is for him to share his opinion on Facebook. The internet, anything – everything is controlled. That's a very important thing. If you need to create a peace treaty in these circumstances; you have to find a way through the social media that does reach the people.

I think you should distinguish between the media and social media. You see that in the media at the moment, IS has stopped spreading pictures of beheadings, except of course for this unfortunate keeper of the temple, the ideologist. They also feel that this is counterproductive. People think this is abhorrent, so they stop. They use social media in a clever way. I'd say, as a negotiator, I would not want the media involved. Because negotiating means: talking on the basis of trust. Convince each other that you can be open, that you can tell things that you do not want to be revealed for the moment because you are testing the other's willingness to make concessions. At the moment when everything is in the newspapers, you stop making those moves. In other words, you always have to bend yourself a little bit, to the other. You say: "if you are willing to do this, I'm willing to concede on that point." From the moment that is in the newspapers, that point is lost. So I think that actual negotiations benefit from media silence. At the moment it is important to get the media on your side, it's a different story.

When I was negotiating to bring back two children that were taken to Syria, I experience the importance of the media. At the beginning, when discussing this issue, I said to the people in the Netherlands, please stay out for a while because I am now in the process of talking to Assad and to his ministers, and each time you make so much noise here, he says: "Ok, you're playing the game that way. We will not negotiate with you any further."

Maybe you need to provide us with some background about these negotiations.

They were about these children that were taken from the Netherlands by their father to Syria without their mother's consent. This was more a general negotiation process, not on war and peace, but these children were taken to Syria, although the judge here assigned the children to the mother, and the mother of course went to the newspapers and wanted her children back. These children managed to flee, to escape from their grandfather's house and they found refuge in the Dutch Embassy in Syria. Then the issue was how do we get them out of the Embassy and back to the Netherlands where they belong. The Syrians said of course that according to their laws, and this is the same in all Muslim countries, the father is the head of the family and the children should be with the father. The minister said: "The children are here to stay, whether they stay at the embassy or with their father." But I said: "No, they are Dutch, the father is also a Dutchman, with dual-nationality, and he said that he would obey the Dutch law." However, while I was negotiating, the mother started a media campaign which was very counterproductive. I told her that, for the time being, it was best that she kept silent if she ever wanted to see her children again so that I could do my work quietly. It took a few months of back and forth discussing with Assad, not about the children but about peace negotiations in Israel, between Israel and Syria, about political matters. In the meantime I talked to the ministers who were responsible for this matter, so I had to make sure that Assad knew what I was also aiming for. In the end, he told me, when we had a discussion about many, many other things, the following: "Ok, I know that you are also very eager to hear what I think: you can have the children". Then I had some final negotiations with a few ministers on the conditions related to bringing them back. It was vital that during that period there was no media. In general, I think that if you really start negotiating, you have to keep the media out. Before you start, you may evaluate the situation and decide whether it is better now to start the campaign, to strengthen your position, with the stick, use the social media. But you cannot stop the social media, that is something that I have learned. People continuously use Twitter and Skype, Facebook, whatever they like. That is a new element in the whole process. It lies within the realm of the unknown how one should deal with that. With the traditional media it's rather clear: if you are seriously negotiating, no media for the time being. Of course, if you want to put some pressure, you can always use a friendly journalist to nicely write something for you but you have to be very careful with that.

The media is such a powerful tool. An expert recently explained that most of the refugees coming from Syria are actually not fleeing from IS, but they're fleeing from Assad's terror. But if you ask a random person in the Netherlands, they will think everybody is fleeing from IS, and that's only because of the way the conflict in Syria is framed in the media.

It's mixed, because I talked yesterday to another negotiator and he said the opposite. He said people prefer Assad, it's not good but they prefer Assad to any other faction group fighting because Assad at least tolerated all the religions. That's what Assad told me that time: "Yes, I want to modernise, and yes, I want democracy. But you do not realise in the west how complex the situation in Syria is. You don't know how many factions, religions, geographical and geological areas we have to take into account." He said: "I know Syria very well, and don't forget we also still have my father's crib around the old die-hards ... and it's not so easy to convert them from one to the other. It's a very slow process." He said: "In Damascus you can buy any magazine you like. There are women in shorts and in blue-jeans, and women who are in every dress that they like. You're free to buy newspapers, that is the process of the last 4-5 years. You have Christians, Muslims, Copts, all living together. And as long as they don't mess up or start a revolution they are free to live here. If they do not behave, then we are a bit tougher than in your country. Because once a rebellion starts here, you cannot stop it anymore. It may be an internal war for years to come." That was very prophetic. It was in 2005-2006 when he said these things. But he's still there. I always said, over the radio a few years ago, that he will not disappear. If there is one person who is going to stay, it's Assad. You cannot get him out of the country. This is something you have to take account of in the negotiations, how to tackle this. I would tackle this with confidence-building measures at the lower level, rather than engage directly with Assad. We will reach a point where we realise that we cannot continue this way and where Mr Assad gets this part of the country, the others get their parts, and together we all fight against IS, for example.

Any last words or suggestions?

We should not forget to look at the successes of the past, and learn from the successes. I hope that the negotiated settlements will stick in Darfur, and in South Sudan. We have accomplished a lot there, so there you can say: negotiations have been successful, the implementation was fairly successful, and now we have the issue of monitoring, which I think is a separate issue. Very complex. Who should do the monitoring: ad hoc groups, internal or regional organisations, with up-to-date knowledge of the situation? But you often see that they need some supervision, because if you're going to leave it exclusively to such regional actors, they make a mess of it. If you want to secure a stable environment, you also need supervision and monitoring.

Thank you.

Epilogue

Are the current situations in Syria, Ukraine and Yemen, to mention just a few of today's hotbeds in international relations, in need of the conclusion of peace agreements? Or can peace sometimes be brokered by international organisations, such as in the cases of Namibia, Cambodia and Iraq-Kuwait, and subsequently be anchored in Security Council resolutions? Can certain principles and procedures be identified in peace-making or is peace-making, in the words of Richard Holbrooke (quoted by Weller, above), "like jazz: you have to listen to the instruments and improvise"?

Peace agreements are agreements concluded by the parties to an armed conflict with a view to end the hostilities between them. Occasionally, they amount to much more than ending "the state of war" and can entail demobilization, exchange of prisoners of war, boundary demarcation, local elections, protection of minorities, constitutional reform, nation-building and other issues which may serve as ingredients for a sustainable peace. It should also be noted that peace agreements can be concluded between two or more States (these are often called peace treaties) as well as agreements between a non-State party to a conflict and one or more States. An example of the latter is the Minsk II agreement of 12 February 2015. Officially, this peace agreement was signed by the Ukrainian government, representatives of the Russian separatists in Eastern Ukraine and the OSCE. This Minsk II agreement was supplemented by a Declaration signed by the Heads of State of France, Germany, Ukraine and the Russian Federation (the so-called Normandy group) in which they pledge to be fully committed, individually and jointly, to the implementation of the agreement and to an exclusively peaceful solution of the conflict. Furthermore, on 17 February 2015 the entire Security Council endorsed the peace agreement, including the cease-fire, in its Resolution 2202 (2015). Later in 2015, the Security Council laid down a framework for peace talks on Syria, and these talks were to be held in 2016 (Resolution 2254 of 18 December 2015). This was a remarkable show of unity in the Security Council, which had been divided over the issue of Syria on so many occasions. This shows that the UN continues to play a key role in international peace brokering, even if expectations are often set at too high a level.

At our conference *The Art of Peacemaking: What Lessons Can Be Learned?* some of the great peace treaties between 1913-2013 were re-

Van Hoogstraten, Schrijver et al. (eds.), The Art of Making Peace: Lessons Learned from Peace Treaties
 ISBN 978-90-04-32123-6. pp. 208-212.

viewed. An attempt was made to bring to the fore the key elements of a number of peace negotiations and peace treaties, irrespective of the fact that these dealt with totally different situations and covered different times in history. This diversity of case studies made it far from easy to distil evidence-based lessons from them. However, some observations could be made which hopefully hold true to a certain extent in the long term.

It makes a big difference, for instance, whether a party, which emerges victorious from a conflict imposes its terms on the losing party, or whether an agreement is established between two more or less equal parties realizing they have to share a common future. The First World War ended with the Treaty of Versailles, in which the allies (the winners) clearly decided which measures to impose on Germany (the loser). Everyone is aware of the consequences of this treaty. The Second World War ended with an armistice, and not with an official peace treaty. Yet the signing of that armistice in Wageningen is still commemorated as one of the great moments of the liberation of the Netherlands. The day on which we commemorate those who died in the war remains an important day for the Dutch people.

That fundamental equality of parties, as a characteristic and essential aspect of holding talks aimed at peaceful relations, is especially evident in the reshaping of the Balkans. Everyone knows that Serbia would never have given up Kosovo voluntarily (it is both historically and culturally viewed as the cradle of their nation), and yet both parties are on speaking terms now, and have concluded an agreement which should make it possible for Serbia in due course to join the European Union. The Dayton Agreement was about ending a war, for which the deployment of military force was a requisite. The mediation by the EU in Brussels between Serbia and Kosovo was subsequently also of great importance.

After Kosovo had declared its independence in 2008, representatives of Serbia and Kosovo met for the first time in 2011. These talks were led by an experienced European (British) diplomat. During these negotiations filmmaker Karen Poulsen made a documentary called *The Agreement*. This documentary also clearly demonstrates that the parties involved should temporarily set aside their respective sentiments in order to discuss in a businesslike manner the remaining disagreements. Mentioning of acts of aggression by the one party, or elaborating on the cruelties of the other, or even making condescending jokes, proved to have a crippling effect on the negotiations. That the peaceful agreement between Serbia and Kosovo about border control in the north of Kosovo (with a considerable Serbian population) was a clear condition for potential future accession of Serbia to the EU, was without a doubt a decisive factor for a conceding attitude of Serbia. This proves once again the major peace-making potential of the European Union. Whereas in Western Europe support for the EU is no longer a matter of course, and the alleged hunger for power of the European institutions has become a benchmark in the national political process, in another part of Europe there is a craving for EU membership, which – strangely enough – in their perception strongly emphasizes national identity. Georgia, Moldavia and Ukraine simply want to be free to conclude association agreements with the European Union, whatever the eye rolling and misgivings this gives rise to in the capital of the former Soviet Union. The equality of the countries after the peace process has ended is a guiding theme in the peace negotiations.

Whether international law plays a major role in peace negotiations is highly doubtful. Of course it is useful to work on the basis of certain minimum standards, such as not turning a blind eye on serious war crimes, the protection of minorities or establishing a constitutional framework. Furthermore, key legal notions like national sovereignty and territorial integrity will always play their part. But holding international negotiations is in essence also an administrative affair during which the importance of concluding an agreement should time and again be weighed against making concessions – which is a requisite for holding constructive talks. The most important negotiations are often those between the peace negotiators and their own government. The negotiator is in the middle of the process and has the prospect of a result, whereas the home front is ruled by political orchestrations vis-à-vis the other party.

In the case of the talks between Serbia and Kosovo demonstrations were held against the pending agreement in each of the two countries, because too many concessions were made to the other party. If the case between Serbia and Kosovo proves anything, perhaps a lesson of a more general nature, it is that a third party – in this case the EU – can play an important, even an historical role in reaching an agreement. And also that agreement is possible without resolving a range of smaller and sometimes even bigger issues, such as border issues. An official agreement between Serbia and Kosovo was reached in Brussels on 25 August 2015, formalizing inter alia the recognition of the rights of the Serbian minority in Kosovo. This agreement will clear the way for the accession of Serbia to the EU in due course.

This dominant position was not used by the EU at the time Cyprus joined the EU. If it had been stipulated that Cyprus could only join the EU once a solution was found for Northern Cyprus (part of Turkey), this may have had a significant and positive effect. In the end, the Greek Cypriots torpedoed the plan of then United Nations Secretary-General Kofi Annan. Negotiator Marc Weller (one of the speakers at our conference) honestly admitted that they had lobbied the wrong party during the process

If we shift our focus to Africa, another question arises. To what extent do NGOs play an important role in achieving a peace settlement? Somewhat to our surprise we noticed that Barney Afako, an experienced negotiator with regard to Uganda, was not very positive about the major role NGOs sometimes claim. Often NGOs have a staff of well-paid legal and other advisors who manage to push the issue into a certain direction, which is not always considered to be supportive. Of course the role of the media is essential. No negotiator can ignore for very long the voice presented in the media "on behalf of the people". Therefore, in our view, in order to reach a settlement, which creates peaceful conditions for an area of conflict, it seems an important condition that negotiators can work in a certain grey area. Whereas normally "transparency" should be a key notion, one not to be challenged, during negotiations about the restoration of peace it should be seen in a different light. Too much involvement of the media is counterproductive in this case, and it harms the atmosphere of trust, which has to slowly evolve around the negotiation table. There should be room both for sudden drama as well as for spontaneous brotherly joy, without being exposed to the limelight of the press. These are only some of the lessons learned on the art of peacemaking.

Steven van Hoogstraten
Nico Schrijver
Otto Spijkers
Anneleen de Jong

About the Contributors

Barney Afako

Barney Afako is a lawyer and practitioner on transition and peace building issues. Among others, he has supported mediation and peace process in Uganda, Sudan and South Sudan. He is an adviser to the African Union High Level Implementation Panel on Sudan and South Sudan. He is a regular commentator on international justice developments in Africa. He sits as a Tribunal Judge in the United Kingdom.

Mohamed Alawad

His Excellency Mr Mohamed Elhassan Ibrahim Alawad is Permanent Representative of Sudan to the Organisation for the Prohibition of Chemical Weapons (OPCW).

Bernard Bot

Dr. Bernard Bot studied law in Leiden, where he obtained a doctoral degree cum laude on international law. He was awarded an LL.M. degree at Harvard Law School. He takes pride in a long career in the diplomatic service; he represented The Netherlands in the European Union, NATO, in Buenos Aires, East Berlin and Ankara. He was Secretary-General in the Ministry of Foreign Affairs, and from 2003 to 2007 served as Minister of Foreign Affairs. Dr. Bot's present positions include the chairmanship of the Board of Governors of the Netherlands Institute of International Relations "Clingendael", Chairman of the Carnegie Foundation, and President of the Executive Board of Netherlands Institute for Multiparty Democracy.

Laurens Jan Brinkhorst

Professor Laurens Jan Brinkhorts is Professor in International and European Law and Governance at the University of Leiden. He has had a long political, European and academic career. He was recently Minister of Economic Affairs and Minister of Agriculture in The Netherlands. He was also a member of the Netherlands and European Parliaments. Earlier in his life, he served as Deputy Minister of European Affairs. With the European Union he served as EU Ambassador to Japan and was subsequently DG for Environmental and Nuclear Safety. He has held chairs at Groningen, Leiden and Tilburg Universities.

Hans Corell

Hans Corell served as Under-Secretary-General for Legal Affairs and the Legal Counsel of the United Nations from March 1994 to March 2004. In this capacity, he was head of the Office of Legal Affairs in the United Nations Secretariat. Before joining the United Nations, he was Ambassador and Under-Secretary for Legal and Consular Affairs in his native Sweden's Ministry of Foreign Affairs from 1984 to 1994.

Joan E. Donoghue

Her Excellency Judge Joan Donoghue has served as a judge on the International Court of Justice (ICJ) since 2010. Prior to her election to the ICJ, Judge Donoghue had a long and distinguished career in the U.S. Government, serving from 2007 to 2010 as the Principal Deputy Legal Adviser of the U.S. Department of State (the senior career attorney). In addition to her government service, Judge Donoghue has taught courses at the University of California, Berkeley, Georgetown University and George Washington University. She also has lectured on investment law in the United Nations regional training course in Addis Ababa, Ethiopia. Judge Donoghue is a member of the Executive Council of the American Society of International Law and is Counselor for the American Law Institute's Fourth Restatement of the Foreign Relations Law of the United States..

Steven van Hoogstraten

Steven van Hoogstraten was General Director of the Carnegie Foundation (Peace Palace) and Treasurer of the Hague Academy of International Law from April 2002 till July 2015. Van Hoogstraten has always been a practitioner with a high interest in the political and international environment of his work. He worked for the Ministry of Foreign Affairs in a position in Brussels at the Netherlands Permanent Representation to the EU, was head of the European legal desk at the Ministry of Agriculture, was a director of Food Policy and Product Safety at the Ministry of Health, and a Deputy DG at the Ministry of Justice involved in international cooperation. In that last capacity Steven van Hoogstraten was charged inter alia with the justice aspects of Netherlands' policy on narcotic drugs. Van Hoogstraten is currently a member of the Supervisory Board of The Hague Institute for Global Justice.

Jaap de Hoop Scheffer

Jaap de Hoop Scheffer graduated with an LL.M. degree at Leiden University in 1974. He worked for the Ministry of Foreign Affairs from 1976 to 1986. For the first two years, he was stationed at the Dutch embassy in Ghana. After that, he worked at the Dutch delegation at NATO headquarters in Brussels until 1980. He became the 11th NATO Secretary General in 2004, and held this post until August 2009. On 1 September 2009 De Hoop Scheffer was appointed to the Pieter Kooijmans Chair for Peace, Law and Security at Leiden University. De Hoop Scheffer focuses on issues in the area of peace, law and security and also lectures in the field of international politics and the practice of diplomacy.

Anneleen de Jong

Anneleen de Jong works as Coordinator for the Hague Academic Coalition, a network organisation of the main knowledge institutions in The Hague. She previously worked as policy-maker at the Carnegie Foundation, Assistant professor at Universidad SEC (Chile) and Coordinator of the Dialogue Among Civilizations Programme at the United Nations Office in Geneva. Mrs. de Jong holds a Masters degrees in Art History, Museography and Art Education, and is interested in the role of art and culture in the promotion of peace. She has published several articles and books on this topic, among which *Representing Humanity. The Art Collection of the United Nations Office at Geneva* (UN, 2001).

Kenneth Keith

His Excellency Sir Kenneth Keith was a Judge at the International Court of Justice from 2006 to 2015. He is Knight Commander of the Order of the British Empire for services to legal education and law reform. Order of New Zealand. He studied law (1956-1965) at the University of Auckland, Victoria University of Wellington and Harvard Law School, qualifying for LL.B. and LL.M. degrees; Honorary LL.D. degrees, University of Auckland 2001 and Victoria University of Wellington 2004. He is a Member of the Legal Division, New Zealand Department of External Affairs (1960-1962); Member of the Office of Legal Affairs (Codification Division) of the United Nations (1968-1970), primarily undertaking research for the International Law Commission and working with the Sixth Committee of the General Assembly, including the Committee on Friendly Relations; student intern in that Division (1965); Member of the New Zealand Law Commission (1986-1996, President 1991-1996). He is Judge of the New Zealand Court of Appeal (1996-2003), and of the newly established Supreme Court of New Zealand (2004-2006); at various times Judge of Appeal in Samoa, the Cook Islands, Niue and Fiji; Member of the Judicial Committee of the Privy Council, London.

Martti Koskenniemi

Professor Martti Koskenniemi is Professor of International Law at the University of Helsinki and Director of the Erik Castrén Institute of International Law and Human Rights. He worked as a diplomat with the Finnish Ministry for Foreign Affairs from 1978 to 1994, representing Finland in a number of international institutions and conferences. As a member of the UN International Law Commission (2002-6) he chaired the Study group on the "Fragmentation of International Law". He has written widely on international law topics and his present research interests cover the theory and history of the field.

Hans Lammers

Professor Johan G. Lammers was previously professor in International Environmental Law at the University of Amsterdam. He has been the Director of the Hague Forum for Judicial Expertise and legal advisor to the Netherlands Ministry of Foreign Affairs, where he participated as a member of the Netherlands delegation in many international conferences on international environmental agreements and acted as agent of the Netherlands in cases in the International Court of Justice and the Permanent Court of Arbitration. Further, Professor Lammers has been an International Legal Expert on several World Bank and other consultantancy missions to Swaziland, Mozambique, Thailand, Laos, Cambodia, and Zimbabwe. He has contributed to a vast array of publications both as author of books and articles and as co-editor of the *Yearbook of International Environmental Law* and the *Hague Yearbook of International Environmental Law*. His areas of expertise include legal aspects of transnational water and air pollution and sustainable development.

Randall Lesaffer

Professor Randall Lesaffer studied law as well as history at the universities of Ghent and Leuven in Flanders, Belgium. He obtained his PhD from the latter university in 1998. In 1999, he was appointed to the chair of Legal History at Tilburg Law School in The Netherlands. He is also part-time professor of European and International Legal History at the University of Leuven and has taught (1999-2010) Public International Law at the Belgian Military Academy. From 2008 to 2012 he served as Dean of Tilburg Law School. His numerous publications include *European Legal History: A Cultural and Political Perspective* and *Peace Treaties and International Law in European History*, both published by Cambridge University Press.

Aloysius Llamzon

Dr. Aloysius Llamzon, A.B., J.D. (Ateneo de Manila), LL.M., J.S.D. (Yale Law School), is an attorney-at-law in the international arbitration group of King & Spalding LLP, New York. He was formerly Senior Legal Counsel at the Permanent Court of Arbitration in The Hague. At the PCA, he assisted numerous tribunals in inter-State, investment treaty, and commercial arbitrations involving States in proceedings conducted at the Peace Palace and elsewhere, including as Registrar or Secretary to the tribunal. He served as Registrar to the Court of Arbitration in the Indus Waters Kishenganga Arbitration (*Pakistan v. India*) and acted as Registrar in the Abyei Arbitration (*Gov't of Sudan v. Sudan People's Liberation Movement/Army*). Among other duties at the PCA, he also assisted the Appointing Authority to the Iran-United States Claims Tribunal. A member of the bar in New York and the Philippines, Dr. Llamzon previously practiced at Skadden, Arps, Slate, Meagher & Flom in Hong Kong, and at Romulo, Mabanta, Buenaventura, Sayoc & de los Angeles in Manila. He is also a professorial lecturer (on leave) at the Ateneo de Manila Law School in The Conflict of Laws (Private International Law), and was formerly a lecturer on international arbitration at The Hague University of Applied Sciences in The Netherlands and on public international law at the University of the City of Manila School of Law. His publications include the monograph *Corruption in International Investment Arbitration* (Oxford, 2014), which won Yale Law School's Ambrose Gherini Prize for best work in public or private international law. He lectures frequently on various aspects of public and private international adjudication and arbitration.

Jamal Mahjoub

Mr. Jamal Mahjoub was born in London in 1960. After living in Liverpool for several years, the family moved to his father's home country. Mahjoub attended Comboni College, run by Italian priests. He subsequently received a grant from Atlantic College in , and continued his studies in geology at the University of Sheffield. While still a student he began publishing his literary texts in magazines. After several changes of location, Northern Europe eventually became his home base – yet his African roots still play a central role in his books. They incorporate stories and history, science and superstition and at the same time discuss the living conditions in which people from different backgrounds live together or in close proximity with each other. The author has been awarded the Prix d'Astrobale for the novel *Travelling with Djinns* (2003) and the

Guardian/Heinemann African Short Story Prize. After spending many years in the Danish city of Aarhus, Mahjoub is now living in Barcelona.

Paul Meerts

Dr. Paul Meerts is a Senior Research Associate of the Clingendael Institute and a Visiting Professor in International Negotiation Analysis at the College of Europe in Bruges (Belgium). He is a Member of the Steering Committee of the Clingendael Processes of International Negotiations (PIN) Program and of the Advisory Board of the *Journal of International Negotiation* (Washington). As co-founder of Clingendael Institute he has been Director of the Department of Training and Education (1983-1989), Deputy Director of the Institute (2000-2006) and Advisor to its Director (2006-2011). Before Clingendael he did research on Dutch Political History at the Universities of Groningen and Leiden (1974-1978) and trained young Dutch diplomats at the Netherlands Society of International Affairs (NGIZ) in The Hague.

Djamchid Momtaz

Studied law in Paris where he obtained a doctoral degree in international law. He is emeritus Professor of international law at Tehran University. Member of the Permanent Court of Arbitration; the Commission for the Settlement of Disputes related to Confidentiality, Organization for the Prohibition of Chemical Weapons; Institut de droit international; Curatorium of The Hague Academy of International Law. Former member of the International Law Commission of the United Nations and of the Group of international Advisers of the International Committee of the Red Cross. Numerous teaching assignments abroad and author of several books and monographs on international human right law, humanitarian law and law of the sea.

Sarah Nouwen

Dr. Sarah Nouwen is University Lecturer in Law, University of Cambridge, and Fellow of the Lauterpacht Centre for International Law and Pembroke College. Dr. Nouwen's research interests lie at the intersections of law & politics, war & peace and justice & the rule of law. Her book, *Complementarity in the Line of Fire: The Catalysing Effect of the International Criminal Court in Uganda and Sudan* (Cambridge University Press, 2013) explores whether, how and why the complementarity principle in the Rome Statute of the International Criminal Court has had a catalysing effect on the legal systems of Uganda and Sudan. In 2010-2011, she was seconded to the African Union High-Level Implementation Panel for Sudan. Before starting her PhD, Sarah worked for the Netherlands Ministry of Foreign Affairs in New York, The Hague and Sudan and for an NGO in Senegal. Sarah holds an LLM (cum laude, Utrecht, with a specialisation in Cape Town), an MPhil in International Relations (Cantab) and a PhD in International Law (Cantab).

Hisashi Owada

His Excellency Judge Hisashi Owada has been a Judge of the International Court of Justice since 6 February 2003; President of the Court from 6 February 2009 to 5 February 2012; re-elected as from 6 February 2012. B.A., University of Tokyo (1955); LL.B., Cambridge University (1956); D. Phil. (*honoris causa*), Keiwa University, Japan (2000); LL.D. (*honoris causa*), Banaras Hindu University, India (2001), Waseda University, Japan (2004), and Groningen University, The Netherlands (2009). Honorary Professor, Leiden University; Professorial Academic Adviser, Hiroshima University; Professor, New York University Global Law School. Associé, l'Institut de Droit international (1995). Membre, l'Institut de Droit international (2001). Member, Permanent Court of Arbitration. Honorary Member, American Society of International Law. President, Asian Society of International Law. Member emeritus, Japanese Society of International Law. Member, Executive Council of the Japan Branch, International Law Association.

Jan Pronk

Professor Jan Pronk has garnered repute as one of the most influential persons in Develpment Cooperation in The Netherlands and internationally, both through his distinguished career as a politician and a prominent United Nations official. He studied Economics at the Erasmus University in Rotterdam where he worked in Research, and has made extensive scholarly contributions to the field of development. In 1971, he took up politics and has since served as the Minister of Development Cooperation from 1973-1977, 1989-1994, and 1994-1998, and as Minister of Housing and Environment in 1998-2002. He was appointed as the Deputy Secretary General of the United Nations Conference for Trade and Development (UNCTAD) from 1980-1986, and served as the Special representative for the United Nations Mission to Sudan for Darfur (2004-2006).

Sir Adam Roberts

Sir Adam Roberts, KCMG, FBA, is Emeritus Professor of International Relations at Oxford University, a Senior Research Fellow in Oxford University's Department of Politics and International Relations, and an Emeritus Fellow of Balliol College, Oxford. He was President of the British Academy from 2009 to 2013. Roberts' interests are in civil resistance, international law, the United Nations and strategic studies. He has published widely, including articles in journals such as *American Journal of International Law, British Year Book of International Law, International Affairs, International Security, Review of International Studies, Survival* and *The Times Literary Supplement.* Previously he held the posts of: Assistant Editor, Peace News (1962-1965); Noel Buxton Student in International Relations, LSE (1965-1968); Lecturer in International Relations, London School of Economics and Political Science (1968-1981); Alastair Buchan Reader in International Relations, Oxford University, and Professorial Fellow of St Antony's College (1981-1986); and Montague Burton Professor of International Relations, Oxford University, and Fellow of Balliol College (1986-2007). Roberts served on the Council of the International Institute for Strategic Studies (2002-2008), on the Council for Science and Technology (2010-2013) and on the UK Defence Academy Advisory Board (2003-2015). He is an Honorary Fellow of the London School of Economics & Political Science, and of St Antony's College Oxford, and has a Guest Professorship at Nankai University, Tianjin, China. He has been awarded honorary doctorates by: King's College London (2010); Aberdeen University (2012); and Aoyama Gakuin University, Tokyo (2012). He became a Foreign Honorary Member, American Academy of Arts and Sciences in 2011 and a Member of the American Philosophical Society in 2013.He was knighted in 2002 for services to the study and practice of international relations.

Nico Schrijver

Professor Nico Schrijver is Professor of International Law and Academic Director of the Grotius Centre for International Legal Studies, Leiden University, and a member of the Senate of the Dutch house of parliament. In the Senate he serves as the chair of the Standing Committee on Foreign Affairs, Development Co-operation and Defence and as the vice-chair of the Senate Committee on European Affairs.

He is also a member of the Royal Netherlands Academy of Arts and Sciences and the chairperson of its Section on Legal Sciences. During 2010-2012 he served as the President of the worldwide International Law

Association. Furthermore, he is a member of the UN Committee on Economic, Social and Cultural Rights, member of the Permanent Court of Arbitration and member of the *Institut de droit international.*

Bernardo Sepulveda-Amor

His Excellency Judge Bernardo Sepulveda-Amor is a Judge at the International Court of Justice, Member of the Court since 6 February 2006-2015, Vice-President 2012-2015. Among other positions, he was Minister of Foreign Affairs of the Republic of Mexico.

Hugo Siblesz

Mr. Hugo Siblesz is Secretary-General of the Permanent Court of Arbitration. Prior to assuming his position as Secretary-General of the Permanent Court of Arbitration, Mr. Siblesz served as Ambassador of the Kingdom of The Netherlands to France, Monaco and Andorra (2006-2012). Secretary-General Siblesz joined the Dutch Ministry of Foreign Affairs in 1973, acting as Director-General for Political Affairs and Director of the Consular Department, among other roles, over the course of his career. The Secretary-General received his law degree from the VU University Amsterdam.

Otto Spijkers

Dr. Otto Spijkers is Lecturer in Public International Law at Utrecht University. He is a member of the Committee on the Role of International Law in Sustainable Natural Resource Management for Development of the International Law Association, and guest lecturer for Amnesty International The Hague. He was guest lecturer at the Association pour la promotion des droits de l'homme en Afrique centrale (APDHAC) of the Université catholique d'Afrique centrale (Yaoundé, Cameroon) and Wuhan University (China) and the Netherlands Institute of International Relations "Clingendael". Previously, he was a PhD candidate and lecturer at the Grotius Centre for International Legal Studies at the University of Leiden. His doctoral dissertation, entitled *The United Nations, the Evolution of Global Values and International Law,* was published with Intersentia in 2011.

Abiodun Williams

Mr. Abiodun Williams was named President of The Hague Institute for Global Justice in January 2013. Prior to this role, he was Senior Vice-President of the Center of Conflict Management (CCM) where he led USIP's work in major conflict zones such as Afghanistan, Iraq, Pakistan, the Middle East, and North Africa. Previously, he also served as director of strategic planning in the Executive Office of the UN Secretary-General during the last six months of Kofi Annan's first term and during the entire five years of his second term.

Marc Weller

Professor Marc Weller is Professor of International Law and International Constitutional Studies, University of Cambridge, Director of the Lauterpacht Centre for International Law. From 2000 to 2009, he was Director of the European Centre for Minority Issues. He has authored, edited, or co-edited twenty books, including *Iraq and the Use of Force in International Law* (OUP, 2010) and *Political Participation of Minorities* (OUP, 2010).

Ida van Veldhuizen

Mrs. Ida van Veldhuizen, a former Dutch ambassador to the OSCE, has been a Member of the Supervisory Board of the Netherlands Institute for Multiparty Democracy (NIMD) since April 2012.

Paul de Waart

Professor Paul de Waart is Emeritus Professor of International Law at the VU University Amsterdam and is the author of many publications on international law and peace and security, human rights and development.

Jaap de Wilde

Professor Jaap de Wilde has been Professor in International Relations and Security Studies, University of Groningen since 2007. He is co-founder of Globalisation Studies Groningen. Since 2013, he has been Chairman of the Dutch Foundation for Peace Research. From 2001 to 2007, De Wilde was Professor in European Security Studies, VU University Amsterdam, and from 1995-2007 senior research fellow in European Studies and IR at the Centre for European Studies (CES), University of Twente. From 1993-1995 he worked as senior research fellow at the Copenhagen Peace Research Institute (COPRI).

Illustrations

Riek Machar (R) is displayed in Juba, South Sudan, on April 14, 2016. Photographer Albert Gonzalez Farran; ©AFP.

P. 122 Sudan negotiations 2016: South Sudan President Salva Kiir (C) holds hands with former rebel leader and First Vice-President Riek Machar (L) and Second Vice-President James Wani Igga (R) after a new unity government was sworn-in, Juba, South Sudan, 29 April 2016. Photographer Albert Gonzalez Farran; ©AFP.

P. 124 Top – Peace keeping Iran-Iraq: UN peacekeeping forces in Khoramshahr, Iran, after UN Security Council Resolution 598 and commencement of ceasefire in the Iran-Iraq War, 18th August 1988. Photographer Kaveh Kazemi; ©Getty images.

P. 124 Bottom – Political prisoners at work in Iran: Political prisoners making clothing for the Iran-Iraq War effort in a workshop at Evin Prison in Tehran, Iran, 10th February 1986. Photographer Kaveh Kazemi; ©Getty images.

P. 138 Mausoleum of the unknown soldier, Baghdad: Iraqi soldiers march pass the Mausoleum of the Unknown Soldier in Baghdad, during a ceremony marking the end of the war against Iran, 08 August 2000. Photographer Karim Sahib; © EPA PHOTO AFP.

P. 158 Top – Great Hall of Justice, Peace Palace, The Hague: On 28 August, 2013 the Peace Palace celebrated its centenary. High level visits, speeches, publications and public events were organized to commemorate the importance of this universal icon for the peace through law endeavour. Photographer Bart Mellink; ©International Court of Justice.

P. 158 bottom – Peace Palace, The Hague: The Peace Palace is the seat of the ICJ, the PCA, The Hague Academy of International Law and the Carnegie Foundation. Photographer Bart Maat; ©Carnegie Foundation.

P. 190 Syria Peace Talks in Geneva, 2016: U.N. mediator Staffan de Mistura attends a news conference after the conclusion of a round of meetings during the Syria Peace talks at the United Nations in Geneva, Switzerland, April 28, 2016. Photographer Denis Balibouse; © Reuters.

P. 192 Sudan Comprehensive Peace Agreement: Soldiers from the Sudanese People's Liberation Army (SPLA) look at a copy of the comprehensive peace agreement on 23 January 2005. Rumbek, Sudan. Photographer Simon Maina; © AFP/Getty Images.

Index

NOTE: Many terms appear numerous – more than 30 – times in the text, and have thus been omitted from this index. Examples include the European Union, United States of America, United Kingdom, United Nations, Security Council, Secretary-General, The Hague, Versailles, adjudication, etc. In view of their primordial significance for the topic of this book, we have made an exception for International Court of Justice (ICJ) and mediation. Others appear only once, as part of a list of examples. See e.g., ILO (on p. 25), or ECOWAS, SADC (p. 176), or crimes against humanity (p. 65), or biological weapons (always mentioned together with chemical weapons). Those have also been omitted.

www.ingramcontent.com/pod-product-compliance
Lightning Source LLC
Chambersburg PA
CBHW071438230926
51846CB00001B/279
* 9 7 8 9 0 0 4 3 2 1 2 3 6 *